D1746052

110,- Gest.

GA ARCHITECT
STEVEN HOLL

G A ARCHITECT 11
STEVEN HOLL

EDITED BY YUKIO FUTAGAWA
INTRODUCTION BY TOYO ITO

企画・編集:二川幸夫　序文:伊東豊雄

A.D.A. EDITA Tokyo

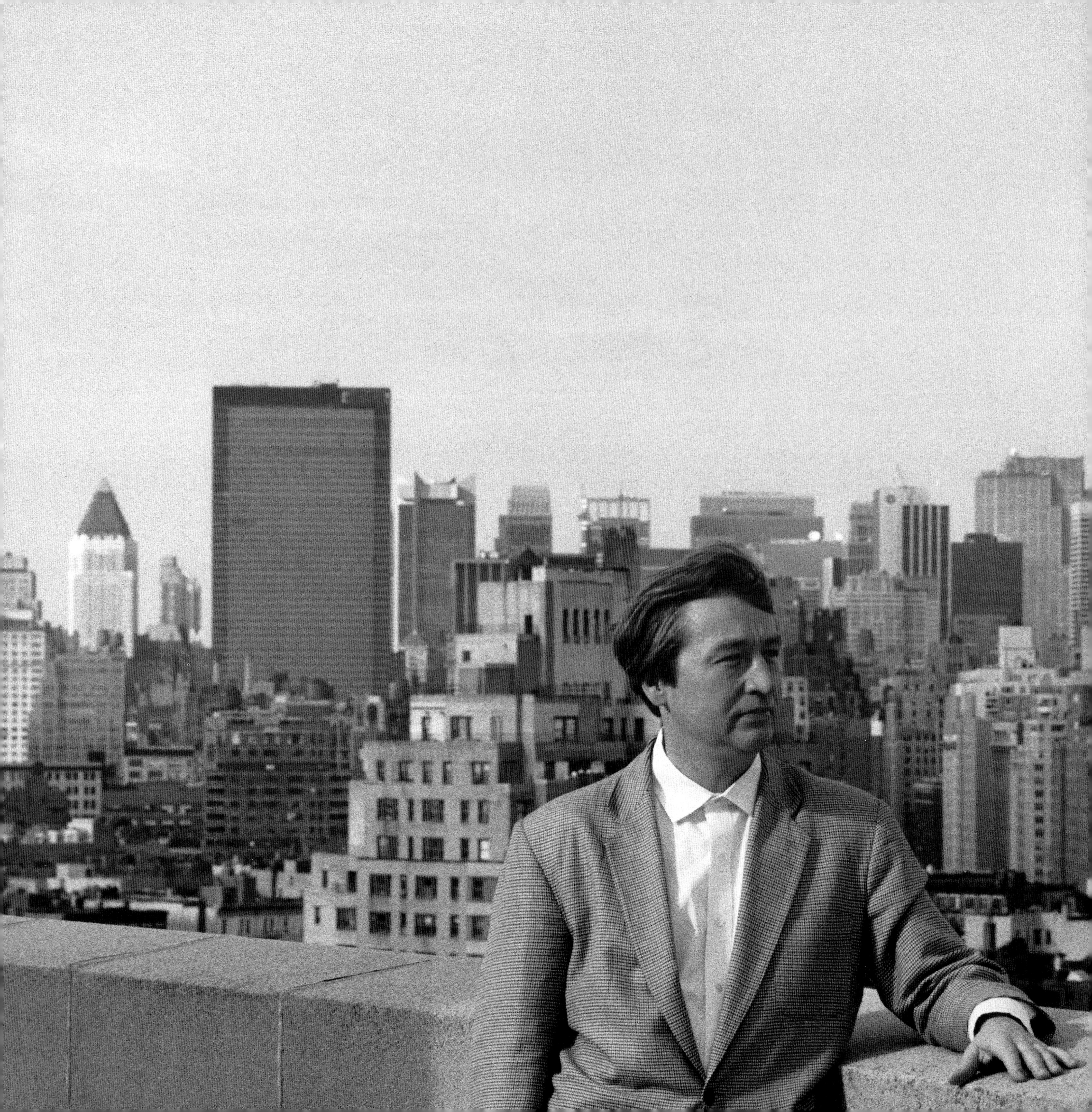

STEVEN HOLL

1947 *Born in Bremerton, Washington*
1970 *Graduates from University of Washington; B. Arch*
1970 *Studies architecture in Rome*
1976 *Post-graduate studies at Architectural Association School, London*
1976 *Establishes Steven Holl Architects in New York*
1981 *Becomes Adjunct Professor at Columbia University*
1989 *Becomes Tenured Professor at Columbia University*
1989 *Publishes "Anchoring"*
1989 *Participates in a two-man show at Museum of Modern Art*
1991 *"Architecture Tomorrow" exhibit at Walker Art Center*
1992 *Receives AIA New York City Chapter Award for Excellence in Design for "Void Space/Hinged Space" Housing, Fukuoka*
1992 *Receives AIA National Honor Award for office renovations at D.E. Shaw & Co., New York*

Photo by Yukio Futagawa

Copyright © 1993 A.D.A. EDITA Tokyo Co., Ltd.
3-12-14 Sendagaya, Shibuya-ku, Tokyo 151, Japan
All rights reserved. No part of this publication may be reproduced,
stored in a retrieval systems, or transmitted, in any form or by any means,
electronic, mechanical, photocopying, recording, or otherwise,
without permission in writing from the publisher.

Copyright of drawings
©1993 Steven Holl Architects

Cover and logotype design: Gan Hosoya

First published, 1993
Reprinted, 1993

Printed and bound in Japan

ISBN4-87140-417-X C1352

Contents
目次

8	An Architecture Adrift in Time: A Message to Steven Holl *by Toyo Ito* 時を漂う建築——STEVEN HOLLへのメッセージ/伊東豊雄	102	Hybrid Building, Seaside, 1984-88 ハイブリッド・ビルディング
12	Phenomena and Idea *by Steven Holl* 現象と理念	112	Town Square, Four Houses and Chapel, Port Ludlow, 1991-92 タウン・スクエア/4つの住宅と礼拝堂
18	Light, Material and Detail *by Steven Holl* 光，材料，ディテール	114	Void Space/Hinged Space Housing, Fukuoka, 1989-91 ヴォイド・スペース/ヒンジド・スペース・ハウジング
20	Cohen Apartment, New York, 1982-83 コーエン・アパートメント	122	Ontology of Institutions *by Steven Holl* 組織の存在論
28	Pace Collection Showroom, New York, 1985-86 ペース・コレクション・ショールーム	124	Berlin AGB Library Competition, Berlin, 1988 ベルリン・アメリカ記念図書館/競技設計案
32	Apartment, Museum of Modern Art Tower, New York, 1986-87 MOMAタワー・アパートメント	132	College of Architecture & Landscape Architecture University of Minnesota, Minneapolis, 1988-91 ミネソタ大学建築/ランドスケープ・アーキテクチュア学部
36	Objects, New York, 1986 調度品のデザイン	136	Palazzo del Cinema Competition, Venice, 1990-91 パラッツォ・デル・チネマ/競技設計案
38	Giada Showroom, New York, 1987 ギアダ・ショールーム	140	Kemper Museum of Contemporary Art, Kansas City, 1991 ケンパー現代美術館
42	Apartment, Metropolitan Tower, New York, 1987-88 メトロポリタン・タワー・アパートメント	142	Edge of a City *by Steven Holl* 都市の周縁
48	D. E. Shaw & Co. Offices, New York, 1991 D・E・ショウ社オフィス	144	Porta Vittoria Competition, Milan, 1986 ポルタ・ヴィットリア計画/競技設計案
52	Houses *by Steven Holl* 住宅	152	Erie Canal Edge, Rochester, 1988 エリー運河畔計画
54	Sokolov Retreat, St.Tropez, 1976 ソコロフ邸の隠れ家	154	Spatial Retaining Bars, Phoenix, 1989 スペイシャル・リテイニング・バー
56	Telescope House, Still Pond, 1978-79 テレスコープ・ハウス	156	Stitch Plan, Cleveland, 1989 ステッチ・プラン
58	Metz House, Staten Island, 1980-81 メッツ邸	158	Parallax Towers, New York, 1990 パララックス・タワー
60	Pool House and Sculpture Studio, Scarsdale, 1980-81 プールハウス/彫刻スタジオ	160	Spiroid Sectors, Dallas/Fort Worth, 1990 スパイロイド・セクター
66	Berkowitz-Odgis House, Martha's Vineyard, 1984-88 バーコヴィツ/オッジス邸	162	List of Works 1975-92 作品リスト
74	Residence, Cleveland, 1988-90 クリーヴランドの住宅		
78	Stretto House, Dallas, 1989-92 ストレット・ハウス		
90	Housing and Hybrid Buildings *by Steven Holl* ハウジングとハイブリッド・ビルディング		
92	Gymnasium Bridge, South Bronx, 1977-78 ジムナジウム・ブリッジ		
96	Bridge of Houses, New York, 1979-82 ブリッジ・ハウス		
100	Autonomous Artisans' Housing, Staten Island, 1980-84 自由な職人のハウジング		

Project description: Steven Holl
English translation: Hiroshi Watanabe
Japanese translation: Kazumasa Tamai

作品解説:スティーヴン・ホール　　翻訳:玉井一匡(和訳)，渡辺洋(英訳)

An Architecture Adrift in Time:
A Message to Steven Holl
時を漂う建築——STEVEN HOLLへのメッセージ

Toyo Ito
伊東豊雄

Dear Steven:

It has been a year since I visited the apartments (with their void and hinged spaces) that you designed for Nexus World. I was impressed then mostly by their extraordinarily delicate beauty, but having had a chance to go through *Anchoring*, the volume of your works that you sent me recently, I now understand that the basic concept of the project in Fukuoka is the product of many years of thought. The qualities that have characterized your projects from the start are, I believe, most fully developed in that building.

The most impressive feature of the Fukuoka project is the open passageway penetrating the five wings of the building. Similar spatial experiences—that is, movements perpendicular to, and through, volumes of the same size located at equal intervals—are offered by the Bridge of Houses (1979-82) built over the regularly spaced blocks of New York, the Autonomous Artisans' Housing (1980-84) for New York's Staten Island, and a portion of the Porta Vittoria project (1986) for Milan.

Is the orderly repetition of mass and void—the preoccupation with formality—an *hommage* to the various urban projects of Le Corbusier? Or is it to be traced back to the agreeable repetition of blocks in Manhattan? I remember sitting through lectures on the planning of public housing as a university student and thinking how tedious the inevitably orderly and formal site plans were, but you have made those qualities a virtue. I feel that is a significant point in considering your architecture.

In other words, up to now our sole concern has been to introduce variety into the homogeneous environments created by modern architectural design and city planning in the early part of this century. You, however, seem to have been attracted precisely to the homogeneity and formality that were beginning then to characterize society.

What is new about the homogeneity and formality of your projects, that is, what distinguishes your site plans for housing from those of Le Corbusier, is their level of abstraction. Le Corbusier's plans are quite abstract and rarefied in drawings, but the realized buildings from not only his later years but even the 1920s and 1930s impress one by their substance and depth. They are characterized by sharp contrasts between massive volumes and voids or between light and shadow. Despite the abstract quality of his work on a conceptual level, Le Corbusier seems to have been drawn to the material and massive qualities of actual buildings, the thickness of walls, the stoutness of columns, and the power or dynamism of spaces scooped out of mass.

To experience a work by Le Corbusier is to wander through spaces defined by weightless lines and planes but to remain conscious at the same time that the structure is firmly rooted in the land. Just as an astronaut in space is sustained by the conviction that he will eventually return to earth and its gravity, we are sustained by the knowledge that ultimately the conceptual weightlessness of architecture will be reconciled with nature. Ultimately, the voyage comes to an

---

Steven Holl 様

Nexus Worldであなたの設計されたアパートメント（void space／hinged space）を見せてもらってから，もう1年経ちました。あの時には異常な程に繊細な美しさだけが印象に残りましたが，最近あなたが送ってくれた作品集『Anchoring』を見て，福岡のプロジェクトの基本的なコンセプトはあなたが長年考え続けてきたことの結実であることがよくわかりました。本当に，あの建築にはあなたがつくり始めてからの数々のプロジェクトに繰り返しあらわれる特質が集大成されているように思われます。

例えば福岡のプロジェクトで最も印象的なのは5つの住居棟を貫く屋外通路です。全く等間隔に置かれた同一サイズのヴォリュームを横断してゆく空間体験，それはニューヨークの規則的な街区を縦断して架けられた「Bridge of Houses」(1979～82)や同じくニューヨークのスタテン島のプロジェクト「Autonomous Artisans' Housing」(1980～84)，或いはミラノのためにつくられたプロジェクト「Porta Vittoria」(1986)の一部などに典型的に見ることができます。

マッスとヴォイドの規則的な繰り返し，その形式性への執着はル・コルビュジエのさまざまなアーバン・プロジェクトへのオマージュに由来するのでしょうか，それともマンハッタンの規則的な街区の繰り返しの心地良さから来るのでしょうか。かつて僕らは大学の住宅地計画のレクチュアで，パブリック・ハウジングに於ける住棟配置のあまりの規則性，形式性にうんざりした記憶がありますが，その退屈さをあなたは徹底的にポジティヴな空間へと置き換えておられますね。このことはあなたの建築について考える時にとても重要な意味を持っているように思われます。

つまり，今世紀初めの近代の建築計画や都市計画にしばしば見られる均質さ，我々は久しくその均質さにどのようなヴァリエーションを与えるかということばかりを考えてきたのですが，あなたはその頃既に今日の社会に浸透しつつある新しい均質さや形式性にこそ魅力を感じておられたのではないでしょうか。

あなたのプロジェクトに見られる均質性や形式性の新しさ，即ちル・コルビュジエの住棟配置との違いは抽象性の差にあります。図面で見る限りはコルのプランもきわめて抽象度の高いドライなものですが，実際につくられた建築は晩年は言うに及ばず，20～30年代の作品でももの自体の持つ実体感や奥行きを感じさせます。それはマッシヴなヴォリュームとヴォイドな部分との強いコントラストや，光と陰の強いコントラストに典型的に示されています。恐らくコルはコンセプチュアルなレベルでの抽象性にも拘らず，実体としての建築の持つ素材感や重量感，壁の厚さや柱の太さ，マッスのなかを繰り抜いたヴォイドなスペースなどの強さやダイナミズムに惹かれていたに違いありません。

したがってコルの建築を体験する時我々は，一方で重さを持たない線や面の空間をさまよいつつ，他方では大地にしっかりと根をはやした構造物への信頼に引き戻されるという両義性を味わうことになる訳です。つまり宇宙に投げ出された宇宙飛行士も必ず重力を持つ地球に帰ってくるという確信に支えられているように，建築という観念内部の無重力状態も常に自然との調和した関係に最終的には到る。結局いつでも旅は終るのです。

しかしSteven，あなたのつくった建築のなかに浸っていると，その空間体験は実に不思議なものです。私はまるで近代建築，特にル・コルビュジエの建築の夢をみているようです。あなたの建築の場合，実作に感じられる存在感の希薄さはむしろ図面や模型以上です。素材の選択やディテールには吟味に吟味を重ねているのでしょうが，それらは消え去って，

end.

However, the spatial experience in your architecture, Steven, is quite unique. It's as if one were dreaming about modern architecture, particularly the architecture of Le Corbusier. In the case of your buildings, the actual work seems to be even more rarefied than the drawings and models. You must study each choice or detailing of material very carefully, but any hint of effort vanishes in the realized building. One is left in an abstract space. There may be a sequence of masses and voids, but it does not offer the sharp contrast of light versus darkness, or of the substantial versus the insubstantial, to be found in Le Corbusier's works. One is always drifting in a weightless world created out of planes without thickness.

The verb "to drift" suits your architecture perfectly. In dreams, space is often weightless, and one travels on a voyage without conclusion. For example, when one steps into the entrance hall of the Fukuoka project one has already embarked on an endless journey. The irregularly articulated and subtly bending sashwork, the crisscrossing brass bars embedded in the terracotta walls, the floor with its slight changes in level and material, and the stairs—all these lead eventually to an open, linear passageway. This passageway, which parallels the street in front and curves gently, is striped by a regular succession of light and shadow. However, this rhythm of light and darkness is a sophisticated surface effect, suggesting a sheet of paper that has been divided into white and gray areas by computer graphics. The facades of the wings that are at right angles to the passageway are, on one side, sheets of corrugated aluminum in a concrete frame, and on the other, finished in exposed concrete. On both sides, windows of diverse sizes establish a light rhythm and create planes without depth. Moreover, these repeated, abstract planes are reflected on the pond and are bathed by reflected light, so that they radiate an extremely delicate light. The water here is also simply a smooth plane without depth like the panels of aluminum.

As one walks down the passageway, the interplay of diverse elements becomes even more complex and subtle. Colors may change, the level may change, and the passageway may bend slightly, but the flow of space never ceases. The windows, which play an important role in giving the exterior space a rhythm, introduce light into each unit from many directions and give even greater variety to the diverse interior compositions of planes.

Your architecture is more aural than visual, more temporal than spatial. An analogy is often drawn between the rhythm of your architecture and the rhythm of sounds. However, when I say that your architecture is aural, I mean that I always sense in your spaces a transparent quality. I sense this transparency not so much in the way void spaces are composed but in the planes. For example, when multiple windows are introduced rhythmically into a single facade, I sense a transparency in the concrete or aluminum wall planes that form the ground for those figures. Like the intervals between sounds in music, the wall planes, be they concrete or aluminum, are fated to vanish in the distance leaving only figural elements.

Your architecture is characterized by such a transparency. Transparency of

あなたの建築のなかで私は抽象的な「空間」のなかにいます。マッスとヴォイドの繰り返しを経ても、その体験は決してコルの場合のようなはっきりとした明暗のコントラストではないし、密実なものと空疎なものとのコントラストでもない。いつでも私は厚さのない面だけが織りなす無重力の世界に漂っています。

正しく、漂うということばがあなたの建築にはぴったりです。夢の空間はしばしば無重力だし、帰結のない旅をしているからです。例えば福岡プロジェクトのエントランスホールに入ると、既にそこはあてどのない旅の始まりです。不規則に分節された微妙に折れ曲がるサッシュワーク、テラコッタの壁面を飛び交う象嵌された真鍮のバー、わずかにレベルや素材を変える床、階段を上ると自然に我々はリニアーな屋外通路へと導かれます。前面道路と平行に緩やかにカーブしたこの通路では光と陰の規則的なストライプが繰り返されます。しかしこの明暗のリズムは白とグレーにコンピューターグラフィックで塗り分けられた紙のように表層的でソフィスティケートされたものです。そして通路と直交して姿をあらわす住棟のファサード、一方はコンクリートのフレームの間にアルミの波板が貼られ、他方はコンクリートの打ち放しで仕上げられていますが、いずれの面もさまざまなサイズの開口が軽やかなリズムをつくりながら奥行きのない面を構成しています。しかも繰り返されるそれらの抽象的な面は池の水に映り込み、或いは水面からの反射光を浴びて繊細きわまりない輝きを放っています。水もまた、ここではアルミパネルと同じように奥行きのない平滑なひとつの面でしかありません。

明るい通路から住戸に歩を進めると、さまざまな要素の絡み合いは一層複雑かつ微妙になります。色を変え、レベルを変え、小さく折れ曲がりながら、空間の流れはとどまることがありません。外部空間で重要な要素であったリズムを織りなす開口は、住居の内部にあってもさまざまな方向からの光を導き多様な面の構成に一層の変化をもたらしています。

あなたの建築は視覚的と言うより聴覚的であり、空間的と言うよりは時間的な建築です。あなたの建築に感じられるリズムはしばしば音のリズムとの類似性を指摘されていますから聴覚的であるのは当然かもしれません。しかし私は聴覚的建築と言う時には、必ずその空間に透明性を感じるのです。それはヴォイドなスペースのつくり方、というよりもむしろ面に感じられる透明性です。つまり例えばひとつのファサードのなかに複数の開口がリズムをつくりながら採られているとすると、地を構成しているコンクリートやアルミの壁面に感じられる透明性なのです。音楽に於ける音と音との間の余白のように、いかにコンクリートであろうとアルミが貼られていようと、その壁面は図を構成する要素の彼方に消え去っていかねばならないのです。

あなたの建築はそうした透明さを備えています。したがっていくらヴォリュームが重なっていようと、それらの質感は消え去って透明な空間のなかに図としての要素だけが浮かび上ってくるのです。そして透明な空間のなかで要素は互いに呼応し合い、響き合って聴覚的な世界を奏で始めるのです。しかしあなたのつくり出す空間は決して不協和音の空間ではありません。要素が反発し合ったり、衝突し合ったり、鋭角的に要素が交差することはありません。各要素はそれぞれに自らの最も心地良い場所を求めて空間を漂い、穏やかな関係の空間を構成しています。

時間的な建築、それはシークエンスの建築です。或る場所から別の場所へ、さらに次の場所へと空間は時間的な経緯を伴ってあらわれ、消えてゆきます。建築は一気に全体像としてあらわれるのではなく、体験する人々とともに現象するのです。

日本を代表する現代作曲家、武満徹はかつて自らの作曲への意志を次のように語ってい

space makes one unaware of the material quality of volumes, no matter how many of them are layered. Only those elements that are figures emerge in the transparent space. In that transparent space, the elements respond and resonate to each other, and create a world of sounds. However, the spaces you create never feature discordant sounds. The elements never repulse, clash against, or pierce each other. Each element seeks the most agreeable place for it and floats in space, composing a space of tranquil relationships.

A temporal architecture is an architecture of sequences. In moving from one place to the next, and then to the next again, space appears and disappears as if marking the passing of time. The architecture does not appear all at once but becomes manifest phenomenally to the people who experience it.

Toru Takemitsu, Japan's best-known composer of contemporary music, once stated his intentions as follows: "Words like harmony and balance do not mean conformity to existing standards. Simple functionalism must be transcended. The objective is to make new discoveries in the world using your own criterion."

He has also said, "I want to free 'sound' from the petty, schematic rules that have bound it and to endow it with a movement that is as true as breathing in and breathing out. I believe the conceptual, inner form of expression that prevails today is not real music. Music ought to be profoundly related to nature; it is at times elegant and at other times brutal."

The architecture you are seeking seems to me to be quite close to what he describes. Many people can sense in your architecture an attempt, not to introduce preconceived schemas into the spatial composition, but to inscribe in that composition a fresh rhythm expressive of the age.

A nostalgia for the vernacular townscape of Italy reappears in the dreamlike, early projects of Aldo Rossi, but with your architecture, Steven, it is as if the modernist spaces depicted by Le Corbusier or Malevich had reappeared in a dream. Just as a dream wanders on the border between reality and unreality, your architecture travels on an endless journey between abstract spaces and palpable spaces. Unlike Le Corbusier, you cannot return to the earth, yet you cannot remain completely in a world of abstraction either. Looking at your projects, I think of a ship that approaches the earth after traveling in space but, unable to penetrate the atmosphere, is adrift on its fringes.

Perhaps that is because you cannot stop trusting architecture or humanity. The reason I believe in you as an architect is that you are sincere. However, our architectural or artistic images are transcending real life and advancing inexorably into an inanimate, unfeeling world. In contrast, our bodies cannot change, and our actions cannot be free of gravity. Our society, in the meantime, continues to abide by conventions so as to maintain order. Our images are alert to the spirit of the era and capture its essence. They rush headlong into a weightless world or a space that is insatiably homogeneous and abstract. As a result, architects like you with a well-honed sensibility are torn between a cutting-edge world of images and the conservative world of the body, which cannot change as easily. You put too much trust in human beings to try to realize the conceptual avant-garde world. To

ます。「調和とか均衡とかいう言葉は，既成の尺に律せられるという意味ではない。それは，たんなる機能主義を超えたものである。自らのモデュールによって世界に新しい発見をすることだ。」或いはまた次のようにも述べました。「図式的なおきてにくみしかれてしまった音楽のちゃちな法則から＜音＞をときはなって，呼吸のかようほんとうの運動を＜音＞にもたせたい。音楽の本来あるべき姿は現在のように観念的な内部表白だけにとどまるものではなく，自然との深いかかわりによって優美に，時には残酷になされるのだと思う。」

恐らくあなたの建築に求めているものはこの言葉にきわめて近いのではないでしょうか。あなたが既成の図式を空間構成に持ち込むのではなく，そこに新鮮な時代の息づかいをリズムとして刻もうとしているのを多くの人々があなたの建築から感じとることができるからです。

アルド・ロッシの初期のプロジェクトにはイタリアのヴァナキュラーな街へのノスタルジーが夢にあらわれる建築のように再現されていますが，Steven，あなたの建築はル・コルビュジエやマレヴィッチなどが描いたモダニズムの空間を夢のなかで再現したかのように感じられるのです。つまり夢が現実と非現実の世界の境界を彷徨するように，あなたの建築も抽象的な空間と現実の生なもので構成される空間の狭間で帰結のない旅を続けているように見えるのです。あなたはコルのように大地に帰還することは出来ない，しかしあなたは虚空に投げ出されたままに，完璧な抽象の世界にとどまることもできない。あなたのプロジェクトを見ていると，宇宙船が地球に近づきながら大気圏に突入し得ないでその周囲を漂っているような印象を受けます。

恐らくそれはあなたの建築への，そして人間への決して裏切ることのできない信頼に因るのではないでしょうか。私がStevenを一人の建築家として信用できるのはあなたのその誠実さです。しかし我々の建築的，或いは芸術的イメージは現実の生活を超えて，非情な世界へとどんどん踏み込んでいってしまいます。我々の生な身体が変わることはないし，我々の行動は重力に逆らうことはできない。また我々の社会は秩序を維持するためには慣習的であり続けようとします。それに対し，我々のイメージは時代の空気を敏感に感じとってひたすらそれを尖鋭化させます。無重力の世界やあくなき均質で抽象的な空間のイメージへと突き進んでいってしまうのです。その結果，あなたのように研ぎすまされた感性を備えた建築家は，イメージの世界での先端性と容易には変わり得ない身体自体の保守性との間の拡大されたギャップに引き裂かれることになるのです。観念内部のアヴァンギャルドの世界を実体化しようと突き進んでしまうには人間を信頼し過ぎている，端的に言えばやさし過ぎるのです。だからこそあなたの建築は虚空の彼方に消え去ってしまうこともなく，かと言って大地に着地することもなく，大気圏の周辺を漂うことになるのではないでしょうか。

今日，新しい均質な空間は魅力的だと言いましたが，私はあなたの国や日本ならば到るところに散在するコンビニエンスストアにそのような性格を感じます。一般的に言えばコンビニエンスストアの空間はきわめて貧しい空間です。大きな冷蔵庫の内部のようにニュートラルなラックに並列された食料品の数々，或いは倉庫の内部のように素っ気なく並べられた日用品の数々，そこには住生活に必要なほとんどすべてのものが取り揃えられていますが，この空間の内部であらゆるものは均質に見えます。それはデパートやブランド品を売る専門店とは全く逆の空間です。デパートや専門店では，各品物は隣の品といかに違うか，それ自体が個性の輝きを放っているかをディスプレイしようとしますが，コンビニエンスストアでは何を食べようが，何を着ようが，掃除や洗濯をするのに何を使おうが，結

put it bluntly, you are too gentle. That is why your architecture neither vanishes into the distance beyond the sky nor lands on the earth but instead floats somewhere at the limits of the atmosphere.

I find the new homogeneous spaces attractive. I feel something of their quality in the convenience stores that are scattered everywhere in both the United States and Japan. Generally speaking, the spaces in convenience stores are quite meager. The food products displayed on neutral racks that suggest the inside of a huge refrigerator, the everyday goods that are arranged matter-of-factly as in a warehouse—practically everything that is needed for everyday life is stocked. Everything in that space seems to be of similar quality. The situation is the very opposite of what one finds in department stores or specialty stores that sell brand products. In department stores and specialty stores, each product is displayed to show how it is different and unique. A convenience store, on the other hand, seems to be saying it is really all the same, no matter what you eat, what you wear, and what you use to clean or wash. The message it seems to be transmitting is that everything is the same quality and neutral, and that the individuality or the difference in quality we set so much store by amounts actually to very little. It is a space that anticipates an ultimate condition of entropy.

This space goes beyond mere rationalization or functionality and gives us a glimpse of the arrangement by which our lives today are controlled. We are drawn, after all, not just to utopian spaces but to their opposite. An image of cool homogeneity in its extreme form always gives us as much a frisson as the universal space depicted by Mies. Only a thin line separates the extreme of poverty from abundance.

Your architecture is adrift in a condition of gentleness, but that cannot continue indefinitely. It must either land on earth or depart, vanishing into emptiness. Awaiting that moment, I give myself up in the meantime to your agreeable spaces.

局すべて同じなんだと言っているように見えるのです。あらゆるものは均質でニュートラルで我々が固執してきたさまざまなものの個性とか質の違いはほんの微差に過ぎないんだ，というメッセージを発しているように思われてしまうのです。すべての運動はエントロピーの究極状態へ向かっているんだという予言の空間のように感じられるのです。

恐らくこの空間は，単に販売の合理性とか機能性といった次元を超えて，我々の今日の生活がどれ程コントロールされたものであるのか，その仕組みを垣間見せているのではないでしょうか。我々はユートピアの空間にのみ惹かれる訳ではなく，その逆にも取り憑かれてしまうのです。かつてミースが描いたユニヴァーサルスペースのように，冷徹な均質さの極限のイメージは常に我々をぞくぞくさせる程の魅力に満ちているのです。貧しさの極致は豊かさといつも紙一重です。

あなたの建築が漂っている状態はやさしさに溢れていますが，このまま永久に漂い続けるわけにはいかないでしょう。それはいつか大地に着地するのか，それとも虚空の彼方に飛び去ってしまうのか，その瞬間を見ることを心待ちしながら，私はあなたの心地良い空間に身を任せています。

Phenomena and Idea
現象と理念

Steven Holl
スティーヴン・ホール

Experience of phenomena—sensations in space and time as distinguished from the perception of objects—provides a "pre-theoretical" ground for architecture. Such perception is pre-logical i.e., it requires a suspension of a priori thought. Phenomenology, in dealing with questions of perception, encourages us to experience architecture by walking through it, touching it, listening to it. "Seeing things" requires slipping into a world below the everyday neurosis of the functioning world. An underground city for which we have keys without locks, it is full of mysteries.

Phenomenology as a way of thinking and seeing becomes an agent for architectural conception. While phenomenology restores us to the importance of lived experience in authentic philosophy, it relies on perception of pre-existing conditions. It has no way of forming a priori beginnings. Making a non-empirical architecture requires a conception or a formative idea. In each project we begin with information and disorder, confusion of purpose, program ambiguity, an infinity of materials and forms. All of these elements, like obfuscating smoke, swirl in a nervous atmosphere. Architecture is a result of acting on this indeterminacy.

To open architecture to questions of perception, we must suspend disbelief, disengage the rational half of the mind, and simply play and explore. Reason and skepticism must yield to a horizon of discovery. Doctrines cannot be trusted in this laboratory. Intuition is our muse. The creative spirit must be followed with happy abandon. A time of research precedes synthesis.

In music one says that something is "meant" by a particular movement. Do architectural thoughts have equivalent "meanings?" Is there a way of thinking in the material of construction? A way of thinking in materials which may yield a coupling of thinking-making specific to architecture? Making architecture involves a thought that forms itself through the material in which it is made. The thinking-making couple of architecture occurs in silence. Afterward, these "thoughts" are communicated in the silence of phenomenal experiences. We hear the "music" of architecture as we move through spaces while arcs of sunlight beam white light and shadow.

In a "zero ground" without site, program, or time, certain types of perception emerge as "phenomenal zones." Experimental territories, these zones of intensely charged silence lie beyond words. In opposition to those who insist on speech, on language, on signs and referents, we strive to escape language-time bondage. To evolve theoretically in active silence encourages experimentation. Silent phenomenal probes haunt the polluted sea of language like submarines gliding along the sandy bottom, below the oil-slick of rhetoric.

Certain physical interactions offer zones of investigation:

Color projection is experienced when light, reflected off a brightly colored surface, then bounced onto a neutral white surface, becomes a glowing phenomena that provokes a spatial sense. Reflected color is seen indirectly; it remains, with a ghostlike blush, the absent referent to an experience. In experiments with these phenomena we have discovered an emotional dimension that suggests a

現象を体験すること——自分の外にある対象として知覚するのではなく、空間と時間の中に身を置くことで得られる感覚——は、建築の「理論以前」の領域に踏み込むことである。このような知覚は論理にかなうか否かを問う以前のものであるから、このときには、演繹的な思考を停止しなければならない。現象学、つまり知覚したことについての問いを抱くという方法は、建築の中を自らの足で歩き、手で触れ、耳で聴くことによって建築を実感しようとする時に、私たちの役に立つはずである。「物を観る」には、機能世界の日常的な神経症的状況の下に隠された世界に入り込むことが欠かせない。私たちが入り口の鍵を与えられている地下の都市は、神秘に満ちているのだから。

思考と観察の一方法としての現象学は、建築を理解するための仲介者となってくれる。哲学の分野でいえば、現象学とは、生きる中で得られる経験の重要性を私たちに再認識させるものであるとともに、まだ実在しない状況を感知しようとするものでもある。したがって演繹的な意味での出発点となるものは持たない。経験主義に基づかずに建築を作ろうとすれば、コンセプト、つまり造形上の理念が必要である。プロジェクトにとりかかる時には私たちはいつも予備知識を集めるけれど、はじめのうちそれらは未整理であるから目的は混乱し計画はあいまいだが、それだけに、材料にせよ形態にせよこの時点では限り無い可能性が残されている。これらの要素のことごとくは煙幕のように、神経質な雰囲気を漂わせながら渦巻いている状態にある。建築とは、このような不確実な状態にはたらきかけた末にやっと作り出される結果なのである。

知覚によって生じた疑問に対して、開かれた状態に建築を置こうとするなら、猜疑心をひとまずおいて、心の半分を占める合理性から離れて虚心に遊びながら探索することだ。理性と懐疑論は、果てしない地平の中で何も発見することなく屈するにちがいない。この実験では、何であれ教条主義に陥ることなく、直観を創造の神にする。独創的な精神には、幸福な放縦がともなう。統合に至る前にまず調査の時が必要なのだ。

音楽では、どの楽章をとっても何かの「意味がある」と言われている。建築でもそれに相当するような「意味」があるだろうか。構造材料についての考え方は確立しているだろうか。考えることと作ることを結び付けるものである素材について考える方法は、建築に特有のものがあるのだろうか。建築を作るにあたっては、それを作る素材を通じて自ずと形成される思想を必要とする。建築について考えることは、作ることと平行して、自然のうちに進んでゆく。のちになって、こうして浮んだ「思想」は現象的な経験のうちに、いつしか伝えられる。太陽の弧を描く白い光とそれぞれが作る影の中、空間を動いてゆくと、建築の奏でる「音楽」が聞えてくるようになるのだ。

敷地もプログラムも時間もない「ゼログラウンド」では、ある種の知覚が「現象ゾーン」として現れる。実験的な領域は、言葉を超越して、沈黙が支配するゾーンである。弁舌や言語や記号や引用などに力をいれる連中とは反対に、私たちは言語と時間の結びつきを避けようとする。あえて沈黙のうちに理論を進化させることによって実験は黙々と進められるからである。現象についての調査は潜水艦よろしく、レトリックが油膜のように水面に浮ぶ下を、汚染された言語の海の底を静かに航行する。

ある種の物理的な相互作用が研究の領域を提供することもある。

色彩の投影を経験するには、鮮やかな色の面で光を反射させて、それを色のない白い面にあてると、白熱する光がにじみだし、それによって空間が実感される。このとき、反射光は間接的にしか見えない。そのぽうっとした明かりは、経験に照らしても思い当るものがない新たな体験である。このような現象を扱う実験によって、私たちは「心理的空間」

"psychological space."

A sponge can absorb several times its weight in liquid without changing its appearance. Cast glass seems to trap light within its material. Its translucency or transparency maintains a glow of reflected light, refracted light or the light dispersed on adjacent surfaces. This intermeshing of material properties and optic phenomena opens a field for exploration. Phenomenal zones likewise open to sound, smell, taste, and temperature as well as to material transformation.

Overlapping perspectives, due to movement of the position of the body through space create multiple vanishing points, opening a condition of spatial parallax. Perspectival space considered through the parallax of spatial movement differs radically from the static perspectival point of Renaissance space and the rational positivist space of modern axonometric projection. A dynamic succession of perspectives generates the fluid space experienced from the point of view of a body moving along an axis of gliding change. This axis is not confined to the x-y plane but includes the x-y-z dimensions manifesting themselves in the other dimensions, gravitational forces, electromagnetic fields, time, etc. Perspectives of phenomenal flux, overlapping perspective space is the "pure space" of experiential ground.

Architecture is born when actual phenomena and the idea that drives it intersect. Whether a rationally explicit statement or a subjective demonstration, a concept establishes an order, a field of inquiry, a limiting principle. The concept acts as a hidden thread connecting disparate parts with exact intention. Meanings show through at this intersection of concept and experience.

A structuring thought requires continuous adjustment in the design process to set manifold relations among parts within the larger whole. As dimensions of perception and experience unfold in the design process, constant adjustments aim at a balance of idea and phenomena.

"Kajitsu"

Japanese Zen poets developed a vocabulary to discuss *Kajitsu* or a poem's aspect and form. *Ka* is the beautiful surface of a poem while *jitsu* is its substantial core. An organic fusion of spirit and intellect opens a path toward inspiration, awareness, and *yugen*, the Buddhist term for "depth of meaning."

Uncovering the elusive essence of architecture, its depth of meaning or substantial core, requires passion and enthusiasm. The search for meaning demands a resistance to empty formalism, textual obfuscation and commercialism. Focusing on ideas early in the design process sets the substantial core ahead of the surface.

If there is life in ideas, a passion for architecture is renewed in the clarification of these ideas. For what is an architectural concept if not the material and spatial expression of spiritual intentions?

Intertwining of intellect and feeling is inherent in thought intuitively developed, thought that seeks clarity rather than possesses truth, thought that searches and is open to the changing field of culture and nature that it expresses. Although

を示唆する情緒の次元を発見したのである。

海綿は，その重量の数倍もの液体を吸い込みながら外には変化を見せない。キャストグラスは，その中に光を閉じ込める。あるいは半透明な，あるいは透明なこのガラスは，反射した光や閉じ込めた光の輝きや，となりあわせた表面で拡散された光の輝きをたくわえる。物質の領域と光学的な領域がこのように重なり合うと，また探求すべき分野が開かれる。現象ゾーンは，物質の変化に対するのと同じように音，香り，味，温度などにも開かれている。

空間の中，身体の位置を動かすにしたがってパースペクティヴが重なり，多くの消失点が生じ，空間の中の視差の状態が開かれる。空間を動く視点から検証されるパースペクティヴな空間は，ルネッサンスの空間の固定した視点とも，現代のアクソノメトリックの合理的実証主義の空間とも根底的な差異がある。パースペクティヴを連続的に移動させることによって，そこには流動的な空間が生じ，すべるように変化する軸に沿って動く身体の視点からそれを経験することができる。この軸はXY平面だけでなく，X, Y, Zの次元を含む諸々の次元，たとえば重力，電磁場，時間などで表される。パースペクティヴな空間に重なるようにして，現象がパースペクティヴに変化すると，そこには実験の場としての「純粋空間」が生じるのである。

現象と，それを動かす理念が交わる時に建築が生れる。合理的で明白な形で表明されるものであれ主観的な主張であれ，コンセプトによって秩序や研究の分野や原則を確かなものにする。コンセプトは表立たずに裏糸のようにして，別個のものであるそれぞれの部分を明白な意図によって結ぶ。このようにして，コンセプトと経験が交わるときに意味が表れるのである。

思考を体系づけるには，デザインの過程で絶えず調整を続けながら，全体をなす大きなものの中にあるそれぞれの部分のうちに多面的な関係をつくりあげてゆくことが必要である。デザインの過程では，知覚と経験の次元が展開してゆくに伴って，理念と現象の間のバランスをとるために常に調整がつづけられる。

「花実」

日本の禅の詩人たちの作ったあるヴォキャブラリーが議論を生んだ。花実，すなわち，詩の伝えるものと形式である。「花」は詩の美しい表面であるのに対して，「実」は本質をなす中心を意味する。精神と知の有機的な融合がインスピレーションや悟りあるいは幽玄（「深くとらえた意味」とでもいった仏教用語）へ至る道を開く。

建築のとらえどころのない本質，深いところにある意味や，本質的な中心を見つけるには情熱と熱中が必要である。意味を探るには，内容のない形式主義に陥ったり，原点に固執する余りに目を曇らせたり，商業主義に堕することは慎まねばならない。デザインの初期のプロセスの中で理念を中心にすえることは，表面よりも，本質的な中心を前にすえるということを意味するのである。

理念が真に生命を持つものであるなら，建築に対する情熱は，これらの理念を明らかにすることでまた新たに再生するはずだ。精神の目指すものが，物質と空間によって表現したものと一致するのでないとしたら，建築のコンセプトなど何の役にも立たなかったことになる。

知と情が織りなされている状態は，直観に基づいて展開された思想，たとえば真実を固定したものとして所有しようとするのではなく明晰さをあくまでも追求しようとする思想，

intuition cannot be explicitly expressed, we cannot condemn intuitive work to ambiguity. Architecture, perhaps more than any other form of communication, possesses the power of uniting intellectual and intuitive expression. Fusing the objective with the subjective, architecture can stitch our daily lives together by a single thread of intensity. It can possess both the core depth and the radiant surface by which to concretize the spirit. We must look beyond the *ka* of a beautiful surface to contemplate the *jitsu* of the core substance.

Soul
Soul is essential to architecture. A building stands in mute solitude, yet receptive individuals silently perceive the soul instilled in the work. Soul lies in attention to detail distilled in space and concretized in the love of construction. This love can take the form of shimmering icicle prisms or perspectives of steel.

In the thirteenth century, Saint Thomas Aquinas developed teachings linking theology and philosophy which held that all knowledge begins with sense perception. The direct connection of soul and perception was taught in "clear sighted penetration of the soul into objects of perception..."

Nourishment of soul begins by allowing greater expression of the language of the imagination, by suspending disbelief in favor of experiment, and by seeing things. Cultivating of a metaphorical sense of reality... a mythopoetic understanding of indefinable experiences and mysteries enriches the soul. Just as the unconscious and the intuitive can be intentionally brought to bear on thoughts and decisions, the intense exploration of a particular locus, together with material, can endow form with greater psychological significance. Like an electrical charge, soul passes from the artist into objects, and through eyes from the object to the viewer.

Reflection on perception in the design process considers all scales, including the micro scale of material properties. Even the most common seemingly inert material must be allowed to "speak" its essence. Kandinsky addresses this approach: "Everything that is dead quivers. Not only the things of poetry, stars, moon, wood, flowers, but even a white trouser button glittering out of a puddle in the street. Everything has a secret soul, which is silent more than it speaks."

Triumphant expressions of life often emerge despite the cycles of death by which they are surrounded. The question of soul is a question of will. The spirit of a community or society as well as that of an individual is often a pathologized territory. New investigations and new projects must be undertaken. Today the urgency of the soul is provoked by unprecedented human coldness.

An inexplicable modern soul unfolds from tragedy and absurdity. Hope rises on the ground of desperate conditions indirectly proportional to the emotional intensity of the situation: in the writings of Franz Kafka, and André Breton, the tragic and seemingly absurd are taken to extremes, yielding a strange existential hope. Humiliating circumstances and absurd predicaments are a part of everyday life in the modern metropolis, yet these conditions fuel the modern soul.

To embrace the unique anxieties of our time, one must avoid false optimism

あるいは文化と自然の領域の変化するありかたを探り，それを受け容れようとする思想などに固有のものである。直観力というものが明確な形で表すことができないとしても，直観に基づく仕事はあいまいなものだといって咎めだてするわけにはゆかない。建築は，おそらく他のどんなコミュニケーションの形式にもまして，知的な表現と直観的な表現を結ぶ力を持っているのだ。建築が客観的な立場と主観的な立場を融合させることができれば，私たちの日々の生活を，丈夫なことこのうえない一本の糸を使って縫い合わせることができるのである。そのとき，建築は深いところにある中心と，精神をにじませて光芒を放つ表面をふたつながらに持つことになる。美しい表面である「花」を貫いて観る目をもって，本質をなす「実」にまで思考を深めねばならない。

魂：ソウル
魂は建築になくてはならないものだ。建築は一言も発するわけでもなく孤独に立っているだけであるけれど，感受性をそなえた人は，そこに潜む魂の存在を無言のうちに感じとることができる。魂は，あるときは空間の中で熟成されたディテールに注がれた思いやりの中に潜み，あるいは建築を作りあげてゆくことへの愛情の中で具体化される。このような愛情は，ほのかに光るつららのプリズムのような形をとることもあれば，時にはスティールが見せるパースペクティヴとなることもある。

13世紀，聖トマス・アクィナスは神学と哲学を結びつけ，あらゆる知識は感性による知覚から始まるのだという教えを展開した。魂と知覚を直接に結び付けることをこう教えたのである。「魂が知覚の対象の中へ，目を見開きながら入り込んでゆくことだ」と。

魂を育てるには，想像をこめた言葉で表現することを認めること，なにごとも実験で確かめるようにする傾向をひとまず描くこと，物事を自分の目で見ることなどから始める。現実の中にメタファーを読みとる感覚を培う——説明のつかない経験や神秘的な事象を神話詩的に理解することが魂を豊かなものにするからだ。無意識や直観力を意図的に思想や判断に持ちこむのと同じように，物質を含む特定のものに焦点を合わせて真剣な探求をすすめれば，心理的な意味を大きくした形態を生み出すことができる。充電をするときのように，魂は芸術家から作品へと移り，作品から観賞者へと目を経て伝えられるのである。

デザインの過程での知覚について考えると，物質の領域での微妙な世界まで含んだあらゆるスケールに及ぶ。たとえ，このうえなくありふれた，浅薄でつまらない物質であれ，その本質を「物語る」ことが許されねばならない。カンディンスキーは，このようなアプローチについてこう書いている。「生命なきものさえ，あらゆるものが身を震わせる。星や月や森や花のような詩的なものたちは言うにおよばず，道端の水たまりでキラキラしているズボンの白いボタンのようなものでもその例外ではない。あらゆるものが秘めた魂を持ちながら語ろうとせずに沈黙を守るのである。」

生命あるものは，やがて巡ってくる死に囲まれながらも，生命のよろこびを示すのである。魂の発する問は意思の抱く問でもある。コミュニティや社会の精神は，人間ひとりひとりのそれと同じように，時には病に至ることが少なくない。それを守るための，新しい研究と新しいプロジェクトが進められるべきだ。今日，魂が追い詰められているのも，かつてない人間の冷たさのせいなのだから。

悲劇や不条理の中で見ると，名状しがたい現代の魂さえも明らかになってくる。希望は，絶望的な状況という大地から芽を伸ばすものだが，それは，状況が感情に訴える強さに間接的に比例したものである。フランツ・カフカやアンドレ・ブルトンの著作では，悲劇やあ

and the phantoms of nostalgia. Our challenge is to make spaces of a serenity and exhilaration that allow the modern soul to emerge. Our everyday lives include the upside-down view of the earth, in a live television broadcast in which figures walk without gravity, or stroll along a sidewalk past barrels of live crabs fighting each other. The modern soul, its unprecedented spirit, must have an architecture.

Meshing Sensation and Thought
If I walk along a shore towards a ship which has run aground, and the funnel or masts merge into the forest bordering on the sand dune, there will be a moment when these details suddenly become part of the ship; and indissolubly fused with it. As I approached, I did not perceive resemblances or proximities which finally came together to form a continuous picture of the upper part of the ship. I merely felt that the look of the object was on the point of altering, that something was imminent in this tension, as a storm is imminent in storm clouds. —M. Merleau-Ponty

Perception of architecture entails manifold relations of three fields; the foreground, middle ground and distant view are united in one experience as we observe and reflect while occupying a space. Mergings of these fields of space bracket very different perceptions. In the intertwining of the larger space with its forms and proportions and the smaller scale of materials and details lies architecture's power to exhilarate. Such phenomenal territory cannot be indicated in plan/section methods. Photography can only present one field clearly, excluding changes in space and time.

The weak link from perception back to inception must be scrutinized and strengthened. The traditional drawing of a plan is a blind notation, nonspatial and nontemporal. Perspectives of overlapping fields of space break this short circuit in the design process. Perspective precedes plan and section to give a priority to bodily experience and binds creator and perceiver. The spatial poetry of movement through overlapping fields is animated parallax.

To work simultaneously in foreground, middle ground, and distant view, an architect must constantly think of the next smaller and the next larger scales. The master plan of a campus space, for example, must consider the space between and within buildings as well as details of materials, glossy or dull or luminescent. Models constructed in plaster, wire, acid-transformed brass, and other construction materials balanced against a range of perspective views set an intermeshing design process in motion.

The phenomenal merge of object and field is accomplished via attention to individual site and situation. The hackneyed terms *contextualism* or *context* have encouraged an operation whereby a new building, chameleonlike, takes characteristics from each of its neighbors without maintaining internal integrity.

Rather, actual experience envisioned in light, perspective and material must be cross-referenced in an analytic process open to a new architecture that may not yet be understood. Architecture inserted into an existing situation may not strive to replicate or to achieve autonomy via contrast. Meshing of site and situation with

からさまな不条理がある限界に達すると，不思議な実存的な希望が湧いて来る。屈辱的な環境や不条理に満ちた境遇は，現代の大都市では日々の生活の一部を占めているのだが，それが，現代人の魂に火を点すのである。

私たちの時代に特有の苦悩と正面から取り組もうとすれば，偽りのオプティミズムやノスタルジアの亡霊に囚われることは避けねばならない。私たちが目指しているのは，静寂に満ちていながら活気を溢れさせて，現代の魂の生れるのを促すような空間を作ることである。日常的な生活の中でも，テレビジョンの生放送では地球の裏側の光景が映し出され，無重力状態で人間が歩いたり，夥しい数の生きたカニが戦いをくりひろげるかたわらの歩道を人がぶらついたりするのだ。このような現代の魂という，かつてなかった精神は，それ自身にふさわしい建築を持たねばならない。

感覚と思考を織り合わせる
「私が渚づたいに或る難破船の方へ歩いて行って，その船の煙突なり帆柱なりが砂丘を縁どる森と溶け合って見えるという場合，やがてこれらの細部が生き生きとその船と合体し，その船に接合される或る瞬間が来るだろう。だが，もっと近づくにつれて私の知覚したものは，この船の上部構造を最後には一つの連続した図面の中に再結合してしまうであろうような，相似または近接の関係ではない。私が感得したところは，ただ，対象の様相が変化して行ったこと，あたかも雲が嵐の逼迫を告げているようにこの緊張が何ものかの到来を告げていたということ，これである。」
——M・メルロー＝ポンティ，『知覚の現象学1』，竹内芳郎，小木貞孝共訳

建築の知覚には，三つの領域相互の多面的な関係を伴う。ある空間の中に立って観賞していると，近景と中景と遠景が結ばれてひとつの経験として残される。三つの空間領域が合体することは，全く異なった知覚を一つに括りこむことである。人を活気づける建築の力は，形態やプロポーションが大きなスペースに，材質やディテールが小さなスケールに織りこまれたところに生まれるのだ。このような現象になると，平面や断面図による方法では伝えることができない。写真にしても，せいぜいひとつの場をはっきりと表現することができるだけで，空間と時間の変容となると手に負えるものではない。

知覚することと，知覚に至るその発端は弱く結ばれているにすぎないことを綿密に調べ，それを強めなければならない。平面図という伝統的な図面は，不十分な表現法であるから空間と時間を伝えることができないが，空間の重なりを表現するパースであれば，デザインのプロセスの中でこのような短絡を断ち切ることができる。平面や断面図の前にパースを描けば身体的な経験を優先させることによって，建築家は作る人間であると同時にそれを感知する立場に立つことができる。重なる領域の中で，動きによって，空間の詩は生き生きとした視差をつくる。

近景，中景，遠景を同時に考えながら作れば，建築家は，常にひとつ小さいスケールから一段大きいスケールまで考え続けることになる。たとえばキャンパスのマスタープランを作るにあたっても，建物の間や中のスペースを考えつつ，細部の材料を艶ありにするか艶消しにするか，それとも発光性のものにするかなどを考えねばならない。プラスターであれワイアや酸化処理をした真鍮であれ，諸々の建築材料を使った模型とある範囲のパースペクティヴとをバランスをとりながら，進行中のデザインプロセスに織り込んでゆく。

物と背景を現象として融け合わせるには，個々の敷地と状況に対する関心を持つことが

an integrally conceived new architecture yields a third condition; a new inter-relation—a new "place" is formed.

Time's Multiplicity
As the imperceptible downward flow of glass in the lower portion of window panes measures the passage of time, architecture also serves as an index of time. Second, minute, hour, month, year, decade, epoch, millennium all are focused by the lens of architecture. Architecture is among the least ephemeral, most permanent expressions of culture.

Nostalgia, an irrational yearning for the return to another time, dominates American architecture today. Preservation of the past continues in the mind in books, in photographs and films, and in the conservation of past construction but simulating the past is a travesty of the present. This return to a romanticized time avoids the existential burden of time—its angst and its joy.

A certain resistance, a "negative capability," is necessary to exist and act in the present. It is important to think and to act on our thinking in the present. We are not merely of our time, we *are* our time. In our time the nature of speed itself has transformed the definition of space. The acceleration of fluctuating trends renders it impossible to meet ever-changing appetites. To last, to endure, is a primary challenge to architecture conceived today.

Strategies transcending the novel and image-driven in architecture counter the ongoing historical time of Western culture with a cyclical time of particular place and individual circumstance. For each distinct situation there is a time, yielding a "multiplicity of times." For example, for Islamic theologians time is not a continuous flow but a galaxy of instants. Space is nonexistent except in points. Alternately, from Bergson's point of view, space is the "impure combination of homogeneous time." Bergson's idea of "duration" includes a "multiplicity of secession, fusion and organization." These two ideas of time—as space or as continuous multiplicity and flow—correspond roughly to the strange cultural conditions of the world today.

While a global movement electronically connects all places and cultures in a continuous time-place fusion, the opposite tendency coexists in the uprising of local cultures and expression of place. In these two forces—one a kind of expansion, the other a kind of contraction—time-space is being formed. A new architecture must be formed that is simultaneously aligned with transcultural continuity and with a poetic expression of individual situation and community.

Expanding toward an ultra-modern world of flow while condensing sunlight or the texture of stone, on a single plot of land, this architecture aspires to Blake's admonition "to see the universe in a grain of sand." Poetic illumination of unique qualities of places, individual culture and individual spirit reciprocally connects to the transcultural, trans-historical present.

Architecture is a transforming link. An art of duration, crossing the abyss between ideas and orders of perception, between flow and place, it is a binding force. It bridges the yawning gap between the intellect and senses of sight, sound,

必要である。紋切り型のコンテクスチュアリズムとかコンテクストといった言葉を使うことですすめられてきた方法といえば、新しい建物をカメレオンさながらに、隣の建物の性格をもらいうけて建てるばかりで、内部から滲み出すそれ自身の性格を守ろうとはしない。

それよりも、光、パースペクティヴ、材料によって思い描いたものの現実の経験を、未知の新しい建築への道を開く分析のプロセスの中で、相互参照してゆかねばならない。そこにあるがままの状況の中に挿しこまれた建築は、周囲を複製しようともせず、さりとて対比をきわだたせて自己主張をしようともしないだろう。敷地と周囲の環境の網目に織り込むように有機的に考えて作られた新しい建築は、第3の状況を産む。新たな相互関係——新たな「場所」が形成されるのである。

時間の多様性
窓のガラスの下の部分では、下に向かうガラスの微細な流れが時間の経過を計るので、建築は時間の指標でもある。秒、分、時間、月、年、10年、一時代、千年という時を建築というレンズによってのぞくことができるのだ。建築は、はかない命とはいい難いものの中でも、最も永遠に近い時間にわたって、文化を表現しつづける。

ノスタルジア、すなわち、過去のある時代に回帰したいという不合理なあこがれが、今日のアメリカの建築を支配している。人間の心の中に、書物や写真やフィルムの上に、あるいは古い建物の保存という形で過去を残そうとする動きは続けられているけれど、過去を模倣しようという試みは、所詮現在のパロディにほかならない。美化された時代に回帰しようという企ては、実存する時間の重荷——その苦悩や歓びを回避しようとするものである。

現代に存在し、行動するには、ある種の抵抗、「負の能力」が必要である。現在という時に思考し行動することこそ重要なのである。私たちは、この時代に属するだけではない、私たち自身が私たちの時代そのものなのだ。この時代は、スピードという性質が空間の定義を変形させてしまった。ますます速度を増して変化をつづける傾向の中では、変化してやまない欲望にすべて応えることは不可能になっている。だとすれば、持続することこそ、今日の建築にとっては主要な挑戦となるのだ。

新しさばかりを追い求めたり、イメージを拡大したりすることで作られる建築を超越しようとするには、西欧文明の歴史を流れている時間に対して、特定の場所と特定の人に固有の、回帰する時間を対置しなければならない。どのような状況の中にも、「時間の多様性」を持つ時間というものがある。たとえば、イスラム教の神学者にとっては、時間とは連続的な流れではなく、無数の瞬間が銀河のように集合したものである。空間は、数々の点でしか存在しないのである。ベルグソンによれば、空間は「均質な時間の、雑多な組み合せ」である。ベルグソンの「時間の持続」という観念は、「離脱と混在と組織化の多様性」を含むものである。時間についてのこれら2つの考え方——空間あるいは連続的な多様性と流れであるという捉え方——は、今日の世界の不思議な文化状況にほぼ合致する。

電子技術を駆使して、あらゆる場所と文化を結び、時間と場所が連続的に混在する世界にしようとする世をあげての動きがある一方で、地方の文化やその場所に固有の表現の反乱という、それとは逆の傾向も共存している。この2つの力——一方は広がってゆこうとし、他方は凝縮しようとする——が抗する中で、時空間は形成されることになる。したがって、新しい建築は、多くの文化の共通項を持ちつつ、同時に、そこだけにしかない状況やコミュニティを詩的に表現するものでなければならない。

and touch, between the highest aspirations of thought and the body's visceral and emotional desires. A multiplicity of times are fastened, a multitude of phenomena are fused, and a manifold intention is realized.

Idea
It is precisely the realm of ideas—not of forms or styles—that presents the most promising legacy of twentieth-century architecture. The twenty-first century propels architecture into a world where meanings cannot be completely supplied by historical languages. Modern life brings with it the problem of the meaning of the larger whole. The increased size and programmatic complexity of buildings amplify the innate tendency of architecture toward abstraction. The tall office building, the urban apartment house, and the hybrid of commercial complex call for more open ideas more imaginative organization of a work of architecture. Organization of overall form depends on a central concept to which other elements remain subordinate.

In the experimental work of tentative investigations we remain explorers. This new freedom produces an anxiety that must be embraced with enthusiasm. The practice of a refined methodology, a technical skill, has now seeped through the osmotic membrane of a narrow profession into the open sea and must be nourished with a passion for discovery. New architectures can only be born if we leave habitual ways of working and reject unthinking methods.

Easily grasped images are the signature of today's culture of consumer architecture. Subtle experiences of perception as well as intellectual intensity are overshadowed by familiarity. A resistance to commercialism and repetition is not only necessary, it is essential to a culture of architecture.

The experience of space, light, and material as well as the socially condensing forces of architecture are the fruit of a developed idea. When the intellectual realm, the realm of ideas, is in balance with the experiential realm, the realm of phenomena, form is animated with meaning. In this balance, architecture has both intellectual and physical intensity, with the potential to touch mind, eye, and soul.

超現代の，流動する世界に向って拡がる一方で，太陽の光や石の肌合いなどを大切にする小さな世界を，ひと切れの土地に作ろうとするこの建築は，ブレイクの「砂のひとつぶの中に宇宙を見る」という言葉を意図している。場所の持つユニークな性格や個人ひとりひとりの持つ文化，ひとりの人間の精神性などの持つ詩的な輝きが，文化の違いを超え歴史を超えた現在といろいろな形で結ばれる。

建築とは，変形させながら結び付ける絆である。頭に抱いた考えと感じとったものの間に横たわる深淵を越え，あるいは流れと場所の間を結ぶ力，持続する芸術である。知性と視覚，聴覚，触覚の間，思想の目ざす高みと肉体の本能的，情緒的な欲望の間の，退屈なまでのギャップに建築は橋渡しをする。多様な時間をまとめ，雑多な現象を融合し，多種多様な意図を実現する。

理念
20世紀の建築では，最も期待できる神話を生むのは，形態でも様式でもない，それはきっと理念の分野だろう。21世紀が建築を送り出す世界は，歴史的な言語では意味をまかなえなくなっているだろう。現代生活は，さらに広範な全体像を必要としている。建築がますます大きくなり，計画の複雑さを増すとともに，建築は抽象化する傾向を強める。高いオフィスビル，都市のアパートメント，複合的な機能を持つ商業施設などは，より開放的な考え方，より豊かな想像力を秘めた建築の構成を求めている。全体の形式の構成は，それぞれの中心に据えられるコンセプトの如何にかかっている。

一時的な研究にすぎないような実験的な仕事では，私たちは探検家であることに安住してしまう。ここで手にいれる新しい自由は，熱情のとりこになるという新たな悩みを生むことになる。洗練された方法論，磨かれた技術の実践は，せまい職能に納まらずに，外海に浸み出すので，発見する情熱という養分を与えられなければならない。我々が，旧態依然たる仕事のしかたを脱し，思考を伴わないやり方を退けようとしないかぎり，新しい建築は生まれない。

容易に手にすることのできるイメージなど，消費におもねた建築の作る今日の文化のしるしにすぎない。そこで感知した微妙な経験は，知的な力と同じように，やがては馴れによって色褪せたものになる。コマーシャリズムや繰り返しに対して抵抗することは必要であるどころか，建築の文化の本質をなすものである。

空間と光と材質の経験は，社会的な問題に対応しうる建築の力と同じように，理念を発展させたことの成果である。知性の領域，すなわち理念の領域が，経験の領域，言いかえれば，現象の領域との間にほどよいバランスを保つことができれば，形態は意味によって生命を与えられる。このバランスがあるかぎり，建築は知的であるとともに物理的な強さを持ち，心と目と魂に触れる力を秘めたものであり続ける。

1 Light, Material and Detail
光, 材料, ディテール

Architecture intertwines the perception of time, space, light, and materials, existing on a "pre-theoretical ground." The phenomena which occur within the space of a room, like the sunlight entering through a window, or the color and reflection of materials on a surface, all have integral relations in the realm of perception. The transparency of a membrane, the chalky dullness of plaster, the glossy reflection of opaque glass, and a beam of sunlight intermesh in reciprocal relationships that form the particular experience of a place.

Materials produce a psychological effect such that mental processes, feelings and desires are provoked. They stimulate the senses beyond acute sight towards tactility. In the perception of details, colors and textures, psychological and physiological phenomena intertwine. Phenomena that can be "sensed" in the material and detail of an environment exist beyond that which can be intellectually transmitted.

The materials of architecture communicate in resonance and dissonance, just as musical instruments in composition. Architectural transformations of natural material, such as glass or wood, have dynamic thought and sense provoking qualities. Analogous to woodwinds, brass and percussion instruments, their orchestration in an architectural composition is as crucial to the perception and communication of ideas as the orchestration of musical instruments is for a symphonic work.

Like a musician's breath to a wind instrument or touch to a percussion instrument, light and shadow bring out the rich qualities of materials which remain mute and silent in darkness. Glass becomes radiant when its functional role is altered in transformed states of the material. Bending induces dazzling variations to a simple plane with the geometric curvature of reflected light. Cast glass with its mysterious opacity traps light in its mass and projects it in a diffused glow. Sandblasted glass, likewise, has a luminescence which changes subtly depending on the glass thickness and type, and the grain size of the silica sand used.

Metals can be significantly transformed by sandblasting, bending and acid-oxidization, to create rich materiality of surface and color. Integral to materials and their weathering change in time, the beauty of various colors and textures of oxidation also gives details a painterly dimension. Cast metals, aluminum bronze and brass also add to the palette of alternative materials, expanding the range of details. A variety of metals, such as copper, nickel and zinc, can now be electronically atomized, and sprayed nearly cold in a thin layer over a surface of a different material, opening up new possibilities for finished and plastic details.

The texture of a silk drape, the sharp corners of cut steel, the mottled shade and shadow of rough sprayed plaster or the sound of a spoon striking a concave wooden bowl, reveal an essence which stimulates the senses.

The experience of material transformations is immersed in the human dimension and the necessity for beauty. Materials form the tools that allow communication of a concept in the experience of an architectural work, regardless of its size. In material and detail, an intensity of quality, rather than quantity, stimulates the perceiver's senses, reaching beyond acute sight to tactility, reviving the haptic realm. The joy of living, and the enhanced quality of everyday life is argued in a quality architecture. It is whispered in material and detail and chanted in space.

(S.H.)

建築では、「理論以前の領域」で時間と空間と光と材料が人に語りかけて、そこにひとつの世界をつくりだす。部屋という空間で生じる現象、たとえば窓から射しこむ日の光、さまざまな材料の表面の色や反射、そうしたものがひとつになって、知覚領域のなかで互いに切り離せない関係が生じるのだ。透けて見える材料、プラスターの落ち着いた白、つややかに光をうつす乳白ガラス、そして一条の太陽光線などが織りなされ、高めあってそこにしかない経験の場をつくりだす。

このようにして材料は、精神作用、感情、欲望をかきたてるほどの心理的効果をもたらす。それらは感覚を刺激し、視覚を超えて、聴覚へと運んでゆく。ディテール、色彩、質感の語るものには、心理的現象と生理的現象が絡み合っている。ある環境を構成している材料やディテールのうちに〈感知〉する現象は、知的に伝達されるものを超えたところにあるのだ。

建築における材料の役割は、ちょうど作曲における楽器のようなものである。ときに美しく響き合い、ときに不協和音をたてる。ガラスや木材のように、自然の材料が形を変えて建築に使われると、思考や感覚を人に惹き起こすような性質を備えはじめる。また、建築にとって種々の材料の組み合わせかたが、設計の意図を感じとらせて、それを伝えることに決定的な意味を持つのは、木管楽器や金管楽器や打楽器などの編成が、交響曲に対して持つ意味と同じようなものである。

演奏家の息が管楽器に吹きこまれ、打楽器に一振りが加えられるときのように、光と影は、さもなくば沈黙の闇に潜まざるをえない素材の持つ豊かな性質を引き出してくる。ガラスが機能的な役割から一歩を踏み出して、素材としての別のありかたをするようになると、自ずから輝きを増してくる。たとえば平面ガラスを曲げるだけで、その表面で反射される光は幾何学的な曲面を浮き上がらせて、眩いヴァリエーションが生れる。キャストグラスは、あたかもその塊の中に光を封じ込めたような、不思議な不透明さのあるひそやかな光を沁み出させる。サンドブラスト加工をほどこせば、ガラスの厚さとタイプや吹きつける硅砂の粒径に応じて微妙に光りかたを変える。

金属の場合にも、サンドブラストや、曲げ加工あるいは酸化などの加工をほどこすことによって生じる著しい変化が、表面や色に豊かな質感を生む。材料の種類に加えて経時変化などが生じると、酸化のもたらす種々の色とテクスチュアによって、ディテールに絵画的な次元が加わることになる。アルミニウム、ブロンズ、真鍮などの鋳物も、材料のパレットに色を加えるので、ディテールはその表現の範囲をさらに拡げてゆく。銅、ニッケル、亜鉛などの種々の金属は、最近ではエレクトロニクス技術によって霧状にすることが可能になり、さほど熱を加えずに他の材質の表面に薄い膜を作ることができるようになって、自由な造型と仕上をもったディテールに新たな可能性が開かれた。

絹のドレープの風合い、切断されたスティールの鋭い角、荒く吹き付けたプラスターのまだらな陰影、あるいは彫り出しの木のボウルにあたるスプーンの音、そんなものを思い浮べれば感覚を刺激するもののエッセンスとは何であるかが明らかになってくる。

材料を変形するという作業は、人間の尺度に合わせつつ美しさを求めるためには欠かすことができない。材料とは、建築の大小を問わず、そのうちにこめられたコンセプトを伝える道具なのだ。材質やディテールについては、量よりも質が人の知覚を刺激して、目に見えるものを超え、触覚の領域を甦らせるからである。生きるよろこびと、日々の生活の質を高めることこそ、すぐれた建築との語らいがもたらすものだが、素材やディテールの中では、ささやかに交されていた言葉が空間という場を得ると、高らかな歌声となって響きわたるのである。

(S.H.)

Stretto House, Dallas ▷

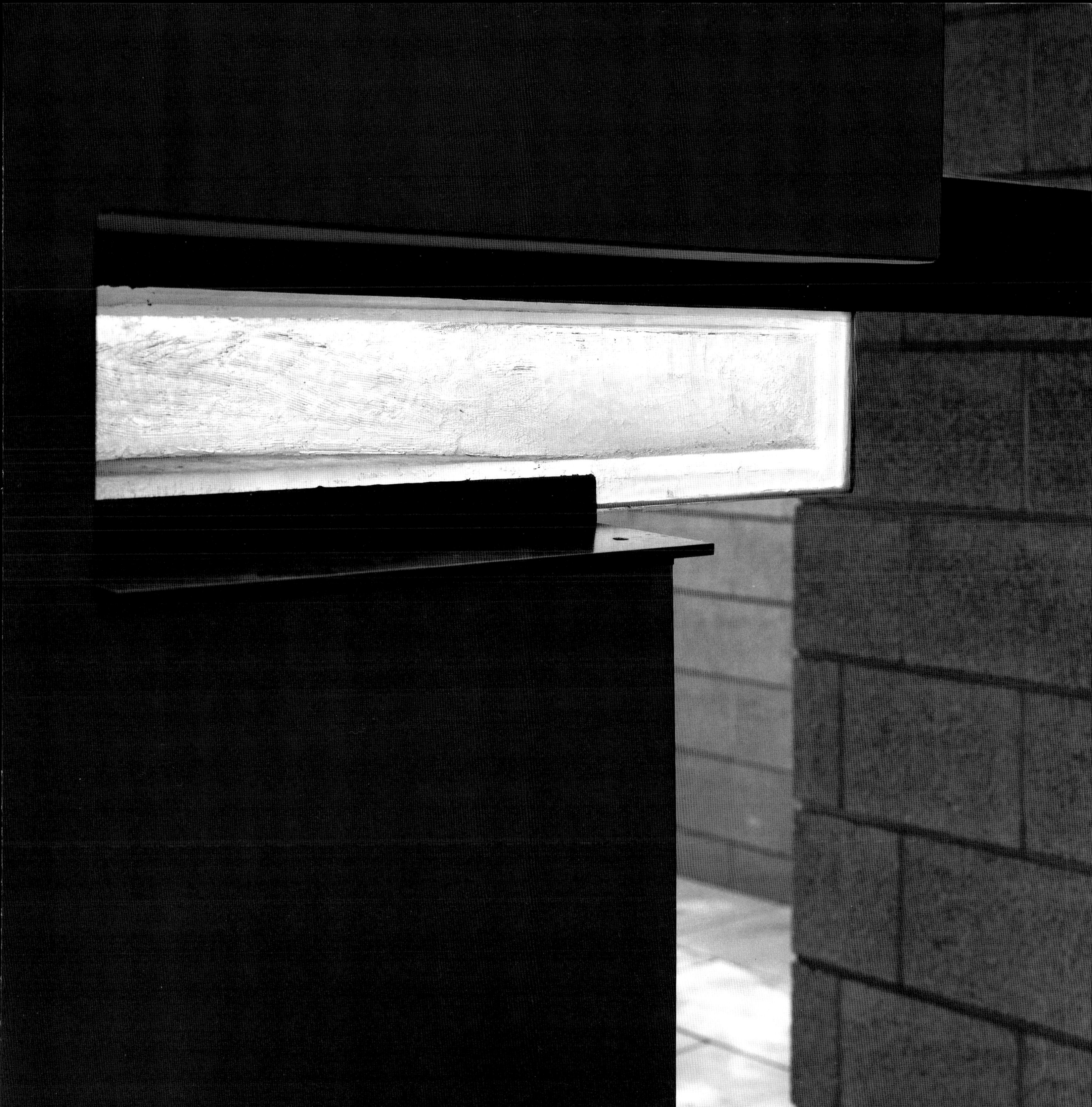

Cohen Apartment
New York, New York
1982–83

The existing rooms were removed, exposing an uneven slab and beam system (1939) in the L-shaped apartment. All views from the apartment are characterized by vertical buildings in the near distance.

A brass channel horizon line is set into the wall all around the "L." Above the channel (which is also a plaster screed), integral-color blue plaster is applied to the random beam and plate configuration, resulting in an Euclidian cloud formation. The plaster sky with flying lamps hovers over a floor of waxed cork. Inside the "L" an investigation of elemental architectural composition is explored in three modes: the linear, the planar, and the volumetric.

The dining area is of a linear mode: a linear chandelier is made of three types of lines, a linear table with four linear chairs sits on a carpet patterned with a great variety of lines.

The living area is of a volumetric mode with stuffed cylindrical sofa cushions, a volumetric coffee table and a volumetric carpet.

The studio and bedroom are in a planar mode with a planar drawing board, planes of walls that unfold becoming doors, and a carpet with woven planar elements.

An L-shaped wall dividing the apartment from the entrance foyer records this investigation in a progression of sandblasted glass drawing: planar, volumetric, linear.

コーエン・アパートメント

部屋は内装を取り除かれ、床はデコボコのスラブで天井には梁が露出している（作られたのは，1939年）という、L型プランのアパートメントだった。外を見ると、垂直にそそり立つビルが間近に並ぶ景観が印象深い。

このL型プランの壁全体に，真鍮のチャンネルを1本，水平に巡らした。このチャンネル（それがプラスター塗の定木の役割も果たした）の上の壁，天井，不揃いの梁の部分にブルーのカラープラスターを塗ると、ユークリッドの雲型模様が浮んだ。プラスターの空を背景にして、照明はワックスがけのコルクの床の上空を翔ぶ。L型平面を，建築を構成する基本要素によって3つに分類して構成した。線と面と立体である。

食堂は直線のモードである。線形のシャンデリアは3つのタイプの線で作られ，線形で構成する椅子を4つ並べた線形のテーブルが，ありとあらゆる線のパターンを織込んだカーペットの上に置かれる。

居間は立体のモードだから、詰め物を入れた円筒形のクッションや、立体感を強調したコーヒーテーブルやカーペットが置かれる。

スタジオと寝室は平面モードである。製図板は平面だし、開けばドアになる壁も平面、カーペットは平面の要素で織ったものだ。

アパートメントを玄関から分かつ「L」型の壁に，こうしたコンセプトをまとめるまでの過程がサンドブラストによってガラスに描かれている。面と立体と線。

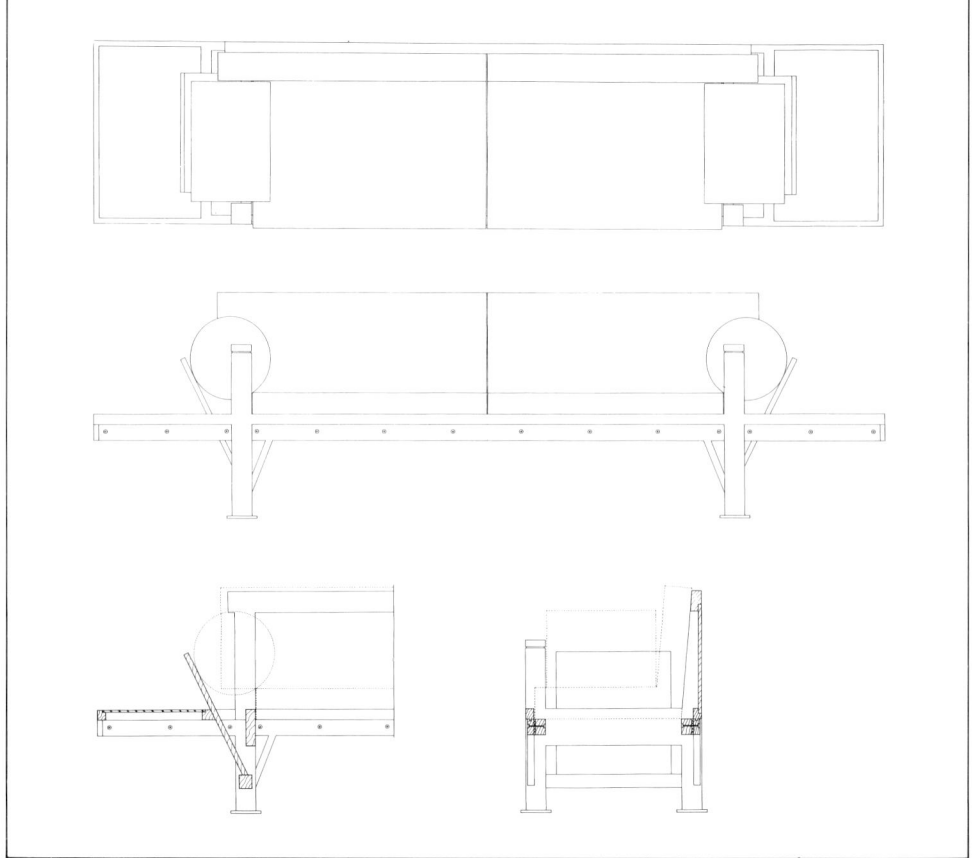

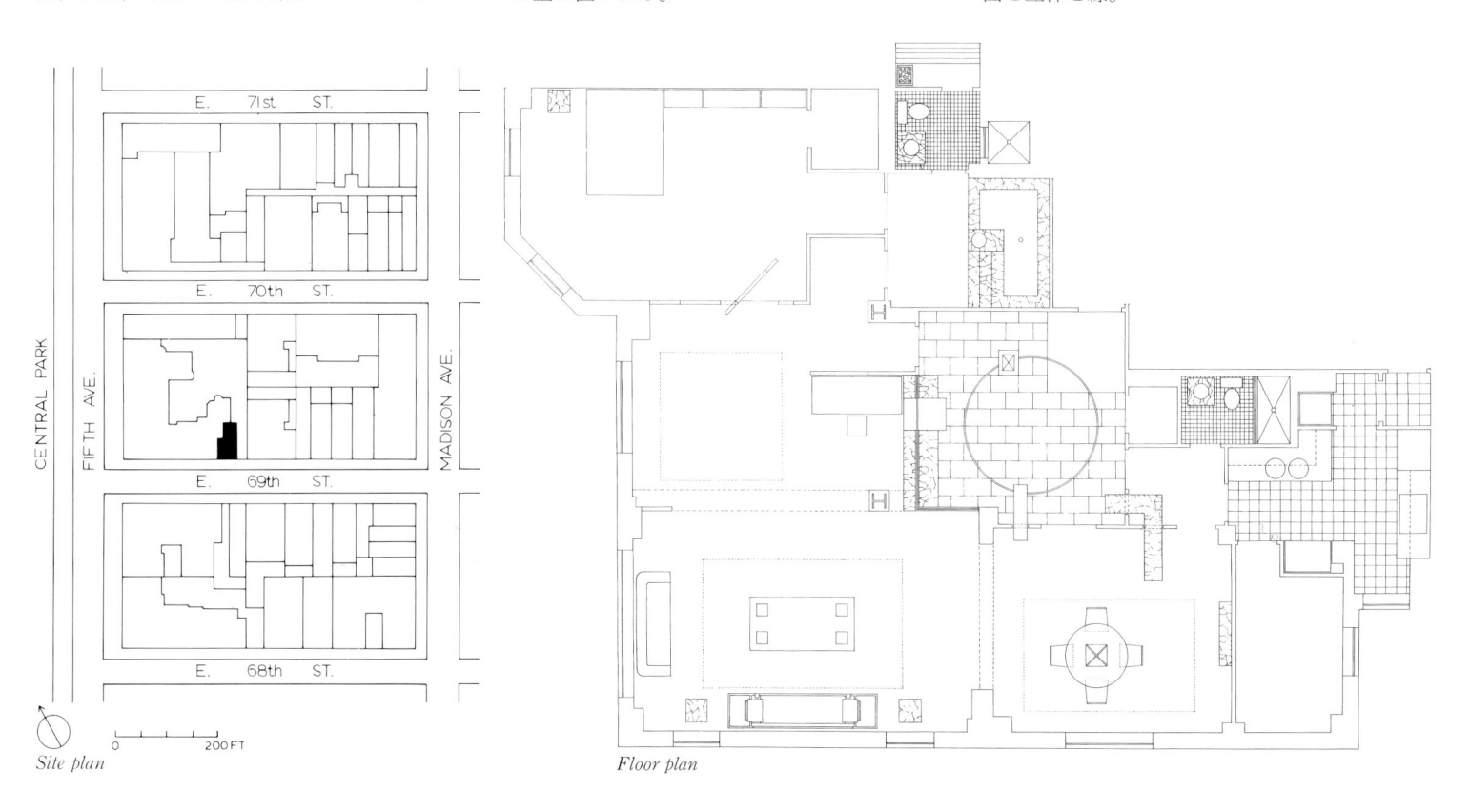

Winged sofa

Site plan

Floor plan

Perspective

View from living area to dining area

Living area and studio (view toward bedroom)

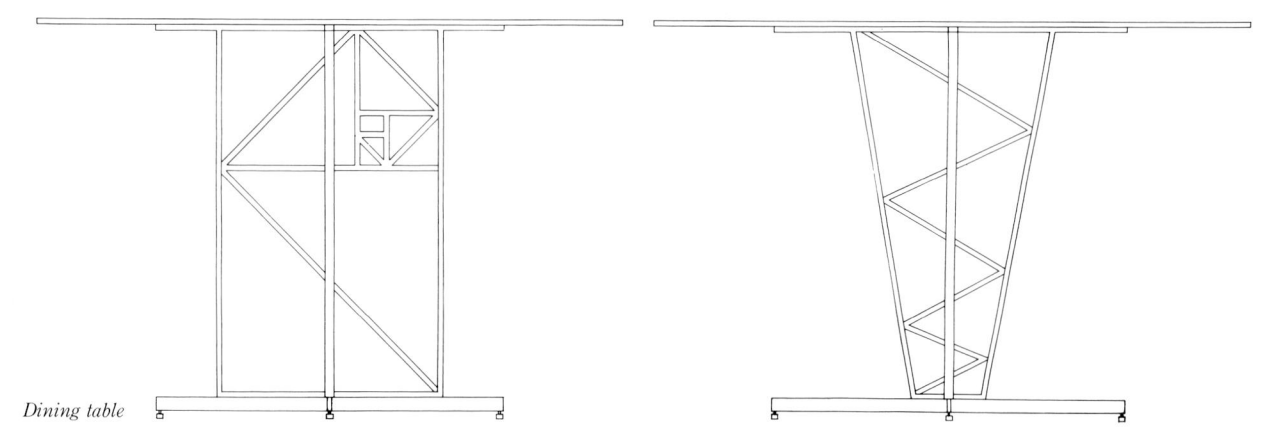

Dining table

Entrance hall

Light fixture

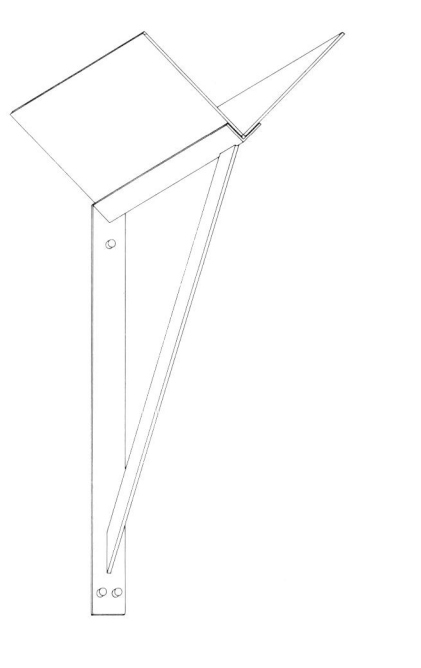

Light fixture

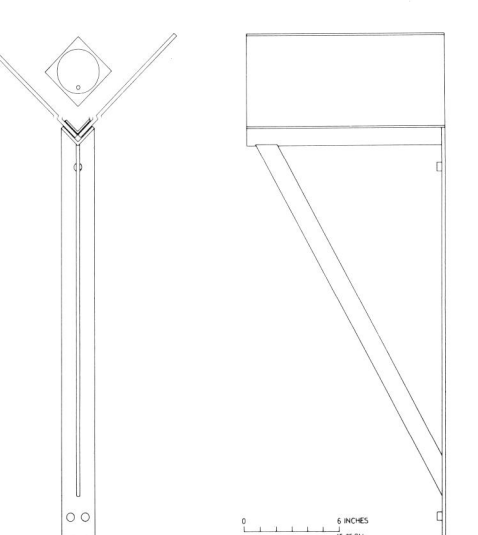

23

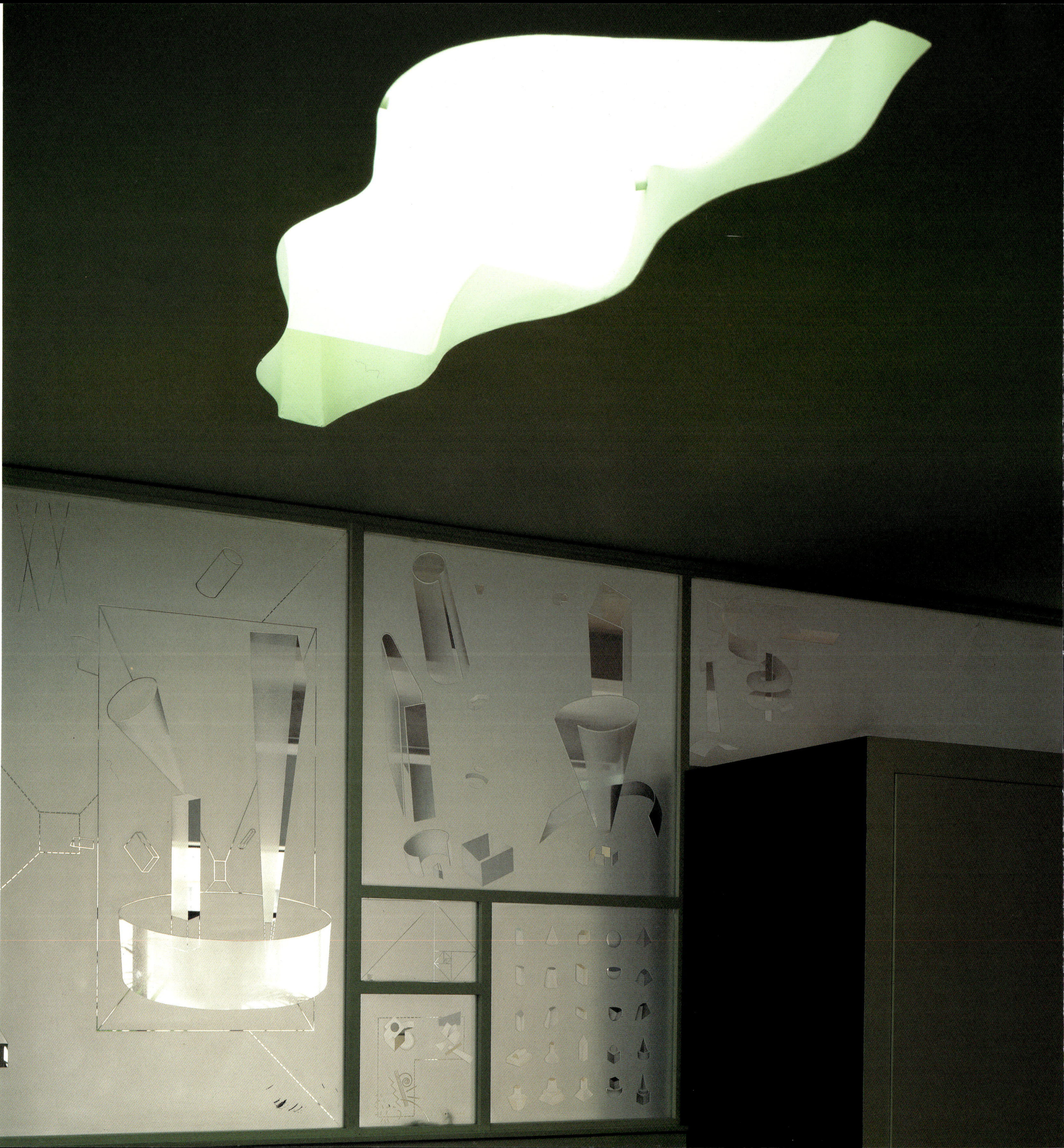

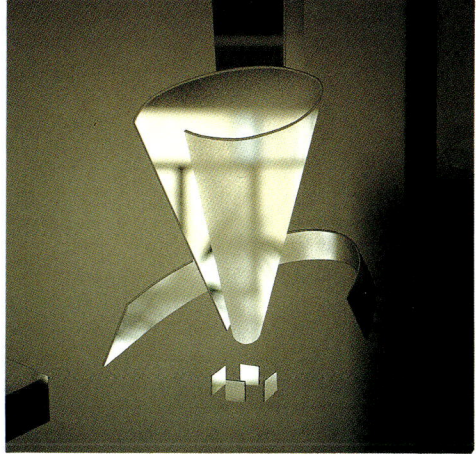

Sandblasted glass

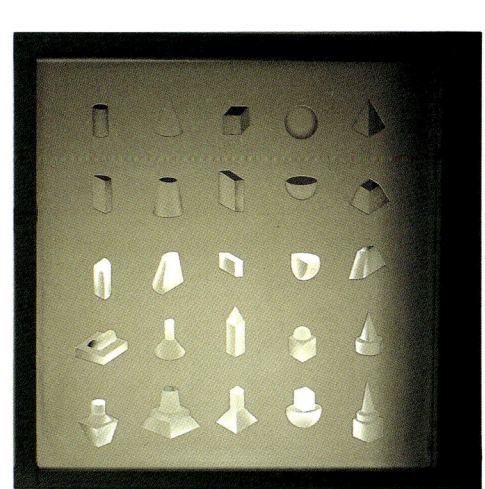

Sandblasted glass

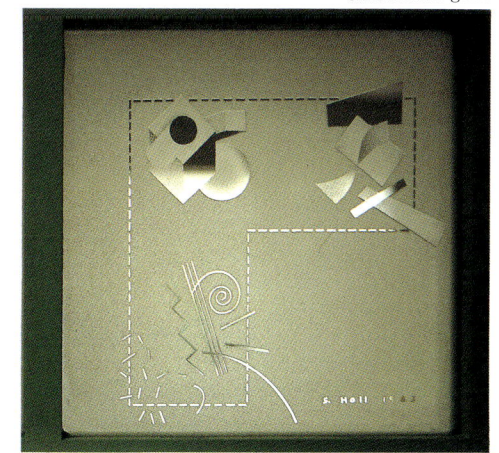

◁ *Ceiling light*　　　*Sandblasted glass*

Dining area

View from bedroom toward study/living area

Bedroom door: closed

Bedroom door: opened

Bedroom

Bedroom shelves

Bedroom shelves

*Pace Collection Showroom
New York, New York
1985–86*

Site plan

East view

North view

The site for the Pace Collection showroom is an existing two-story limestone structure with the corner of the building sliced back. A new foundation at the edge of the urban grid was set for the new showroom, completing the corner with a steel-mullioned window affording the maximum showroom glass.

An individual standing on a corner of a Manhattan intersection like Madison Avenue and 72nd Street is exposed to a hyperactive view of alternating forces of movement. The intersection is a counterpoint of one thing against another—fast against slow, stop against go—with the ominous command from the metropolitan authority, "Don't block the box."

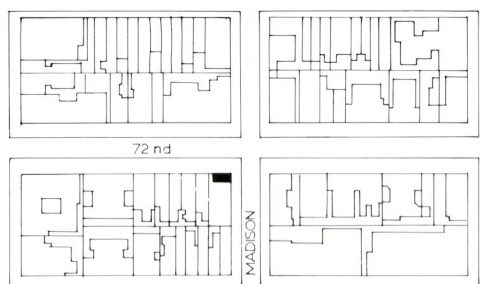

An idea of counterpoint (note against note) characterizes the essentially linear architecture. Small sandblasted amber glass panels are set against the horizontal steel bars of the main mullions. Along 72nd Street, the bars are predominantly horizontal, while along Madison they are predominantly vertical. The sandblasted glass drawings carry the contrapuntal idea to the detail scale. Along Madison Avenue, these drawings are in lines, while the 72nd Street facade shows the same drawings extruded into planes. It is as if the shop itself were a block of wood with end grain and edge grain differentiation. Each glass drawing freely interprets counterpoint in a different way, contrasting two kinds of lines, straight against curved, free-form against arc, arc against zigzag, arc against chord, etc. The awning is a curve against the straight lines of the mullions. Inside, the idea is carried further in the guardrail where a curve fuses against simple horizontal bars dislocating them vertically to miss connecting along the curve. The ceiling is a free contrapuntal arrangement of rectangular voids (containing lighting and A.C.) set against the flat horizontal plane.

ペース・コレクション・ショールーム

ペース・コレクションのショールームが入るのは，角のところが切り取られて後退している2階建の石灰岩の既存の建物である。区画の縁にそって新たに基礎を作り，スティールの方立でそこを包んで最大限のガラス面を確保した。

マディソン街と72丁目の交差点のような，マンハッタンの街角に立つと，ひきもきらず行き交うとてつもない動きと力にさらされる。こうした交差点はものとものの対位法の場なので——素早く動くものと緩やかなもの，停止と前進——そこには，「交差点をふさぐべからず」などという市当局のご託宣がある。

そこで，対位法(音と音の対比)に則って，この建築の線形という性格を表現することになった。細かく割り付けたアンバー色のガラスパネルを，主方立の水平のスティール・バーにはめ込む。72丁目側では，水平方向が強く，マディソン街に面するところでは垂直線が強調される。サンドブラストによるガラスのドローイングは，ディテールのスケールに至るまで対位法の考え方が一貫している。マディソン街側のドローイングは線で描かれるが，72丁目側のファサードは同じドローイングが面に形を変える。さながら，この店が木のかたまりで，一方には木口の年輪を見せ，他方が柾目を見せているようなものだ。ガラスに描かれた各々のドローイングは，2種の線でそれぞれに異なる形で対位法を表現する。曲線に対して直線，円弧に対比する自由曲線，ジグザグに円弧，直線の弦には円弧といった具合だ。庇は，方立の直線に対置する曲線である。内部に目を転ずれば，これが手摺にも表われて，曲線がシンプルな水平線にとけこみ，それが垂直方向に位置を変えて曲線とのつながりを断つ。天井には長方形の掘り込み(照明や空調が納められる)が散在する。これも水平に対する対位法なのである。

View from mezzanine

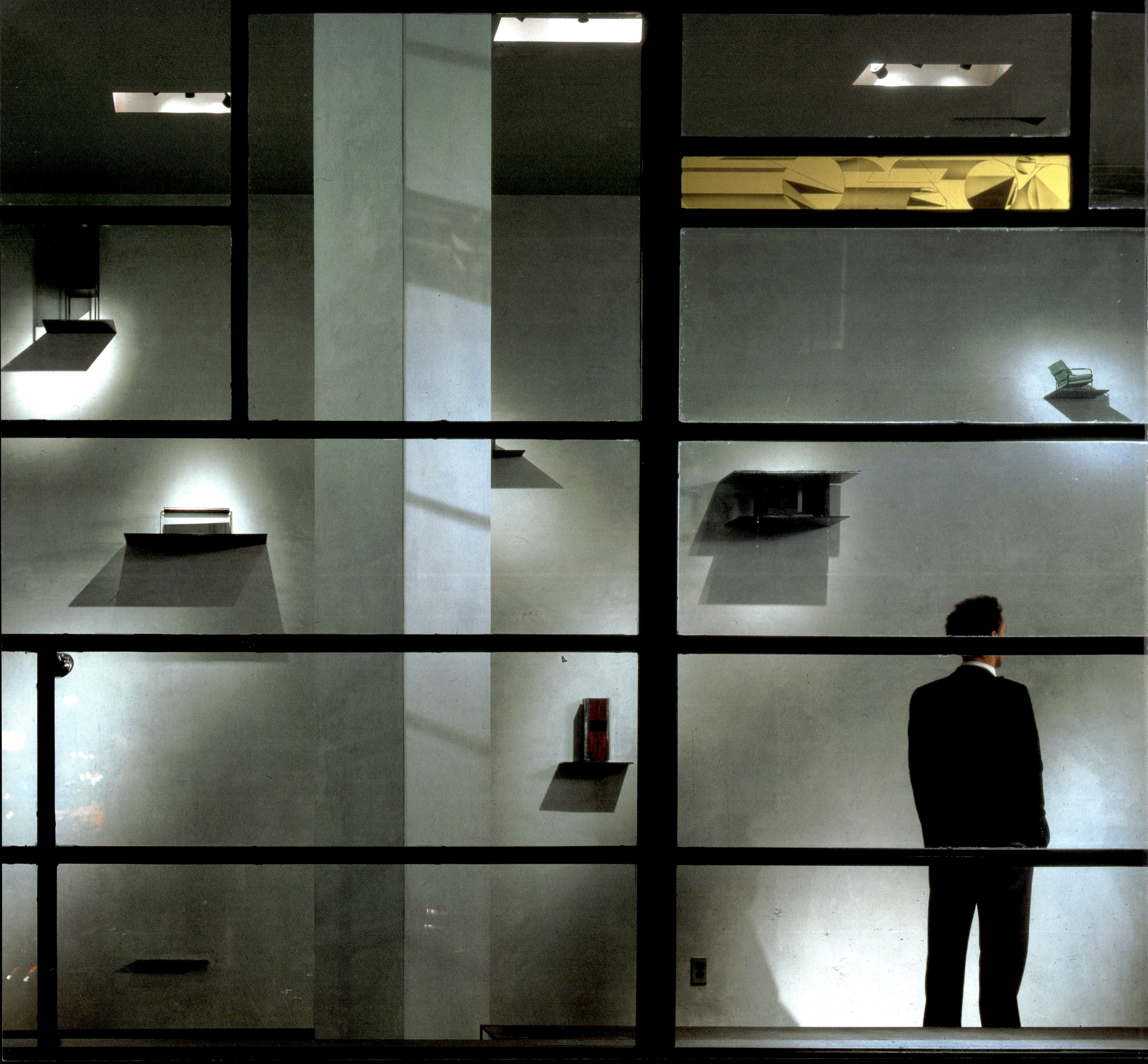

Plan

Section

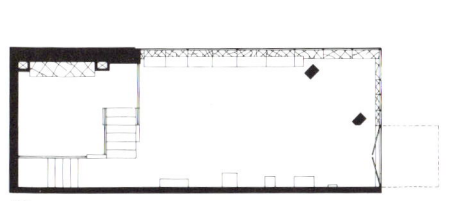

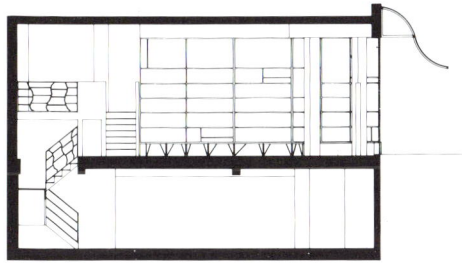

Second level

◁ *Night view*   *Staircase*

View toward mezzanine level

31

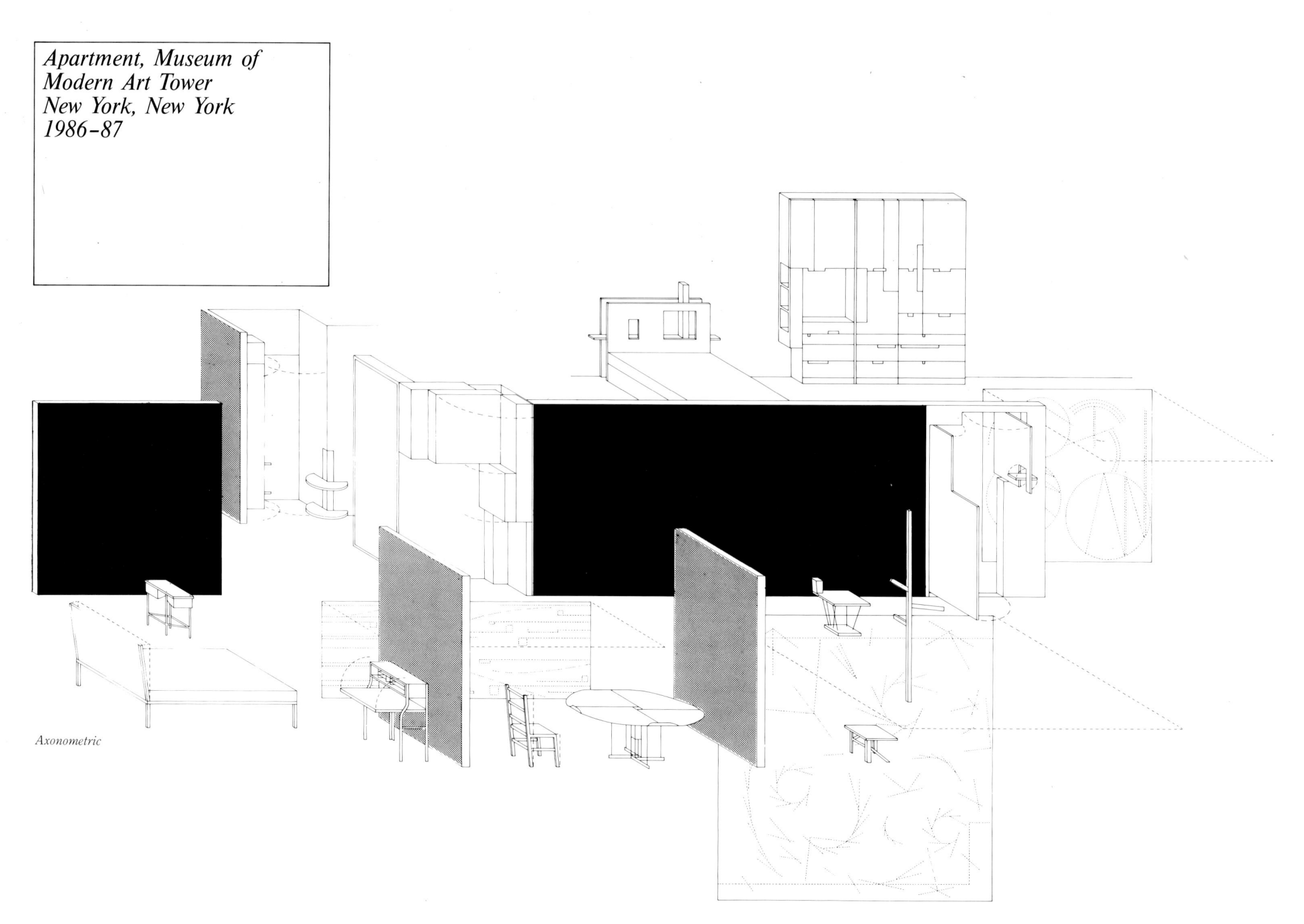

*Apartment, Museum of
Modern Art Tower
New York, New York
1986–87*

Axonometric

The interior renovation and design of fixtures and furniture began with a simple concept arrived at during the first encounter with the Manhattan site. The apartment tower rises directly up from its lot line, intensifying the experience of the Manhattan grid. Standing in the front corner window, the north/south and east/west geometry of the urban perspectives outside are particularly emphasized by the vanishing point in the Z (vertical) dimension. (From here the tower appears to be leaning over 53rd Street.)

This experience inspired the organization of all the elements in the apartment according to a lyrical illumination of the X, Y, and Z directions.

Plaster walls in the X direction are charcoal black integral color, while plaster walls in the Y direction are yellow. The Z dimension is emphasized in a long narrow corner lamp at the entry, in an intersected pole lamp near the main corner window, and in linear verticals in the furniture. Three wool carpets are fabricated for the apartment, one based on the X, one on the Y, and one on the Z dimension. Furniture specially designed for the apartment includes a dining table in which the XYZ dimension is emphasized at its steel center while its edges are vaguely free form.

The elements present the original idea in a variety of ways—literal, poetic, systematic, intuitive. Seen together they do not become a collection of more or less equivalent examples; the differences in means prevent this. Their association is less didactic and more mysterious; the elements serve to form a ground for each other. Only in this indirect way does the original XYZ idea prepare a relation between the parts.

This relation is spatial. That which is the object in one position is the reference in another. Their common result is a kind of suspension—a consequence of the suspended site, the vertiginous view.

MOMAタワー・アパートメント
設備や家具のデザインを含んで、インテリアを改装するためのデザインは、マンハッタンのこの場所にはじめて立った時に胸に浮んだシンプルなコンセプトが始まりだった。このアパートメント・タワーは敷地の境界線から直かに立ち上ってマンハッタンの街路のグリッドを強調していた。道路側の角の窓際に立って外に目を向けると、この都会のもつ、東西と南北に走る街路の幾何学的パターンのパースペクティヴが、とりわけZ(垂直)方向の消失点によってますます強められるのが感じられる(ここから見下ろすと、タワーは53丁目の通りに倒れかかっているように感じられる)。

このような体験がもとになって、このアパートメントのあらゆる要素にX, Y, Zの3つの方向性を用いた叙情的な光をあてることでデザインを構成しようと考えたのである。

X方向の壁はチャーコール・ブラック、Y方向は黄色のプラスターを塗った。Z方向の要素は細長いコーナーランプが玄関に、コーナーウィンドウのそばには照明を直交させてつけたポールランプがあるし、家具では垂直線が強調される。3カ所に敷かれたウールのカーペットは特注で織った物で、それぞれX, Y, Zの3つの次元にもとづいてデザインされている。家具も、この住いのためにデザインされた。中でも食卓は天板の周辺部分は自由な形態だがスティール製の中央部分では、X, Y, Zの方向性が強調されている。

様々な要素が、中心となる考え方を様々な形で表現する——あるものは文学的に、詩的に、あるいはシステマティックに、時には直観的に。それらをひとつのまとまりとして見ると、同等のものの単なる集合には感じられない。やり方がそれぞれに違うからだ。それら全体の、ひとつのまとまりとしての印象は、何かを伝えてく

View from bedroom

Furniture

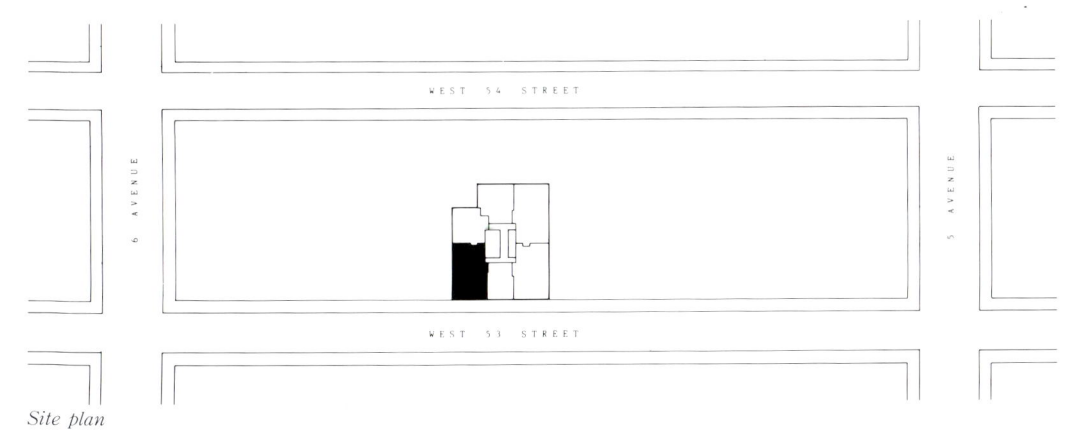

Site plan

Floor plan

るというのではなく,神秘的なものである。各要素が,それぞれ互いに他の背景となるのだ。このような間接的な形で,X, Y, Zという基本概念が,部分部分を関係づけるのである。

この関係は空間的である。ある所では主役を演じるものが,別の場では引立て役をつとめる。その結果,常に浮遊状況が生じる。マンハッタンに浮遊したこの場所と目も眩む景色がそれを生んだのだろう。

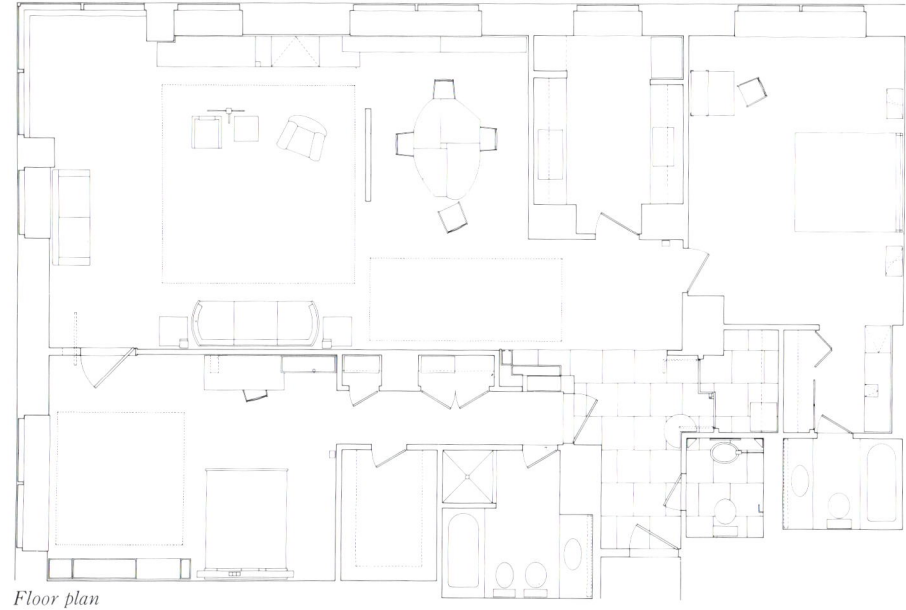

Bookcase

Dining area

Dining area

Door

Concept sketch

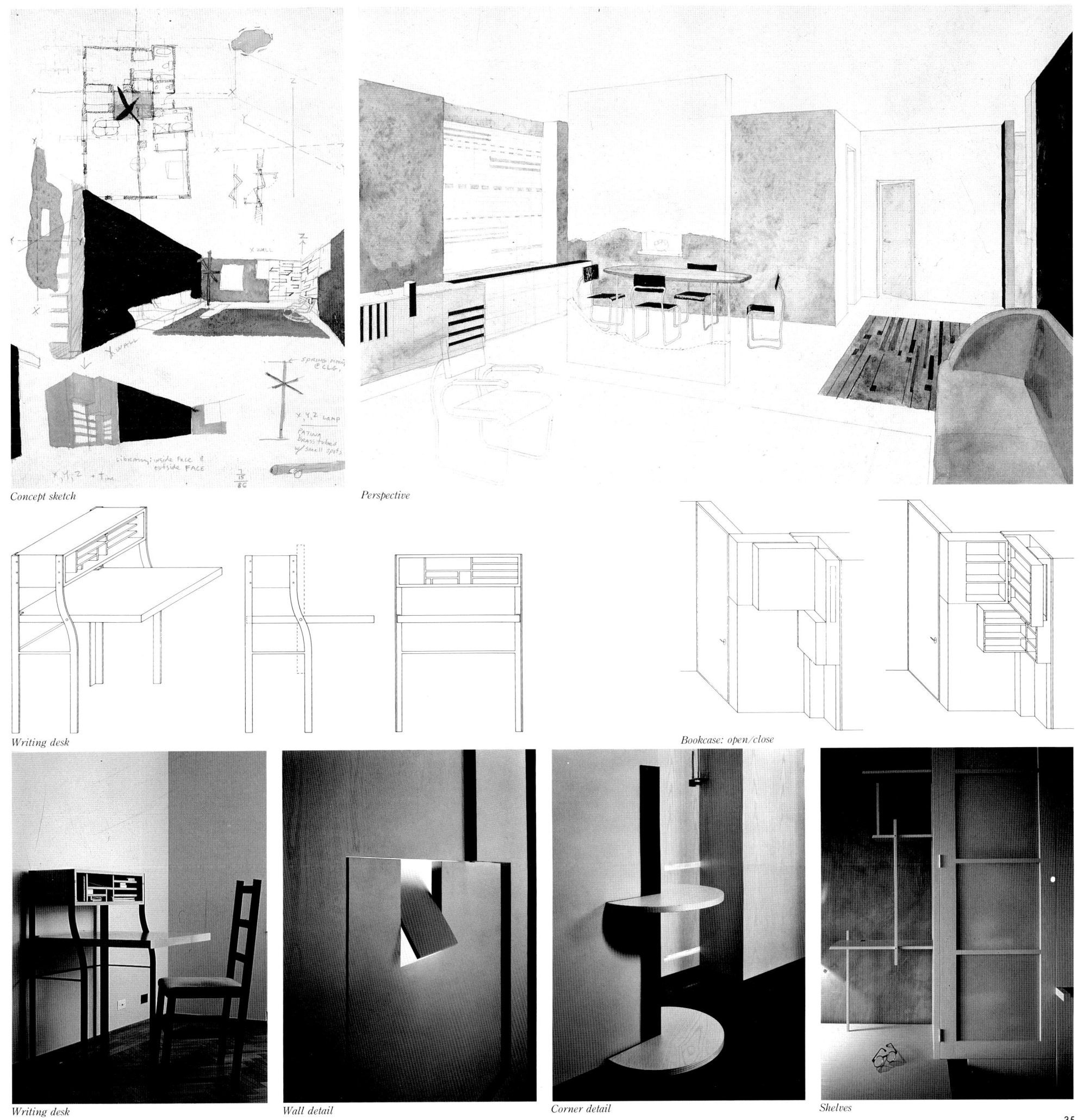

Perspective

Writing desk

Bookcase: open/close

Writing desk

Wall detail

Corner detail

Shelves

*Objects, Swid Powell
Carpets, V'Soske
New York, New York
1986*

As an exercise in elemental composition from line to plane and volume, several household objects were designed, and produced by Swid Powell beginning in 1984. An open language of composition from micro to macro implies a shift in scale. Possible combinations of lines, planes, and volumes in space remain disconnected, trans-historical and trans-cultural. They float about in a zero-ground of form without gravity but are precursors of a concrete architectonic form. They are proto elements:

Lines
Stems of grass, twigs, cracks in mud, fissures in ice, veins in a leaf, woodgrain, nodal lines, spiderwebs, hair, ripples in sand... the astonishing Gothic stone tracery of King's College Chapel, of Westminster Abbey, or of Gloucester Cathedral. The steel linearity of Paxton's Crystal Palace...

Planes
Ribbons of seaweed, palm leaves, cabbage, sediments, stone, elephant ears, sheets of water, wings, feathers, papyrus... the planar wall architecture of ancient Egypt; the temple of Luxor. The wonderful superimposed lyrical planarity of Terragni's Casa Giuliani-Frigerio or of Rietveld's Schröder House.

Volumes
Nautilus shells, pumpkins, watermelon, tree trunks, icebergs, endomorph crystals, cactus, the volumetric intensities of Roman architecture, the stone drums, the pure pyramid of Cestius or the Romanesque interior volumes of St. Front at Périgueux.

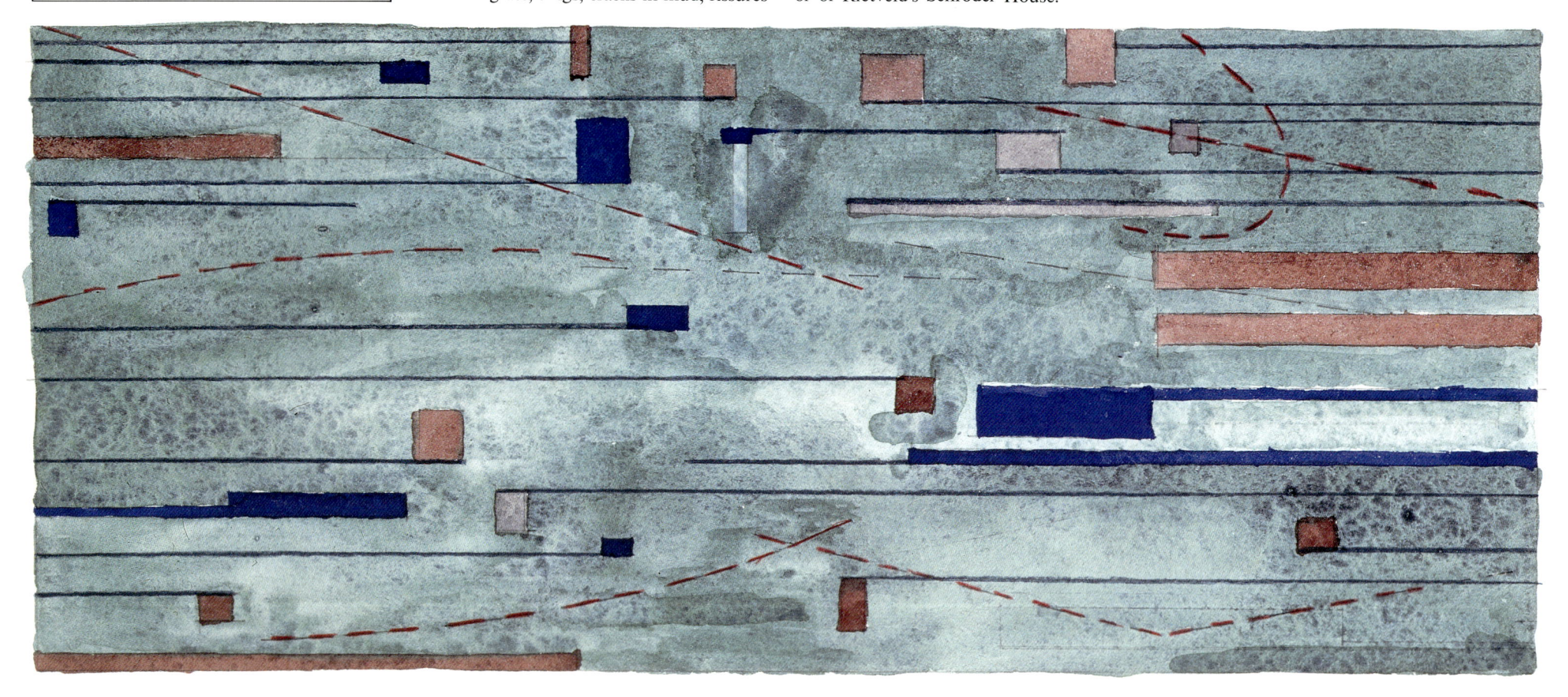

Studies for carpets

調度品のデザイン

線から面，面から立体へと至る基本的な構成の習作として，いくつかの家庭用品をデザインし，その製品化がスウィッド・パウエル社によって，1984年に始められた。ミクロからマクロまでの様々な構成が作る言語は，そのまま種々のスケールを物語る。空間の中で，線と面と立体のそれぞれが組み合わされたものを，あらゆる歴史と文化にわたって無作為に並べると，これらは重力のない形態のゼログラウンドに漂っている。けれどもそれが，具体的な建築形態を生む萌芽，つまりプロトエレメントなのである。

線——グラスの脚，小枝，乾いた泥地に走るひび，氷の裂け目，葉脈，木目，波紋，クモの巣，髪の毛，砂の風紋……キングスカレッジのチャペル，ウェストミンスター大聖堂，そしてグロスター・カテドラルなどの，石でつくられた驚くべきゴシックのトレイサリー。パクストンのクリスタルパレスを支えるスティールの細長い構造体……。

面——リボンのような海草，ヤシの葉，キャベツ，水の底に降り積もった堆積物，象の耳，水の膜，翼，羽根，パピルス……古代エジプトの建築の平らな壁，ルクソール寺院。テラーニのジュリアーニ・フリジェリオ邸やリートフェルトのシュローダー邸の，面が重なり合って詩的に語りかけるすばらしさ。

立体——オーム貝，カボチャ，西瓜，木の幹，氷山，内に結晶を秘める水晶，サボテン，宇宙に浮かぶ惑星，古代ローマ建築のヴォリュームのある力強さ，ドームを支える石造のドラム，セシウス神殿のピラミッドの純粋な幾何学的形態，ペリグーにあるサン・フロン聖堂のロマネスク様式による内部空間の造形。

Frame/clip box/vase

Volumetric plate

Linear plate

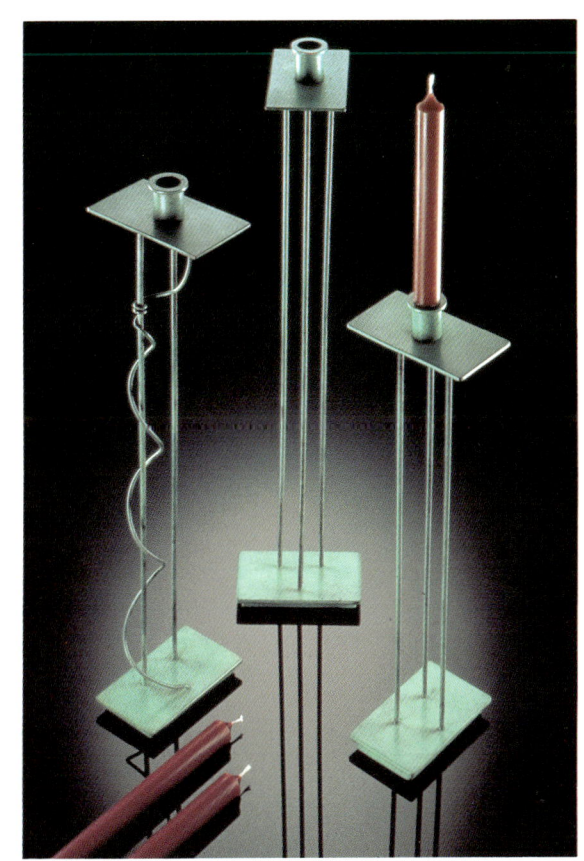

Candle stands

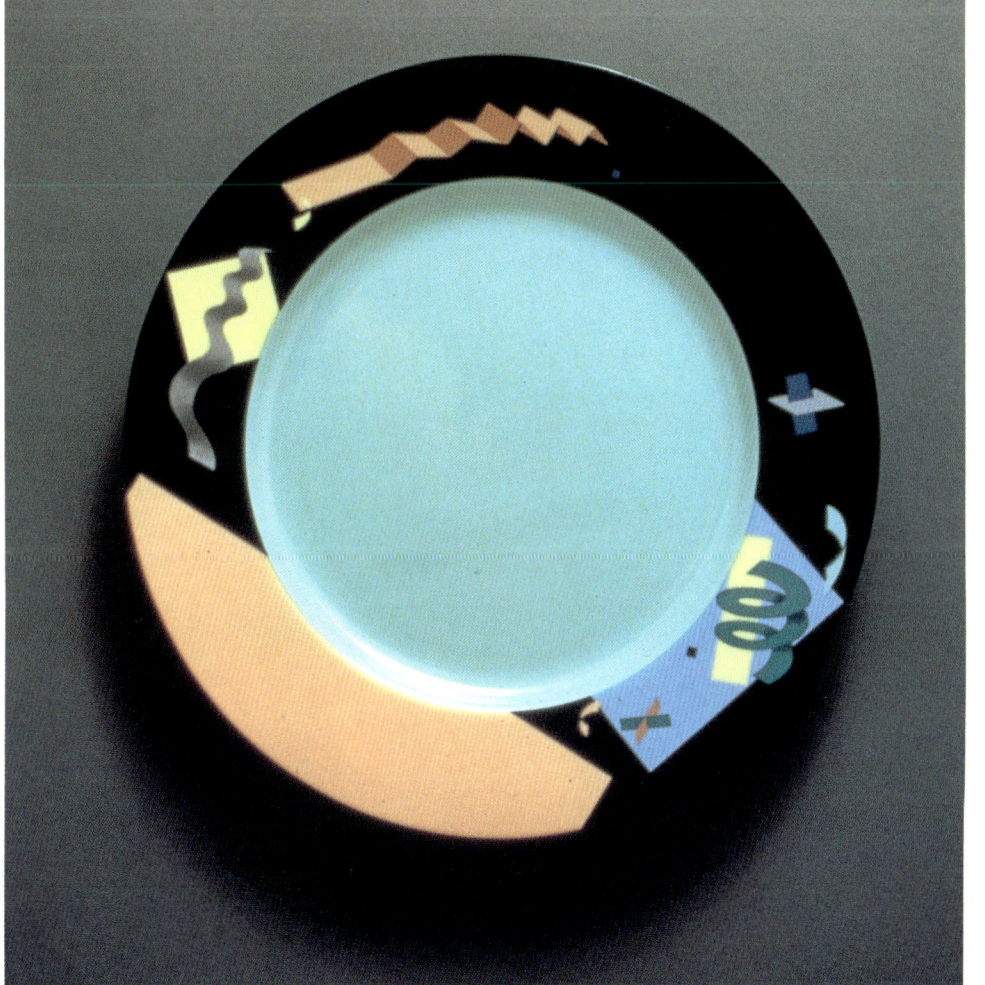

Planar plate

*Giada Showroom
New York, New York
1987*

The site is on a busy section of Madison Avenue, midblock between 72nd and 73rd Streets. The absolutely compressed condition of the 14- by 30-foot shop is situated with a large building above bearing down with more than gravitational force; economic pressure and time pressure together act like an invisible vise grip pressing the space in a psychological densification. The idea was to express the compression on the exterior and relieve it on the interior. All proportions are organized according to a logarithmic spiral of relations to the section.

On the exterior, cast glass, three-inch slab glass, and brass plates express densification. The brass plates that contain and define the front are acid-etched to a dull red with flathead and round-head screws spaced according to conceptual pressure. Bulging and bending shapes are heavy in contrast to interior elements.

Interior materials, bronze wire screen, brass mesh, and spun aluminum, express the lightweight. An eight-inch void below a "floating" terrazzo floor in cloud-like, hand-sprinkled terrazzo has pockets and trap doors opening up for various exhibit devices. When the wire skeleton mannequins with their cast glass shoulders are moved from pocket to pocket, the spaces below are being activated as anti-compression devices. Light ash doors at the changing rooms turn inside-out when not in use, giving their interior volumes back to the overall space.

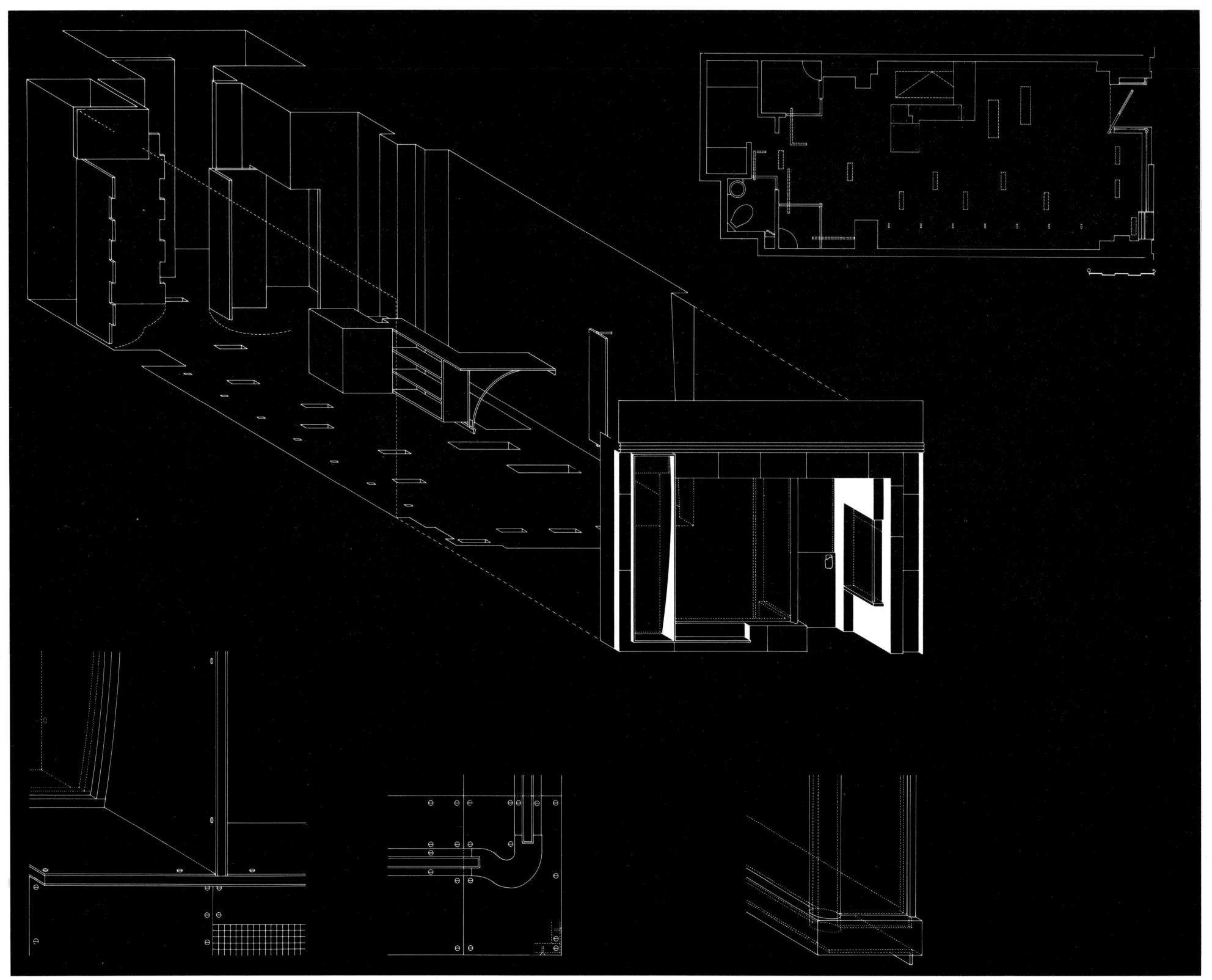

Floor plan, axonometric and details

ギアダ・ショールーム

敷地はマディソン街の72丁目と73丁目に挟まれるブロックの中央というにぎやかなところにある。14フィート×30フィートの広さに圧縮されたこの店が支えているその上の巨大なビルの重さは、ただの物理的な重力だけではない。経済的な圧力と時間の圧力がもろともに、さながら目に見えぬ万力のように締めつけては心理的な密度をあげるからだ。そこで、外部に対してはこの圧力を表現しながら、インテリアではそれを解き放つという意図でデザインを進めることにした。プロポーションはすべて、対数曲線に基づいて断面を決定し、構成した。

エクステリアでは、3インチ厚のガラスと真鍮板が密度を表現する。正面の一部を構成する真鍮板は酸で表面を腐蝕させて、沈んだ赤味を帯びさせ、そこに皿ビスや丸頭ビスを取付け、その間隔を想像上の圧力に対応させた。外部に膨らみながら傾いた形は、インテリアの要素と強いコントラストを示す。

インテリアは、ブロンズ・ワイヤのスクリーン、真鍮の網、削り出しのアルミなどの材料を使い、軽やかさを表現する。下に8インチの隙間をとって浮ぶ、雲状の模様をちりばめたテラゾーの床には、そこここにポケットやはね上げ戸を配した。様々な催しが行われる時にはそこを開けて利用する。たとえば、針金の胴体にガラスの肩を持つマネキンが、ポケットからポケットに移動されるとき、床下のスペースは圧力に対抗するしかけとして働く。試着室の軽いトネリコのドアは、使われない時には裏を出して開けておけば、そのスペースも全体空間の一部となる。

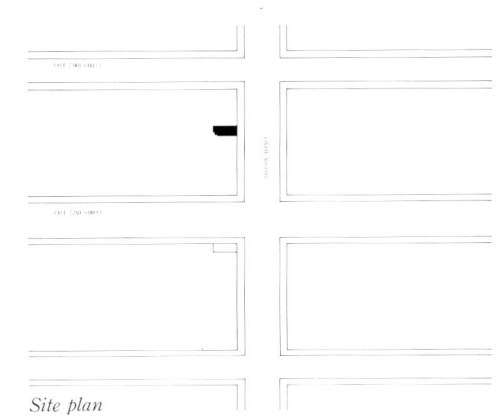

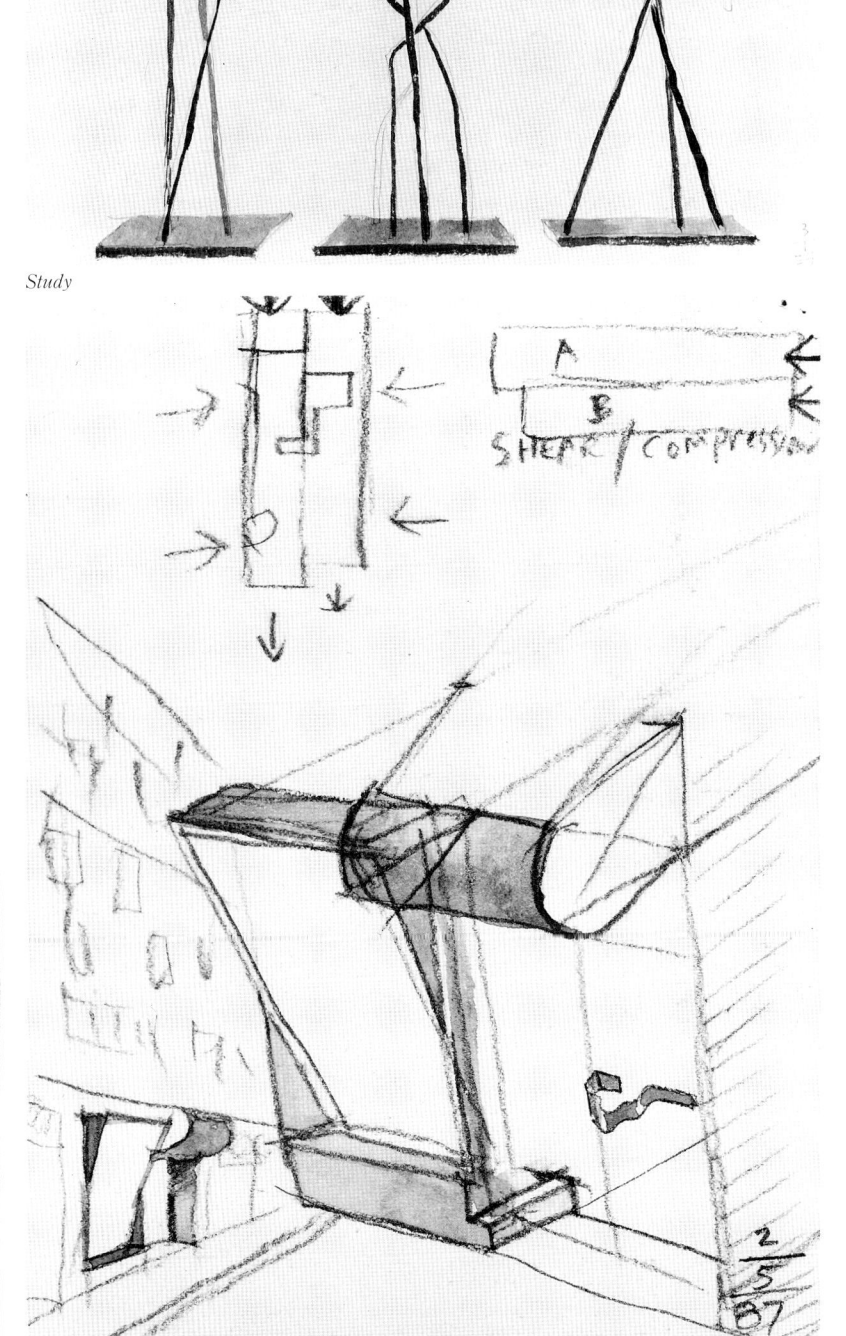

Site plan

Storefront

Study

Study

Storefront

Storefront

Interior view

Interior view

Sweater shelf

Display stands

Sweater shelf: chain link

Door pull

Window detail

Door detail

Sweater shelf: chain link

*Apartment
Metropolitan Tower
New York, New York
1987–88*

In the gridded city of Manhattan, ruthless economic forces have inserted a tall, sharp-pointed wedge of glass midblock between 56th and 57th Streets. The point that rises up from the street edge becomes the crucial character of the interior, its shrill angle of 40 degrees analogous to a shrill sound high in pitch (high in elevation).

The interior design is an intensification of this event or condition rather than a criticism or negation. No apparent traditional domesticity, no static rectilinearity or symmetry should attempt to reverse the direction already taken. Rather, what has started can take a more lyrical tone, increasing its non-rectilinearity and indeterminacy. A free floating spatial tilting is characterized by the four-degree tilt of walls that accompany the acute angle of the existing plan. A floating cloud-like black and white terrazzo floor underlies the new free-form walls. The slight folds in the curved walls are like folds in a paper airplane. In a range of sandblasted glass fixtures, interior night-lighting is diffused and indeterminant. An ultra-light curved wall fragment constructed in basswood and airplane silk is a kind of "Icaran wing" dividing the sleeping (dreams) area from the conscious area. Carpets are drawn from an intuited version of a piece of music, "Landscapes of the Mind," based on a painting by Georgia O'Keefe, "Sky Above Clouds." A floating cloud-like habitat striving for immateriality, this dwelling is in the evaporative dream state above the metropolis.

Site and floor plan

Concept sketch

Perspective drawing

Dining area

メトロポリタン・タワー・アパートメント

マンハッタンの格子の都市の只中,仮借ない経済の力学ゆえに,高くそびえる鋭角をもったガラスのくさびが56丁目と57丁目の間のブロックの中に差し込まれている。道路の間際から立ち上がるくさびの先端にこの部屋があるということで,内部空間が性格づけられた。その40度という鋭角は,高く鋭い音(エレベーションの高い所に位置する)のアナロジーかもしれない。

このインテリアデザインは,このようなできごと,もしくは条件を,あえて批評もせず否定もすることなく強調することであった。

伝統的な家庭らしさや静止的な直交性や対称性といったもので,すでに存在している方向を転換しようなどとするべきではない。むしろ,そこにある条件は,詩的な調子をさらに加え,非直角性と不確定性を増幅するという方向をとることのできるものだ。自由に漂う空間の傾斜は,平面のなす鋭角に加えて4度というわずかな壁の傾きで強められた。空に浮かぶ雲のような黒地に白のパターンを散らしたテラゾーの床が,新たに構成された自由な形態の壁の足元に広がる。曲面をなす壁には,紙飛行機の折り目のようなすじがある。サンドブラストのガラスの照明器具が放つ光で,夜の光は拡散されおぼろに広がる。曲線を描く非常に軽い壁の一部は,しなの木と飛行機用のシルクで作られているので,「イカルスの翼」を思わせながら,眠り(夢)の空間を覚醒のエリアから分かつのである。カーペットの模様は,ジョージア・オキーフの「雲の上の空」と題する絵をもとに作曲された「心の景色」という音楽の一部を感覚的に表現したものだ。空を漂う雲のような非物質性を,あくまでも追い求めたこの生活空間は,メトロポリスの上空高く浮かぶ,儚い夢の国の住いなのだ。

View from entrance hall

Living/dining area

Living/dining area

Wall detail

Wall detail

Bedroom corner (view toward Central Park)

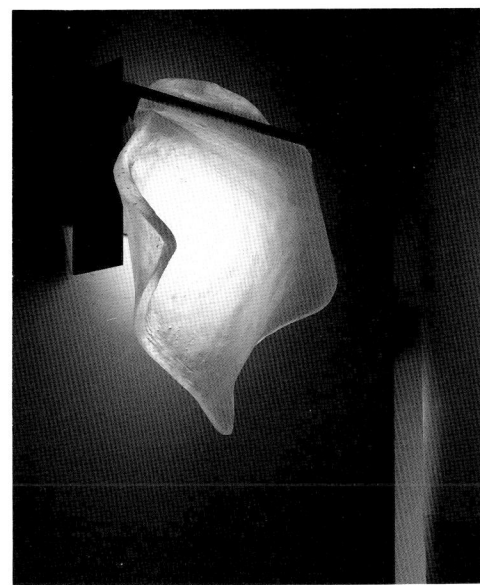

Cast glass light fixture

Living area

Furniture

Furniture

Reception

D.E. Shaw & Co. Offices
New York, New York
1991

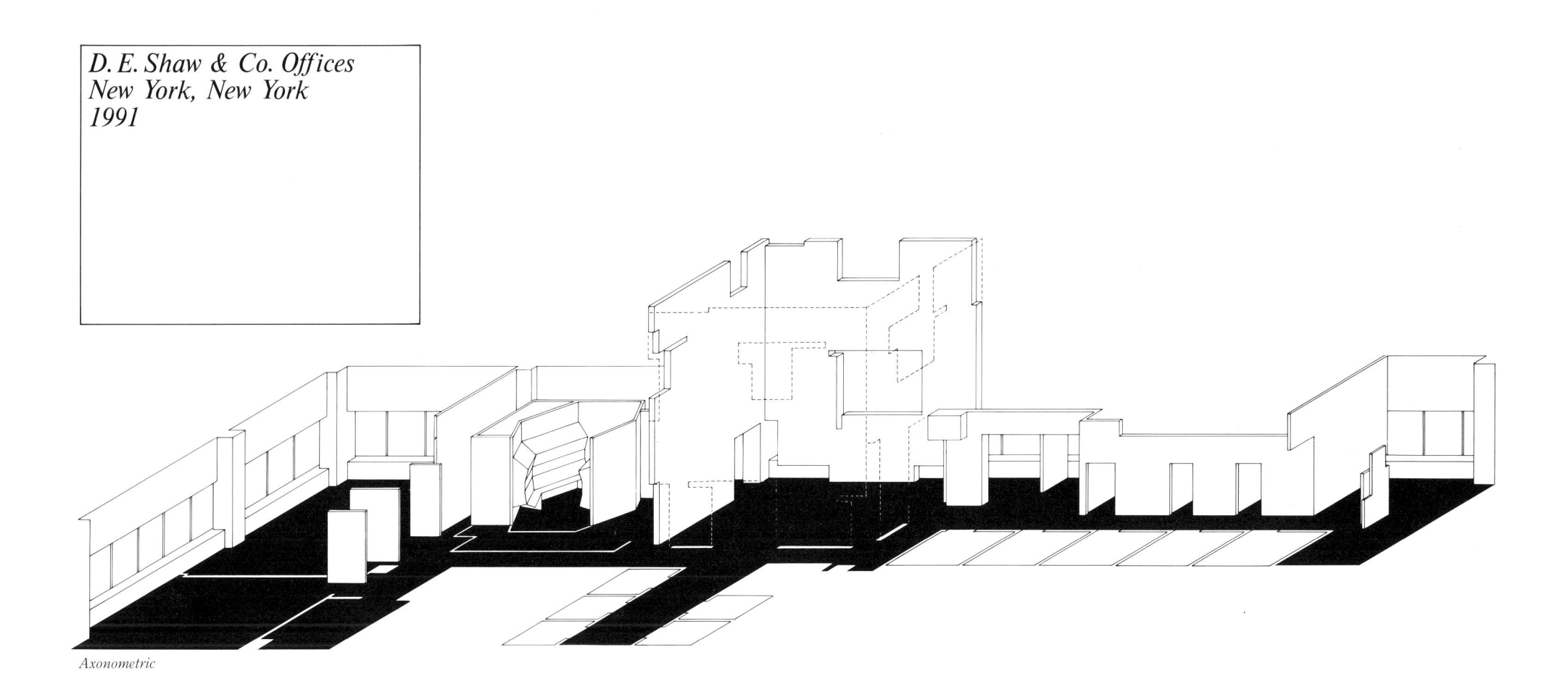

Axonometric

The top two floors of a skyscraper, mid-block between 6th and 7th Avenue on 45th Street, are the site of an experimental project exploring the phenomena of spatial color reflection or "projected color."

D.E. Shaw & Co., a young company founded and invented by a doctor in physics, works with the miniscule drift of numbers and percentages as measured in short intervals of time. Their extensive series of computers are hooked up by telephone lines and working $22\frac{1}{2}$ hours per day, at rest only between the time the Tokyo exchange has closed and the London exchange has not yet opened. One room in the facility contains more than 200 small computers. This curious and invisible program was given a parallel in the design concept of the interior. The metal framing and sheet-rock with skim-coat plaster was carved and notched at precise points around the central 31-foot cube of space at the entry. Color was applied to the backsides of surfaces, invisible to the viewer within the space. Natural and artificial lights project this color back into the space around walls and fissures. As the phenomena greatly reduces the intensity of the color being reflected, a range of fluorescent colors could be utilized on the unseen surfaces. One consequence of the exploration was the presence of the project seen from the street as a fluorescent green backside on the top floors of the tower.

The interior has a mysterious calm glow with surprising views as one moves around observing one field of reflected color through another and vice versa.

D・E・ショウ社オフィス

6番街と7番街の間の45丁目，超高層ビルの最上階の2層を使って，色彩を空間に投射して，「投影された色彩」という現象を探求する実験的な計画のための場が作られた。

ある物理学博士が創設した若い会社であるD・E・ショウ社では，ひっきりなしに流れてくるこまかい数字やパーセンテージを扱っている。彼等のコンピューター・ネットワークは電話回線で結ばれて，一日のうち22時間半動き続け，東京の株式市場が閉まりロンドン市場が開くまでの間だけが束の間の休止時間である。この施設のある部屋には200をこえる小型コンピューターがある。コンピューターの目に見えぬプログラムが，このインテリアデザインのコンセプトのもとになった。金属の下地にプラスターボードを張り，プラスターの薄塗を施して入口のスペースの中心に置いた31フィートの立方体の周りには，厳密に決定した位置に模様をつけV形の溝を刻んだ。立方体の外側の面に色彩を塗るので，スペースの中にいる人には直接目に触れない。自然光や人工照明の光がこの色を塗った裏側の面にあてられると，光はまわりの壁や割れ目から入りこんでくる。色は反射されて漏れて来るにすぎないからすっかり弱められてしまうので，見えないスクリーンには蛍光色が使われる。この実験の結果，街路から見ると蛍光色のグリーンに塗られた壁の背面がタワーの最上階にあらわれた。

中に入って反射光をうける場所を観察しながらひと巡りすると，神秘的で静けさをたたえた光芒の醸し出す光景に驚かされる。

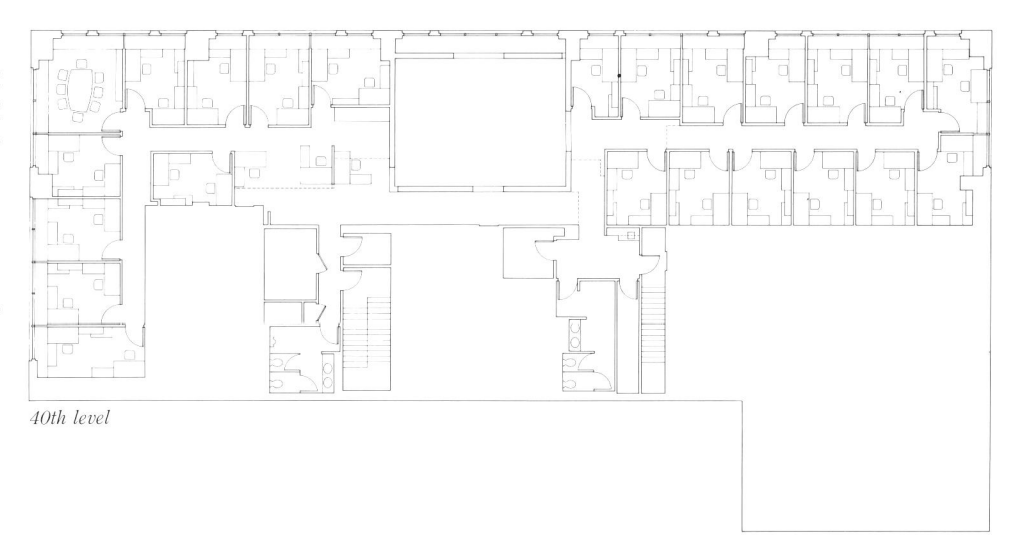

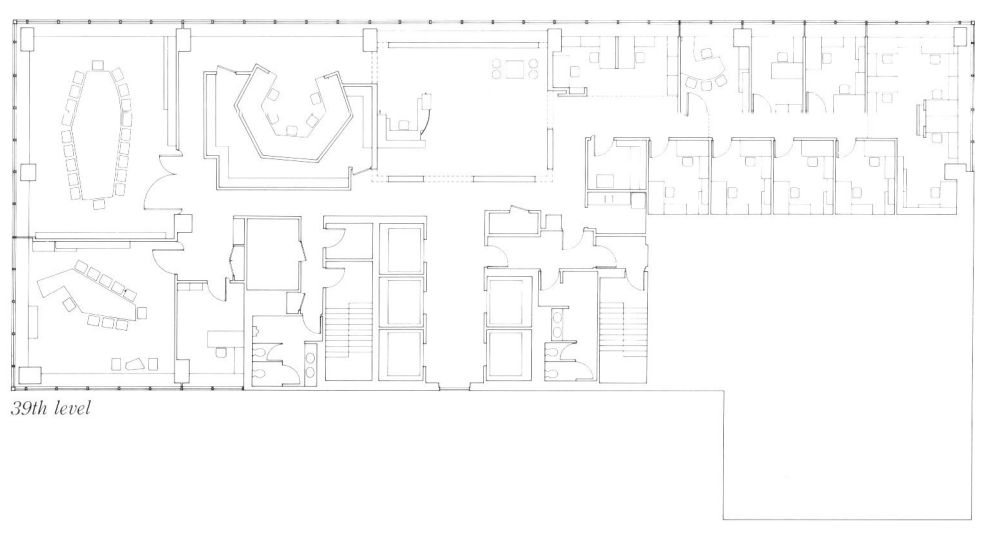

40th level

39th level

Reception

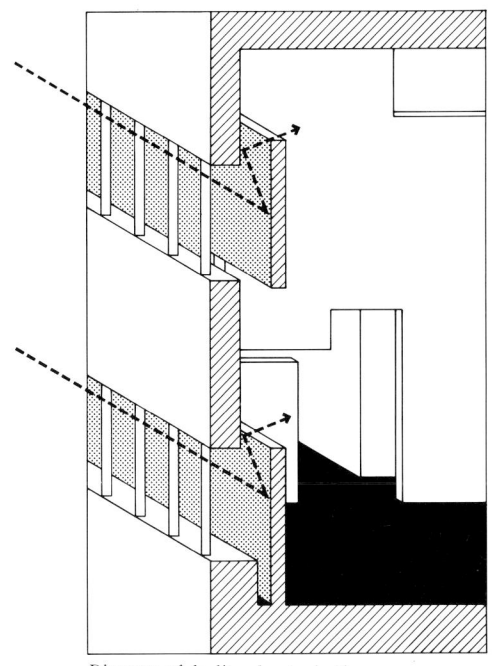

Diagram of daylit color projection

Upward view

Conference

Reception

2 Houses
住宅

The challenge of designing houses depends on the particular intensity with which characteristics of place, spatial and material ideas are developed. Experiencing the poetry of light and space is a confirmation of the exhilarating potential of architecture as a vessel for everyday life. From meditative spaces to inspiring details, architecture holds the potential to change the way we live.

Space is a plastic medium. From the absolute stillness of the underwater chambers of the 1976 Sokolov Retreat, which drift in a wash of gently moving sunlight to the cubic shift of space in the Metz House of 1980, and the sheared space of the Residence in Cleveland, 1988, architectural space and its unique relation to site is explored.

With a pairing of Solid and Void, or Cavity and Mass, the Metz House is an exploration of a program where concavities become convexities. Here, space is conceived as blocks of ice shearing past one another, yet overlapping—a study in principles which Adolf Loos developed in the "Raum Plan."

Space becomes fluid in the 1989 Stretto House in Dallas, Texas. The reading of the existing stream and pools of water created by dams on the site is transformed into "aqueous space." A light steel and glass structure "flows" through four concrete-block "spatial dams." An obsession with the relation of music and architecture has shown promising ground for research since the "Music and Architecture" design experiments were begun in the fall of 1984 at Columbia University. The Stretto House, constructed as an analogue of Bela Bartok's *Music for Strings, Percussion, and Celeste,* concretizes liquid spatial concepts and explores new possibilities for domestic space.

"Hinged Space," or the space of "participating walls," was developed as a means of opening cramped interiors in Manhattan Apartments in the 1983 Cohen Apartment renovation. Lightweight hollow core doors and pivot hinges allowed the transformation of interior spaces by the inhabitants. This dynamic spatial shifting was taken to a large scale in "Void Space/Hinged Space" housing in Fukuoka, Japan in 1990.

The space of the oceanic horizon embraced in the body of the house became a point of departure for two ocean-front houses designed in 1984. In the Leucadia Oceanfront House, the central portion of the house is removed to form a void which brackets the Pacific Ocean horizon. The Martha's Vineyard House is the metaphor of a skeleton. The horizon is always seen through the delicate ribs of its linear structure. In each of these projects, an economy of means fuses with the desire for a spiritual connection to the site.

The house is a home for the soul, the heart and the spirit. It is a container for the day's light, from the pale yellow of dawn to the deep blue of twilight. It is a box for the existential objects of life. It is a vessel for imagination, laughter, and emotion . . . and a silent space for the poetic sense of life.   *(S.H.)*

住宅の設計に挑戦するには，場所の持つ特性や，空間と材料についての思考を展開することに，並々ならぬ熱意を注がなければならない。光と空間の詩を体験するということは，日常生活の器としての建築の，人を鼓舞する能力を知ることである。瞑想的な空間から，生気に満ちた空間にいたるまで，建築には私たちの生き方を変える力が秘められている。

空間とは，造型的なメディアである。1976年のソコロフ氏の隠れ家の水面下の部屋のように，おだやかにたゆたう日の光に洗われて漂う孤絶の中の静寂から，1980年のメッツ邸でのキュービックな空間への転換，1988年の，切り分けるような形でつくったクリーヴランドの住宅に至るまで，建築空間と敷地との間のユニークな関係のあり方を探求して来た。

虚と実，あるいは，空洞とマッスを組み合わせるプランニングによって，凹面が凸面に姿を変えてゆく構成を求めたのがメッツ邸であった。ここでは，空間を，互いに切り込まれ重なり合う氷の固まりと考え，アドルフ・ロースが「ラウム・プラン」で展開した原理の演習を試みた。

1989年のテキサス州ダラスのストレット・ハウスでは，空間が流体になる。敷地を流れる小川と，それをせきとめて作られていた池を読みとって，それを「水の空間」という形にした。軽量鉄骨とガラスの構造がコンクリートブロックでつくられた4つの「空間ダム」を「流れる」のである。1984年の秋，コロンビア大学で始めたデザイン実験以来とりつかれてきた，音楽と建築の関係の探求に明るい地平を開くことができたのがこの住宅である。ベラ・バルトークの「弦楽器と打楽器とチェレスタのための音楽」になぞらえてつくられたストレット・ハウスは，流体空間というコンセプトを実現して住空間の新たな可能性を探るものである。

「ヒンジド・スペース」あるいは「参加する壁」のある空間は，1983年のコーエン・アパートメントの改装で，マンハッタンのアパートメントの狭く閉ざされた内部空間を開放する手段として考え出されたものだった。軽いフラッシュドアとピボットヒンジを使うことで，住人が自分の手で内部空間を変えることを可能にした。この動的な空間転換の仕掛けを大規模に試みたのが1990年の福岡のハウジング，〈ヴォイド・スペース／ヒンジド・スペース〉である。

外洋の水平線を住宅の中に抱き込む空間をつくろうという意図が出発点になって，外洋に面する2つの住宅が，1984年に設計された。リューカディア・オーシャンフロント・ハウスでは，住宅の中央部を取り去って，その中から見ると太平洋の水平線を開口の端から端にかけわたしたように見える空間をつくった。マーサズ・ヴィンヤードの家は，骨格のメタファーとして作られた。直線で表現したこの家の，肋骨のように並ぶ細い列柱を通して，常に水平線が望める。この2つの住宅はいずれも，費用を切りつめることが敷地との精神的な結びつきを求めることと，うまく融合したものだった。

住宅とは，魂と心と精神の拠り所となるものだ。夜明けの青みを帯びた淡黄色からはじまって，たそがれ時の深い青に至る，日の光の容れ物でもある。生活のための物たちを仕舞う箱。想像力と笑いと感動のための器……そして生活の中の詩的な感覚に捧げられた静謐な空間。

(S.H.)

Stretto House, Dallas ▷

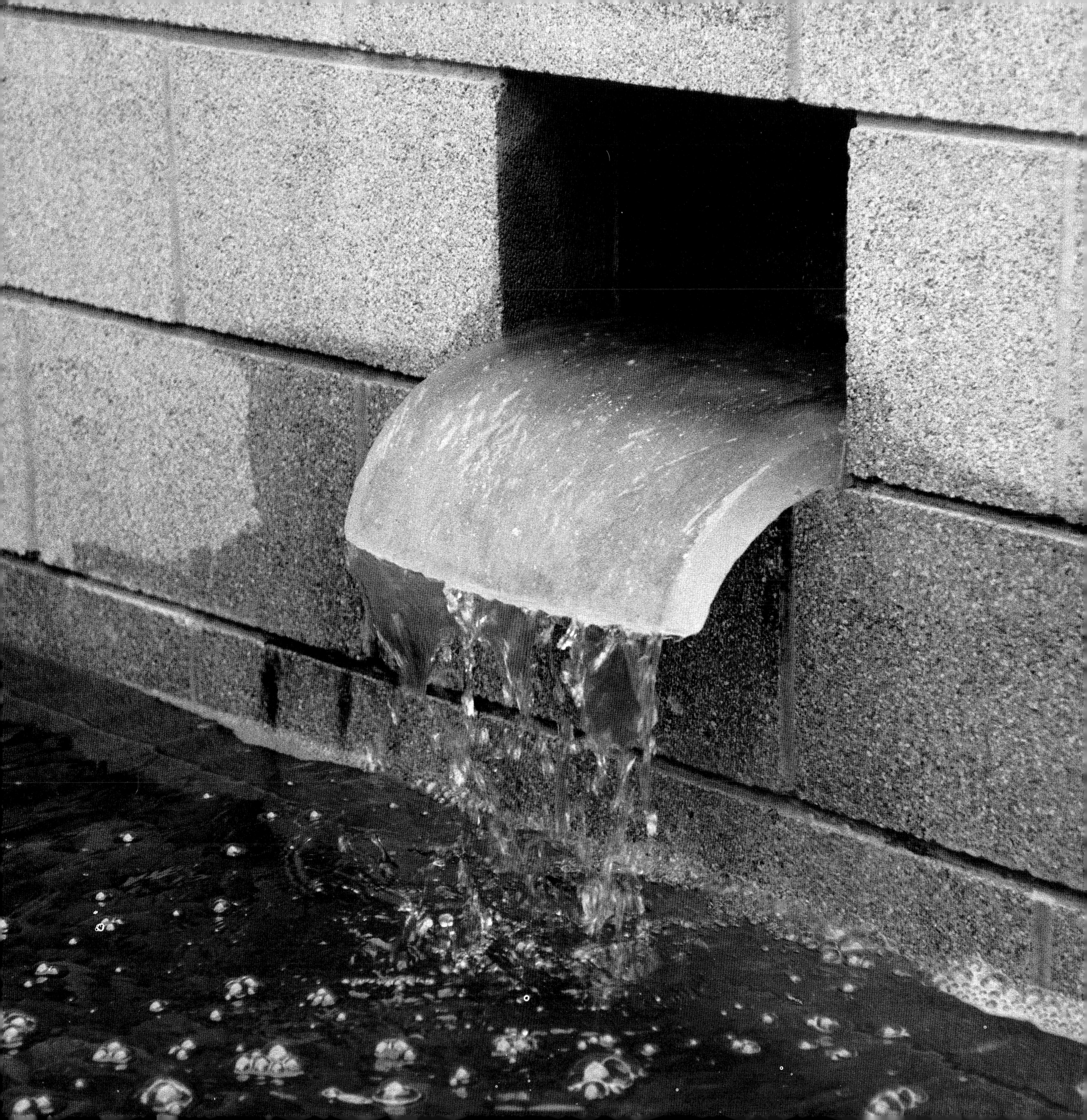

Sokolov Retreat
St. Tropez, France
1976

The noise and confusion of vacation crowds in the harbor of St. Tropez suggested the need for a retreat from a vacation house. The retreat is easily accessible from the client's waterfront house. Silence and solitude are primary concerns.

The retreat is underwater, anchored in front of the existing house at the edge of the harbor. Floating four centimeters below the surface of the water, the chamber is invisible except for the hollow glass block towers for light and air. The towers extend upwards to guard against waves and to increase air circulation via the principle of the chimney draft.

The effort required for entry contributes to the sensation of a retreat; one must row from the mainland, secure the rowboat, and, with shoes off and trousers rolled, cross the submerged deck to the tower containing the entry stair.

The area of the plan stretches into a cruciform, like a catamaran leaning in two directions, to minimize rocking. Within the plan, one can retreat toward the ends to the hammocks or sit in the central meeting area, which has a glass bottom. The hollow glass block towers are at the endpoints of the plan for the best distribution of light and air. One tower is equipped with a ladder allowing eccentric guests the opportunity to dive off into the bay.

The structure is resin-coated ferroconcrete, a thin shell construction with layered wire mesh. Automatic sump pump and adjustable ballast in the double bottom maintain flotation and protect against overloading and listing. The towers are steel-secured glass block with silicone joints and acrylic rain flaps. Floors and walls are polished pigmented concrete. The hammocks are uncolored canvas.

ソコロフ邸の隠れ家

サントロペの港の喧騒と混乱のほどは，別荘からさらに引きこもることのできる隠れ家が欲しいという要望にうなずかせるに充分なものがあった。隠れ家へは，海辺に建つクライアントの別荘から，たやすく行くことができる。そこでは，静けさの中で孤独にひたれることが，すべてに優先した。

隠れ家は水面下にあって，港のはずれにある別荘の目の前に繋留される。水面下4cmに浮ぶ部屋は外からは見えない。水面の上には光と空気を採り入れるガラスブロックの塔が立つのが見えるだけだ。上にのびる塔は，寄せる波をかわし，煙突効果で空気の循環を促すのである。

ここに辿り着くまでには，多少の手間をかけねばならないために，いっそう隠れ家らしさが増すことになった。岸から漕いでやって来たボートを舫うと，まず靴を脱ぎ，ズボンのすそを折り上げてから水面下にかくれたデッキを渡って，階段のある塔にゆく，という具合なのだ。

平面形は十字をなし，さながら双胴船のように2方向に伸ばすことで揺れを軽減させるのである。中に入ると，ハンモックを吊った奥の方に潜むか，中央の，ガラス張りの床の居間に腰を下ろす。十字型プランの各先端に立つガラスブロックの中空の塔は，光と空気をできる限り行きわたらせようとしている。そのひとつには梯子があって，変り者の客が湾に飛込みたいなどと言い出しても，要望に応えることができるというわけだ。

構造は，レジンを塗ったフェロコンクリートの薄いシェル構造体で，ワイヤメッシュを重ねて入れる。2重底の中にある自動揚水ポンプの働きとバラストの増減によって浮力を安定させ，荷重の超過や減少による転倒を防ぐことができる。塔は，鉄筋で補強したガラスブロック。目地にはシリコンのコーキング，アクリルの雨よけも備える。床と壁は，コンクリートに光沢のある塗料を塗る。ハンモックは，生成りのキャンヴァスである。

Model

Section

Roof plan

Floor plan

Site plan

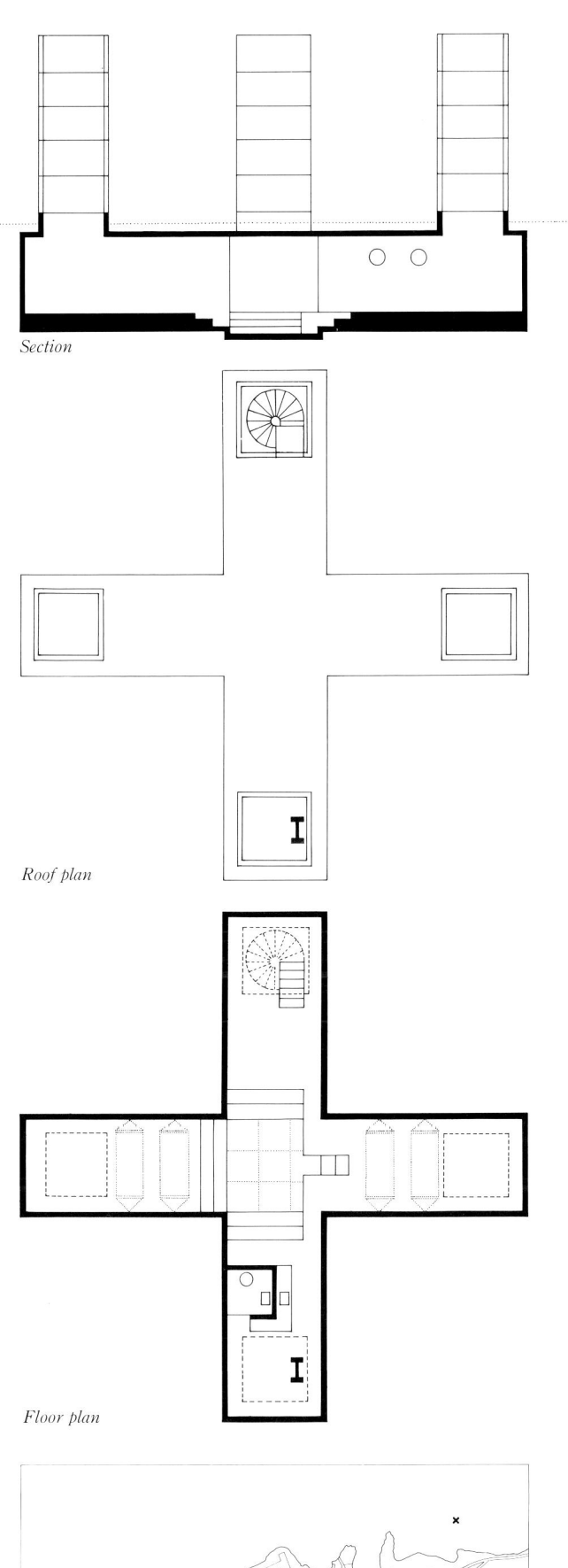

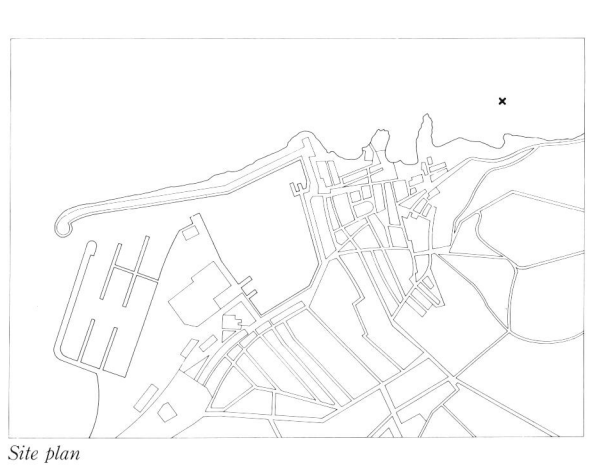

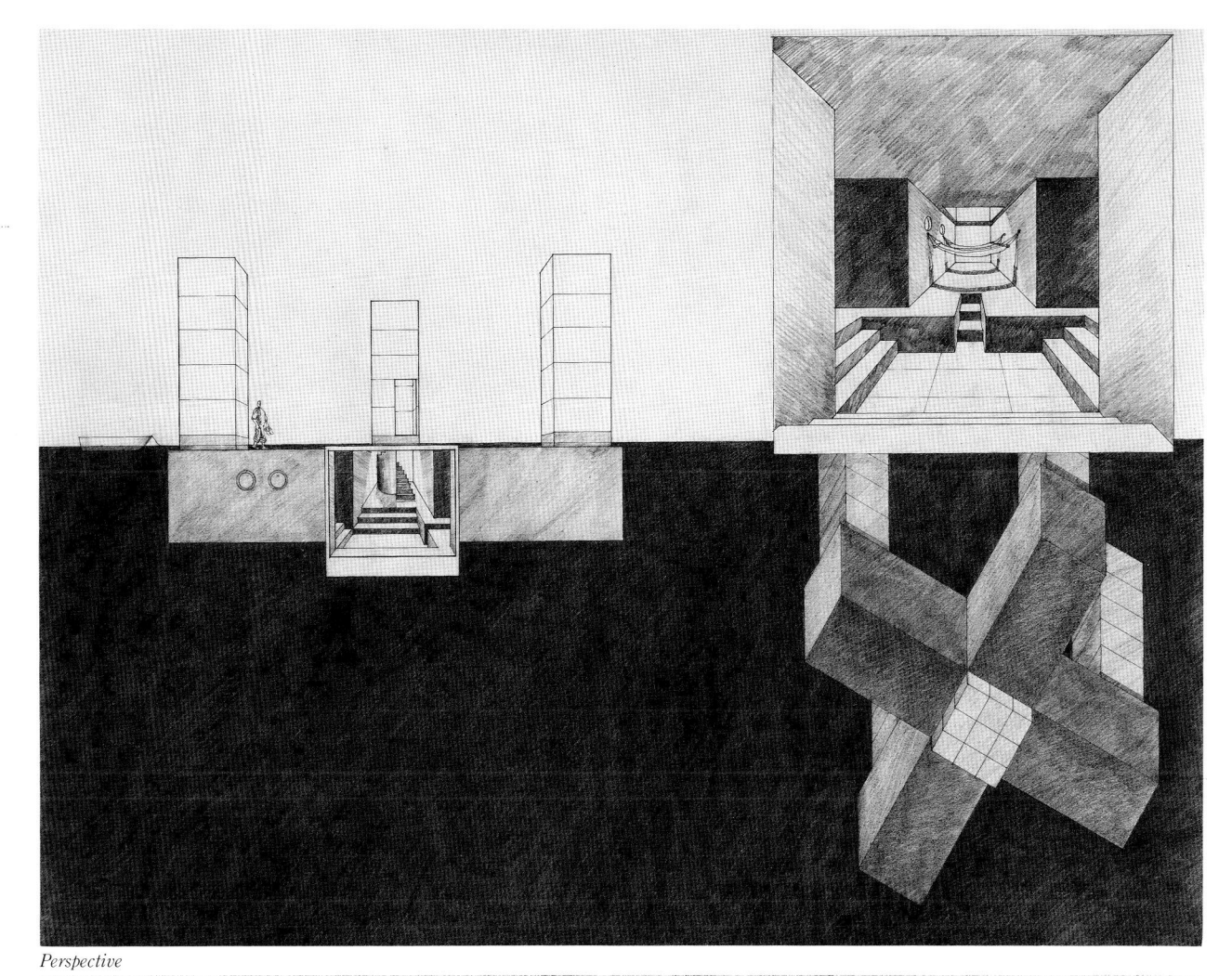

Perspective

Night view

55

*Telescope House
Still Pond, Maryland
1978-79*

With this project we launched our debate against eclecticism and against the importation of history. Eclecticism provokes the fragmentation of the past and the obfuscation of the present. This project is for us its opposite; it is a kind of distilled modern interpretation of certain cultural developments.
—Excerpt from exhibition, Yale University 1979

A retired couple with a very narrow site on Chesapeake Bay required a house in portions that could be closed off when not in use. This coincided with certain configurations observed in the history of Eastern Shore architecture. We fused a model of a particular type, the telescope house, with the program. Telescope houses, evolving since the early 1700s, received their name from their external appearance resembling a spyglass or telescope. Some were built large section first, descending, some small section first, ascending, and some, all sections at once.

The proposed house is in three portions corresponding to frequency of use: a) the basic house for two persons, used year round; b) the formal entertainment rooms for visiting family; and c) the guest rooms, closed off when not in use.

The plan responds to a thin lot (160 by 493 feet) which is narrowed further by a 60-foot setback from the water edge and from the street. The house is approached from a long driveway framed with trees, which offers a glimpse of the bay before passing parallel to the house and court. Walking through the court onto the screened front porch, a grid of steel windows with double doors leads to the entrance hall and sitting room beyond. Moving through the house gives a feeling of crossing strips of sunlight aligned with views of the water, as each major room has both north and south windows of identical exposure. The second level observatory can be reached by an interior stair or by way of the roof that ascends parallel to the water's edge. Magnificent vantage points facing the bay and the wildlife preserve on the adjacent site can be found along the roof, in the observatory, and along the deck overlooking the courtyard. The house does not so much fill the site as create a new, synthetic one, looking over the trees to the Chesapeake.

The structure is of stained concrete block with wooden roof and floor joists. The rubber-membrane roof is of the type developed for commercial construction, eliminating the need for any roof flashing. Windows are painted steel with insulated glass. The cerulean blue concrete pavers of the entrance court lead to an entrance hall of honed marble slabs, which gives way to an assymetrical black slate stair leading to the observatory.

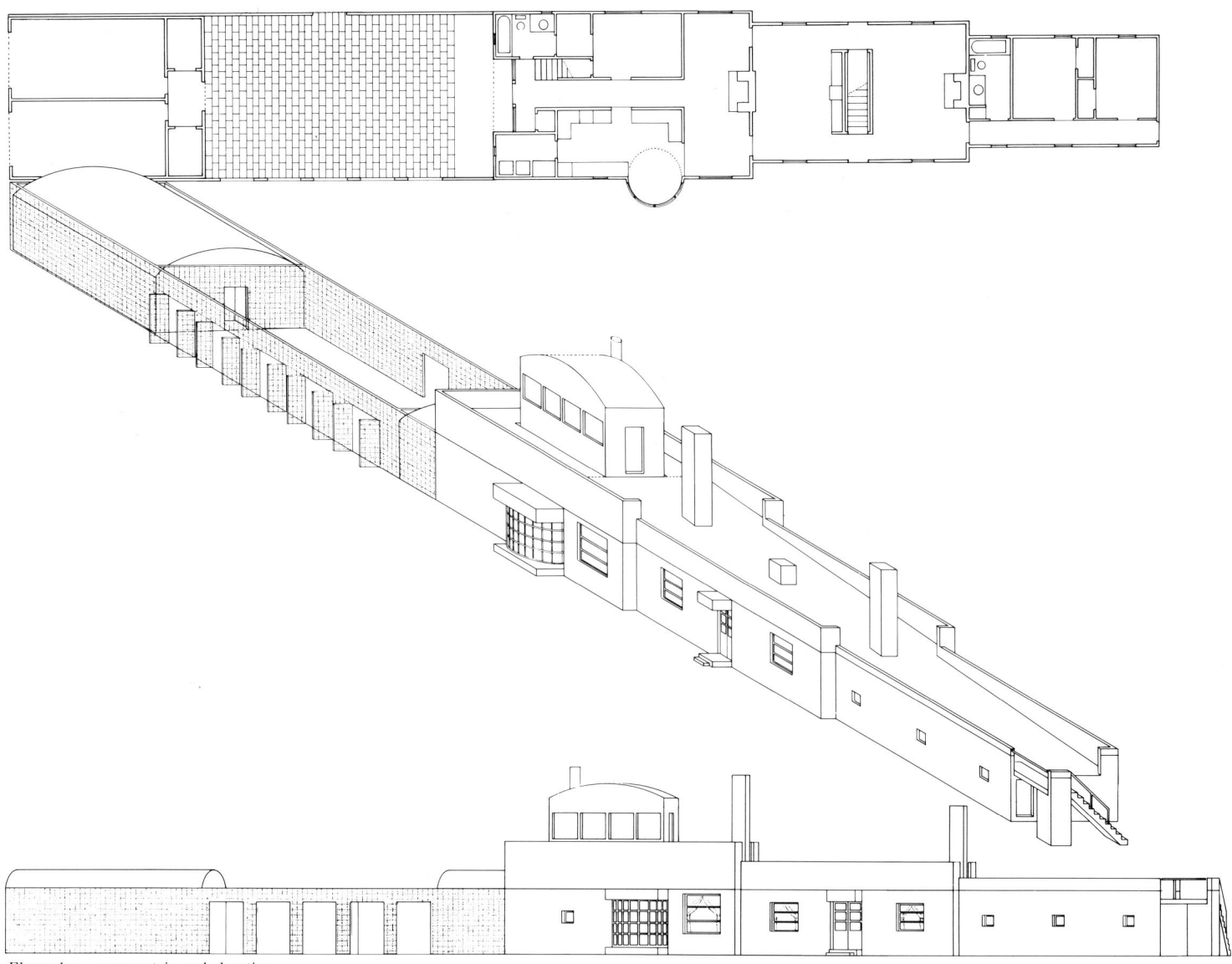

Floor plan, axonometric and elevation

テレスコープ・ハウス

このプロジェクトで、私たちは折衷主義と歴史の転用に対して議論を挑むつもりだ。折衷主義は過去を切り刻み、現在を曖昧なものにする。それに対してこのプロジェクトは、私たちに言わせればそれとは対極にあるものだ。つまり、発展の過程にある文化に対して、現代という時点に立って解釈を加え、それを精製したものなのである。(1979年イェール大学に於ける展覧会より)

チェザピーク・ベイに細長い土地を持つ、引退した夫妻は、家の一部を、使用しない時には閉め切ることができるよう希望した。東海岸の建築の歴史には、このような形式にぴったりのものがあるので、私たちはテレスコープ・ハウスと呼ばれる形式をこの住宅にあてはめることにした。これは、1700年代の初頭から始まったものだが、その名はスパイ・グラスや望遠鏡に似た外見から取ったものだ。あるものは大きい部分をはじめに作って、徐々に小さい部分に移り、またあるものは逆に小さい部分をはじめに手がけてから大きい方へとりかかったし、中には全ての部分を同時に作りあげるものもあった。

この住宅の計画案では、使用頻度に応じて全体を3つの部分に分けた。a)一年を通じて使われる、2人の住み手のための、住宅の中心をなす部分、b)家族づれの来訪者を迎えるための、正式なもてなしの部屋、c)使用されない時は締め切っておくゲストルームである。

もともと細長い敷地の形(160フィート×493フィート)から、水際と道路の両方から60フィートのセットバックを取ると、平面はなお狭められた。樹木に囲まれた車回しを抜けて走るアプローチの途中、家と中庭に平行な方向に向きを変えようとする時に、湾を垣間見ることができる。中庭を経て、スクリーンで囲われた玄関ポーチに至ると、格子状のスティールの窓の中に設けられた両開きのドアから、玄関ホールと、その奥の居間へと続く。家を通り抜ける途中、片側に太陽の光、片側に水面の景色があるので、連続する光の帯をつぎつぎに通りすぎるような思いを抱かされる。主な部屋は、そのどれもが南北両面に同じ大きさの窓があるからなのだ。2階の展望台へは室内の階段、もしくは湖面に平行に高さを変える屋根づたいに行くことができる。湾や、隣接する野生生物保護区を一望にする絶好の見晴しは、屋根の上にも展望台にも、中庭を見下ろすデッキにも、こと欠きはしない。この住宅では、敷地いっぱいに建てるというよりも、木々の梢越しにチェザピークを望めるような、敷地との新しい関係をつくりだそうとした。

構造はステイン塗りのコンクリートブロックに木造の屋根と床梁を架けたものだ。ゴム系の屋根材は商業建築のために開発されたもので、水切などを必要としない。窓はスティールに塗装、ペアグラスを入れる。セルリアン・ブルーのコンクリート舗装を施されたエントランス・コートから水磨きの大理石の玄関ホールにつづき、それが、展望台への非対称のスレート張の階段へ至る。

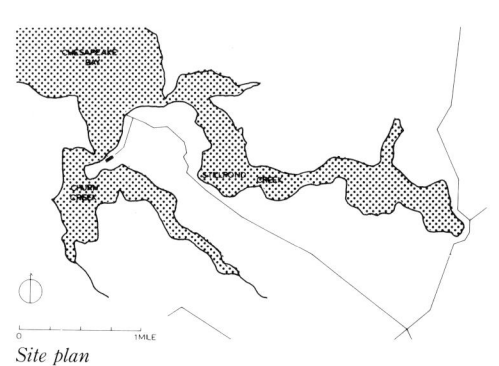

Site plan

Model

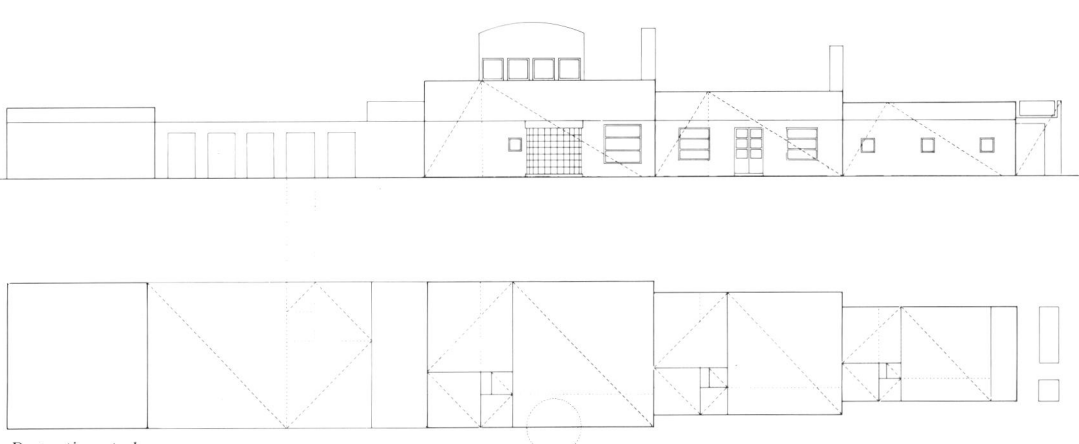

Proportion study

Model

57

*Metz House
Staten Island, New York
1980-81*

The site for this project is a thickly wooded lot on Staten Island overlooking a forested ravine. It is an inexpensive house for a young couple, both artists. Conventional living and dining rooms are excluded in favor of two larger studios and a large kitchen. The studio's requirements reflect the nearly opposite sensibilities of the two artists: husband (sculptor) and wife (painter). She makes floral paintings, loves sunlight and plants, and has several cats. He makes black concrete sculpture, hates cats and house plants, and doesn't care to have natural light in his studio as he works mostly at night. One bedroom is for a teenage daughter who desires privacy. The client expressed dislike of the suburban image of local developments, favoring an approach that leaves all natural vegetation on the site untouched.

The house is a dialectic of two parts based on a traditional U-type courtyard plan. An introspective outdoor court opens to the sun and a view of the ravine. The analogy of an urban building type, like an island in the forest, is carried out in all the elevations: the front facade is articulated in integral color concrete blocks, the side walls are painted black like the party walls in a city, and the courtyard is painted white for maximum light.

Each wing of the "U" contains one of the studios, whose character is expressed by the contrast between the two wings. In the right wing is the painting studio with skylight providing indirect light. Above the monitors is a ramp to the solitude of the study. In the lower part of the left wing is the sculpture studio, opening to the grotto and outdoor work area. The grotto receives light from cylindrical glass block elements cast in the slab of the courtyard. In the center of the main level are the common areas of the kitchen/dining and entrance foyer. The teenager's bedroom has a special roof, giving her the feeling of being in a separate little house.

Construction is insulation-filled concrete block with plaster interiors applied directly to the block. Floors are industrial grade pine with an oiled finish. The roof is insulated wood framing with composite roll-roofing. Interior stairs in the entrance foyer are black slate alternating with white marble, creating an effect like the black and white keys of a piano.

メッツ邸
この計画の敷地は、スタテン島の樹影の濃い峡谷を見下ろす土地である。いずれも芸術家である若いカップルのための、工費を抑えた住宅である。居間や食堂といった伝統的なものは作らず、大きめのスタジオを2つと広いキッチンが求められた。スタジオについての要求には、2人の芸術家は正反対というほどの感性の違いを示した。夫は彫刻家、妻は画家である。彼女は花を描くので、日の光と植物を愛し、猫を何匹も飼っている。夫は黒いコンクリートの彫刻を作る。こちらは猫も、園芸植物も大嫌いで、スタジオに自然光はいらないという。ほとんど夜に制作するからだ。ひとつしかない寝室は、プライバシーを欲しがるティーンエイジャーの娘の部屋だ。クライアントは、地元のディベロパーの作るような郊外風を嫌って、敷地にあった植物を全て残すよう望んだ。

この住宅は、伝統的なU型の中庭型プランをもとにして、その両翼を発展させたものである。内省的な中庭は太陽を抱き入れ、渓谷の景色に向って開いている。森の中に浮ぶ島のような家を作るつもりで、都市の建物のようにしてエレベーションを作っていった。正面のファサードは、カラーコンクリートブロックで作り、側面の壁は、都市の建物の隣地との共用壁であるかのように黒く塗り、中庭にはできるだけ光を採り入れるために白い塗装を施した。

U型をなす2つのウィングは、それぞれにひとつずつスタジオがあって、その性格がそのまま2つのウィングの対照的な形にあらわれている。右のウィングには、間接光を取入れるスカイライトのついた、絵画用のアトリエがある。屋根の上のスロープは、独立した書斎に続く。左のウィングの下の階は彫刻のスタジオである。ここは、グロットと屋外作業場に続く。グロットには、その上の中庭の床スラブに埋め込まれた円形のガラスブロックを通して光が落ちてくる。メインレベルの中央には、キッチンとダイニングそして玄関がある。ティーンエイジャーの寝室には特別の屋根が載せられているので、独立した小さな家にいるようだ。

構造は断熱材を充填したコンクリートブロックに、内部は直かにプラスターを塗る。床は量産の松の板にオイルフィニッシュ。屋根は木造で、断熱を施したうえ長尺の合成屋根材で仕上げる。玄関ホールの階段は玄昌石の黒と大理石の白が交互に混り、ピアノの黒鍵と白鍵を思わせる。

Site plan

Axonometric

Courtyard elevations

Sections

Exterior elevations

Roof and study

Entry level

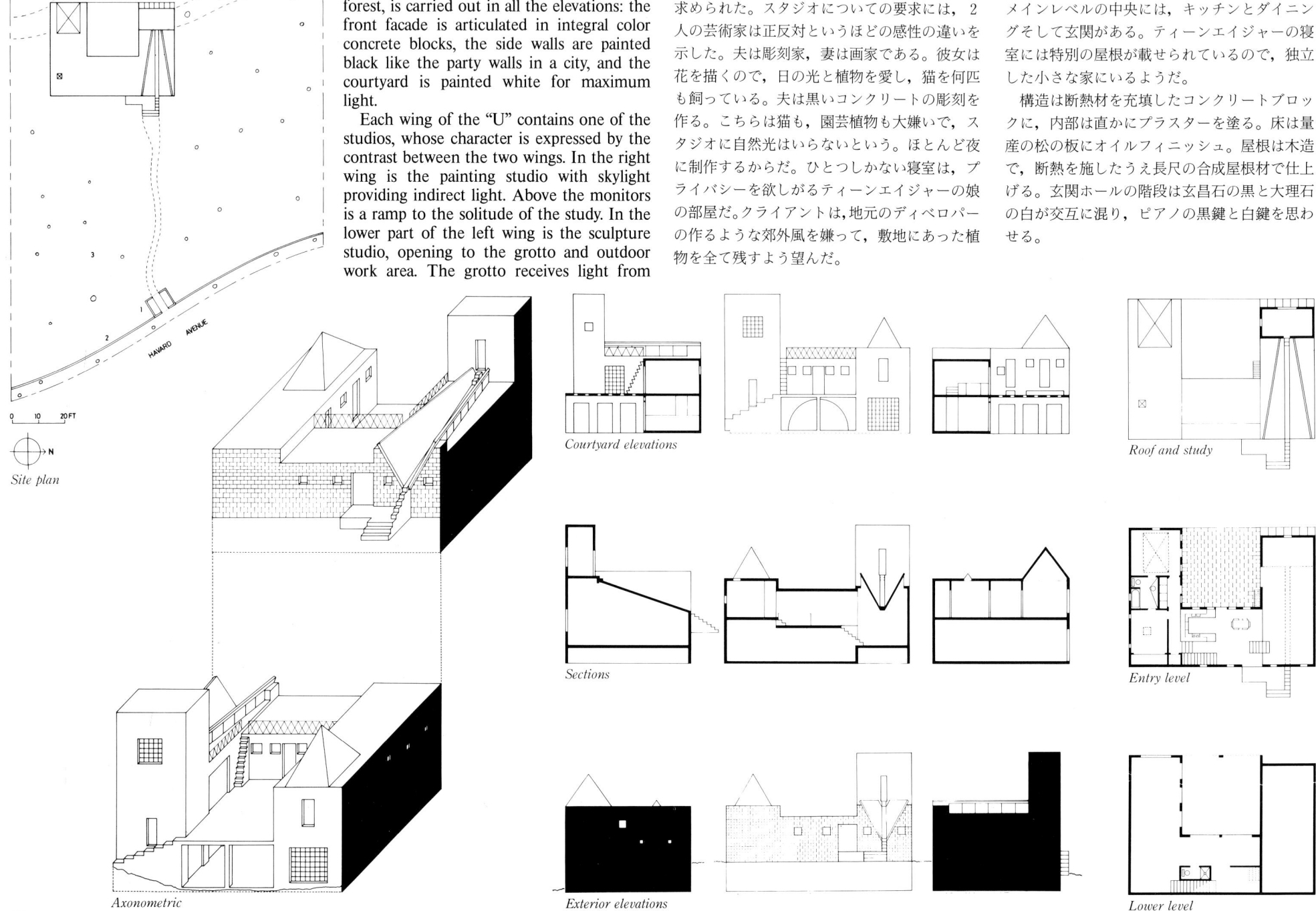

Lower level

Model

Model

Cutaway perspective

View from west

59

Pool House and Sculpture Studio
Scarsdale, New York
1980–81

Second level

First level   10'/3m   N↑

A sculpture studio and a bathhouse are sited next to an existing swimming pool. The bathhouse provides both a changing and refreshment area near the pool. The sculpture studio is situated adjacent to the bath house to enable it to function occasionally as a guest room.

The site in Scarsdale, New York has a history that dates from the transference of property rights by King George in the early eighteenth century. The land is marked by stone walls that were used to define its boundaries.

The project is organized with the idea of *walls within walls*. New walls enclosing the existing pool form a courtyard recalling the ancient stone boundary wall around the site. On the north wall of the new court, the pool house and sculpture studio form a two-story pavilion. The sculpture studio on the upper level receives light from two major windows and a pyramid skylight, which also marks the major axes on the site.

Construction is of insulation-filled concrete block with smooth plaster interiors and luminous gray stucco exteriors. Red integral-color concrete pavers in the courtyard provide contrast with the dark green marble of the details and countertops. The floor of the bathhouse is flesh-colored marble. The white ceramic tile of the shower room is broken by a green marble water column with brass shower fixtures. Glass openings in the lower doors have sandblasted drawings carved in them that relate to the history of the site and the architectonic ideas.

プールハウス／彫刻スタジオ

彫刻のスタジオ／バスハウスがプールの脇に作られた。バスハウスはプールの近くにあるので着替えにも、休息にも使うことができる。彫刻スタジオはバスハウスのすぐ上にあるので、必要とあらば時にはゲストルームとして使われる。

ニューヨークのスカーズデイルにある敷地は、18世紀のジョージ王朝による土地所有権の移譲まで遡る歴史をもっている。この土地は、かつて境界を表示するために使われた石積の壁で囲われている。

計画は「壁の中の壁」という考え方によって作られた。既存のプールを囲む新しい壁は中庭を形作り、敷地の周囲の旧い壁を思わせる。この新しい中庭の壁の北側の一部を構成してプールハウスと彫刻スタジオの2階建のパヴィリオンがある。2階の彫刻スタジオは2つの大きな窓とピラミッド型のスカイライトから採光する。このピラミッドは、敷地の主要な軸をなす。

断熱材充填のコンクリートブロックに、内部はプラスター塗り、外部は光沢のあるグレイのスタッコ仕上である。中庭の床に使われたカラーコンクリートの赤は、ディテール各部とカウンターの天板に使われるダークグリーンの大理石とコントラストを示す。バスハウスの床は肌色の大理石。シャワールームの白いタイルは、真鍮のシャワーをとりつけた柱のグリーンの大理石がひきたてる。1階の開口部のガラスにはサンドブラストのレリーフで、この地の歴史と、この建築の理念が描かれている。

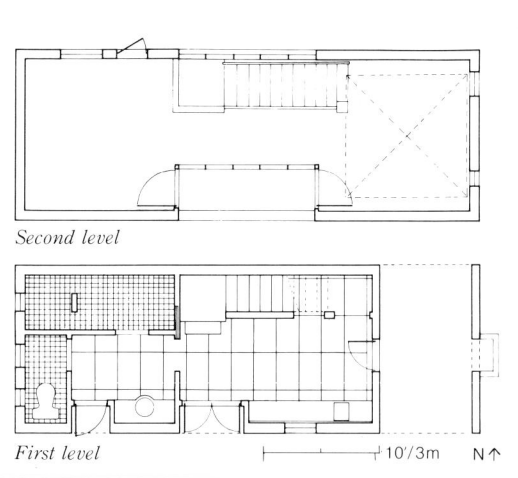

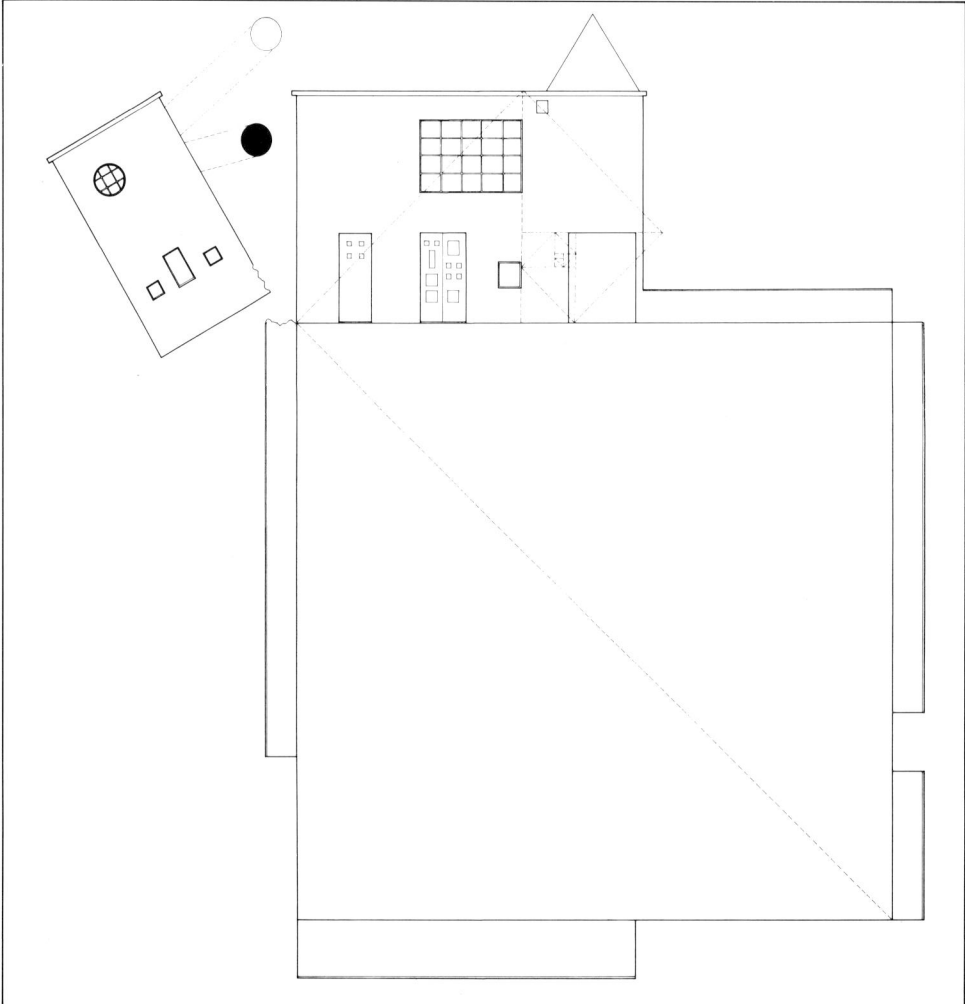

Proportion study

Overall view from east

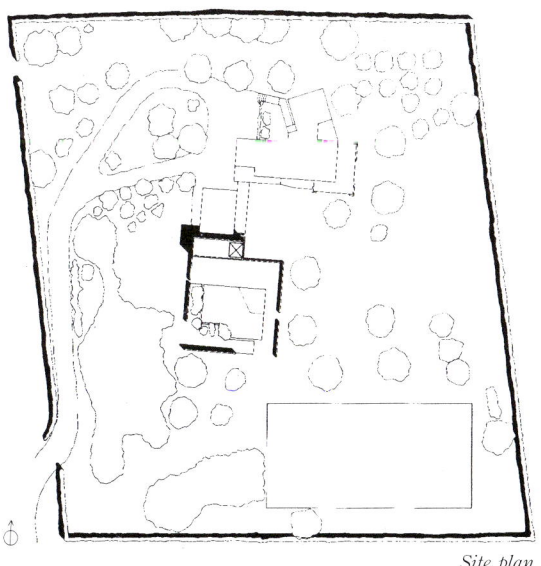

Site plan

Detail

View toward entrance

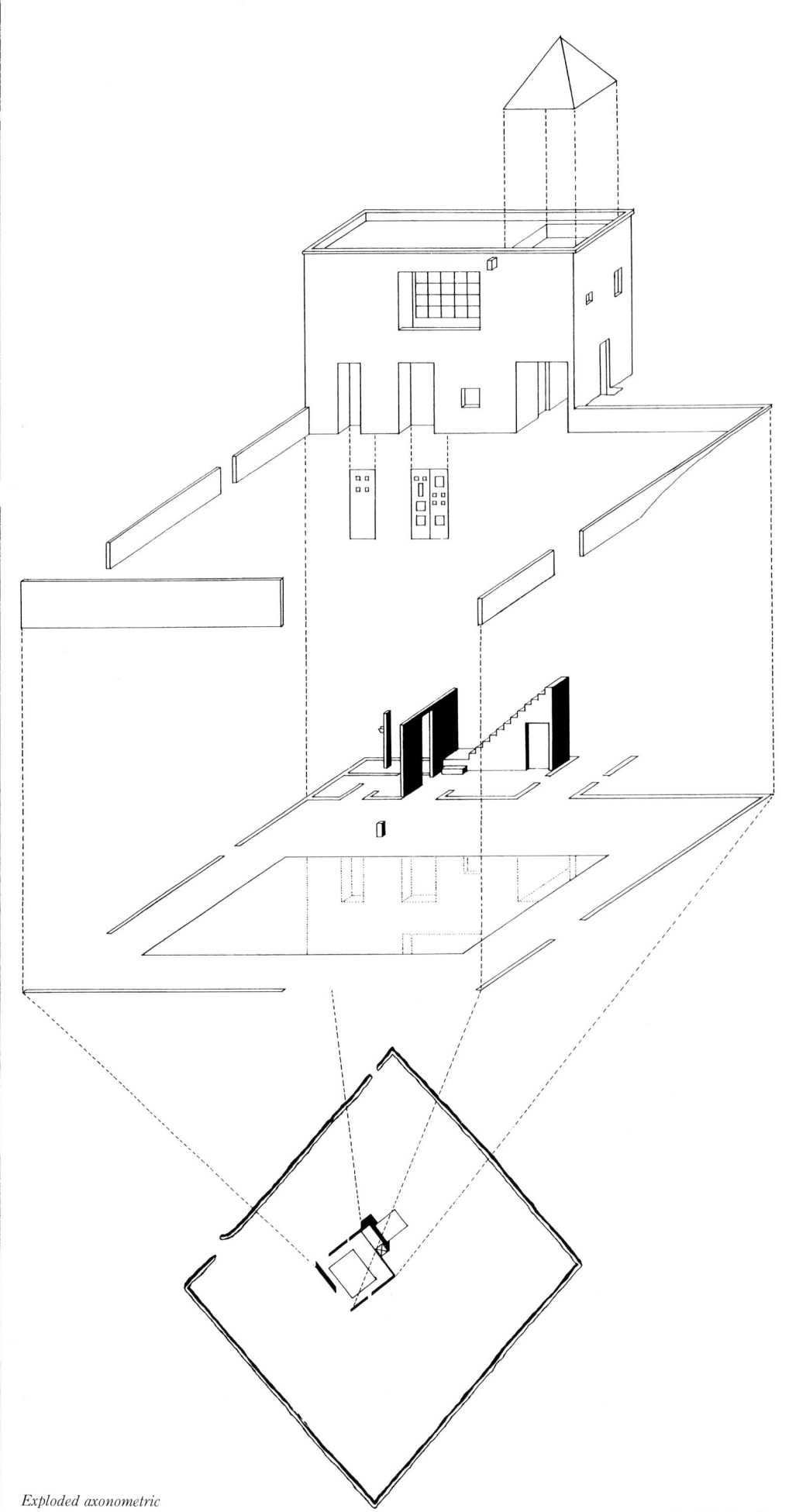

Exploded axonometric

▷ *Poolside facade*

62

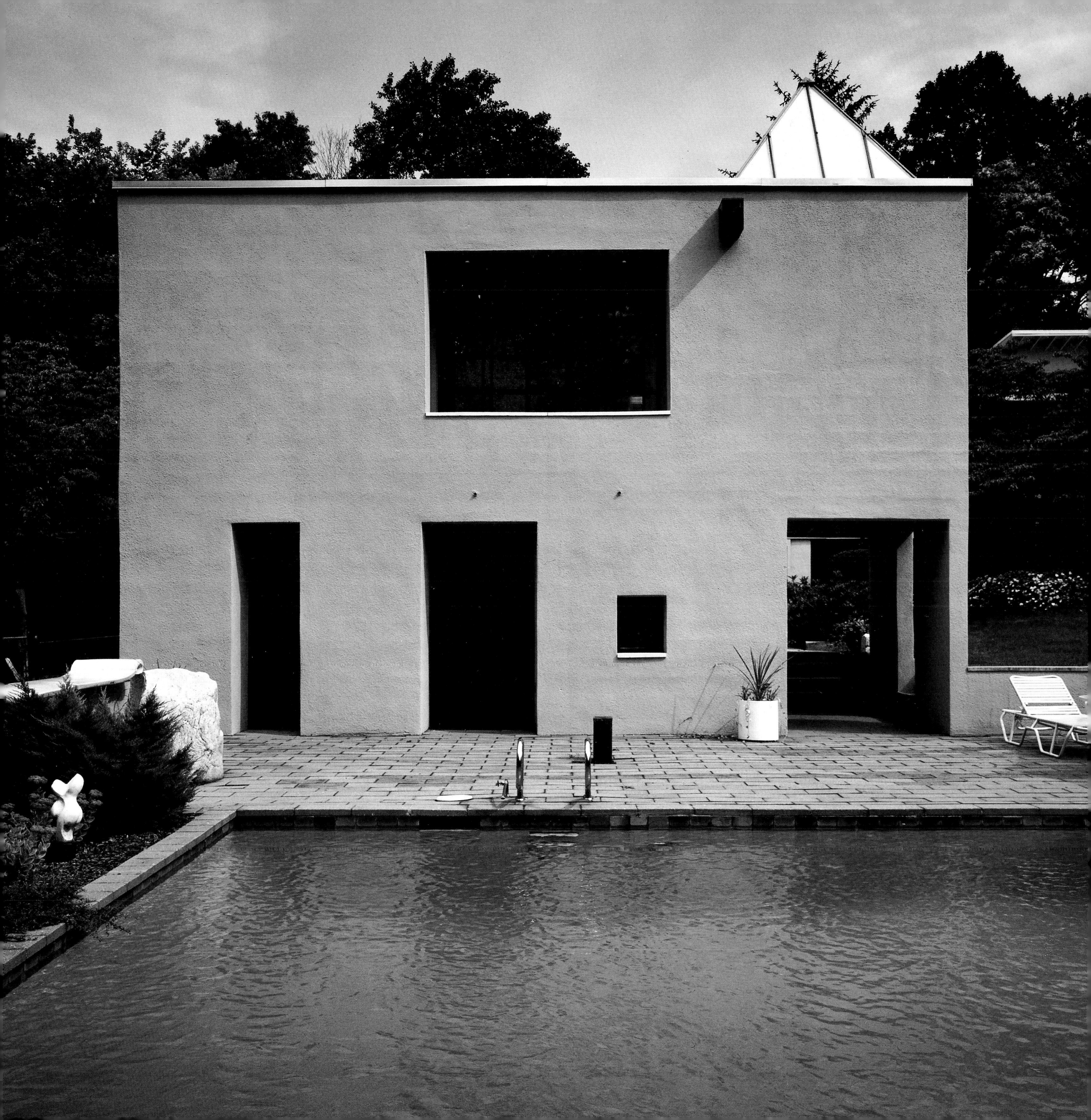

Sculpture studio

Sandblasted glass

Entrance door

Sandblasted glass

Sandblasted glass

View on second level

Berkowitz-Odgis House
Martha's Vineyard, Massachusetts
1984–88

In looking at things spiritual, we are too much like oysters observing the sun, through the water, and thinking that thick water the thinnest of air.
—H. Melville, *Moby Dick*

The site is a hill overlooking the Atlantic Ocean. The ground, densely overgrown with brush, is cut by a gully that descends to an unobstructed bog. The steep terrain and other building restrictions strictly limit the siting and construction material as well as the building height for the vacation home.

According to Melville's *Moby Dick*, the Indian tribe that originally inhabited Martha's Vineyard created a unique dwelling type. Finding a whale skeleton on the beach, they would pull it up to dry land and stretch skins or bark over it, transforming it into a house.

The house is an inside-out balloon frame of wooden construction: a skeleton house whose modern bones define a veranda. Along this continuous porch, wooden members receive the natural vines of the island, which transform the straight linear mode of the architecture.

The structural frame exposed inside and out meets the undisturbed sand dune on point foundations rather than on a common perimeter footing. Roofing is a rubber membrane unrolled over the frame, analogous to the skins over the whale skeleton.

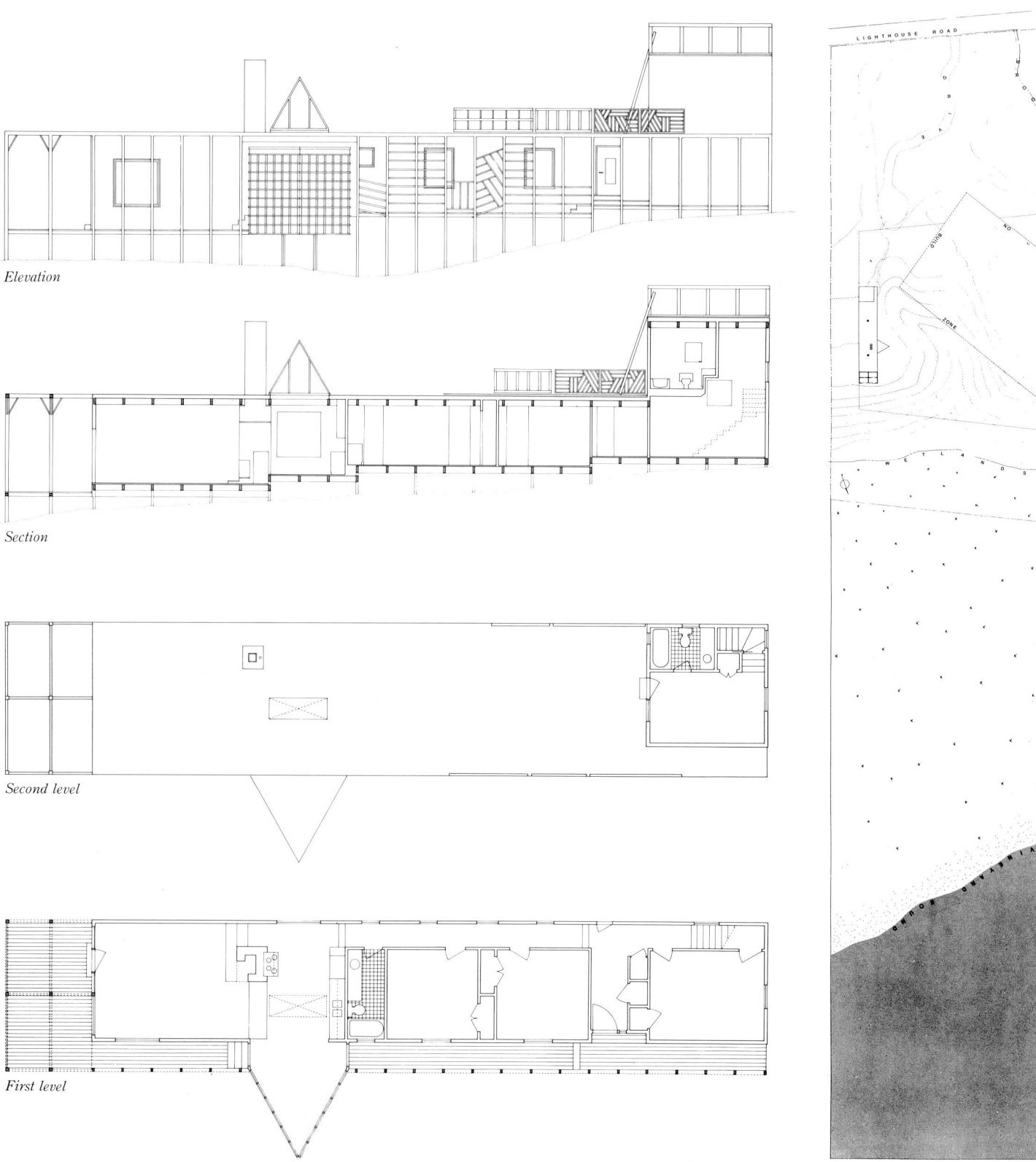

Elevation

Section

Second level

First level

Site plan

バーコヴィツ／オッジス邸

「おれ達が霊的な物事をながめる時において，まるで牡蠣が水の底から太陽を覗きながら，どろどろした水を澄明な空気だとおもっているようなものかもしれないぞ。」
―― H・メルヴィル，『白鯨』，阿部知二訳

敷地は，大西洋を見下ろす丘にある。地表はびっしりと潅木が生い茂り，一方は削りとられたような斜面が沼地に向い，景観を遮るものはない。土地の傾斜のきつさに加えて建築規制があるために，この別荘は高さはもとより，配置や構造もすこぶる限定されることになった。

メルヴィルの『白鯨』によれば，マーサズ・ヴィンヤードの先住民だったインディアンの部族が考え出したすこぶるユニークな住いがあるそうだ。海岸に打ち上げられた鯨の骨格を見つけると，彼等はそれを乾燥した土地まで引き上げて毛皮や樹皮を張って家に変身させたのだという。

この住宅は，バルーンフレームを裏返しにしたような木造建築である。現代製の骨がベランダの周囲を包む，骨組の家だ。周囲を巡るこのポーチの柱や梁にこの島に自生するツタがからみ，建築の直線的な性格を変身させてしまうのである。

あるいは内側に，あるいは外に露出する構造体は，布基礎に代えて使われた円柱形の独立基礎だけで整地しないままの砂丘と接する。屋根には長尺のゴム系の屋根材を，さながら鯨の骨の上にめぐらした皮のように張った。

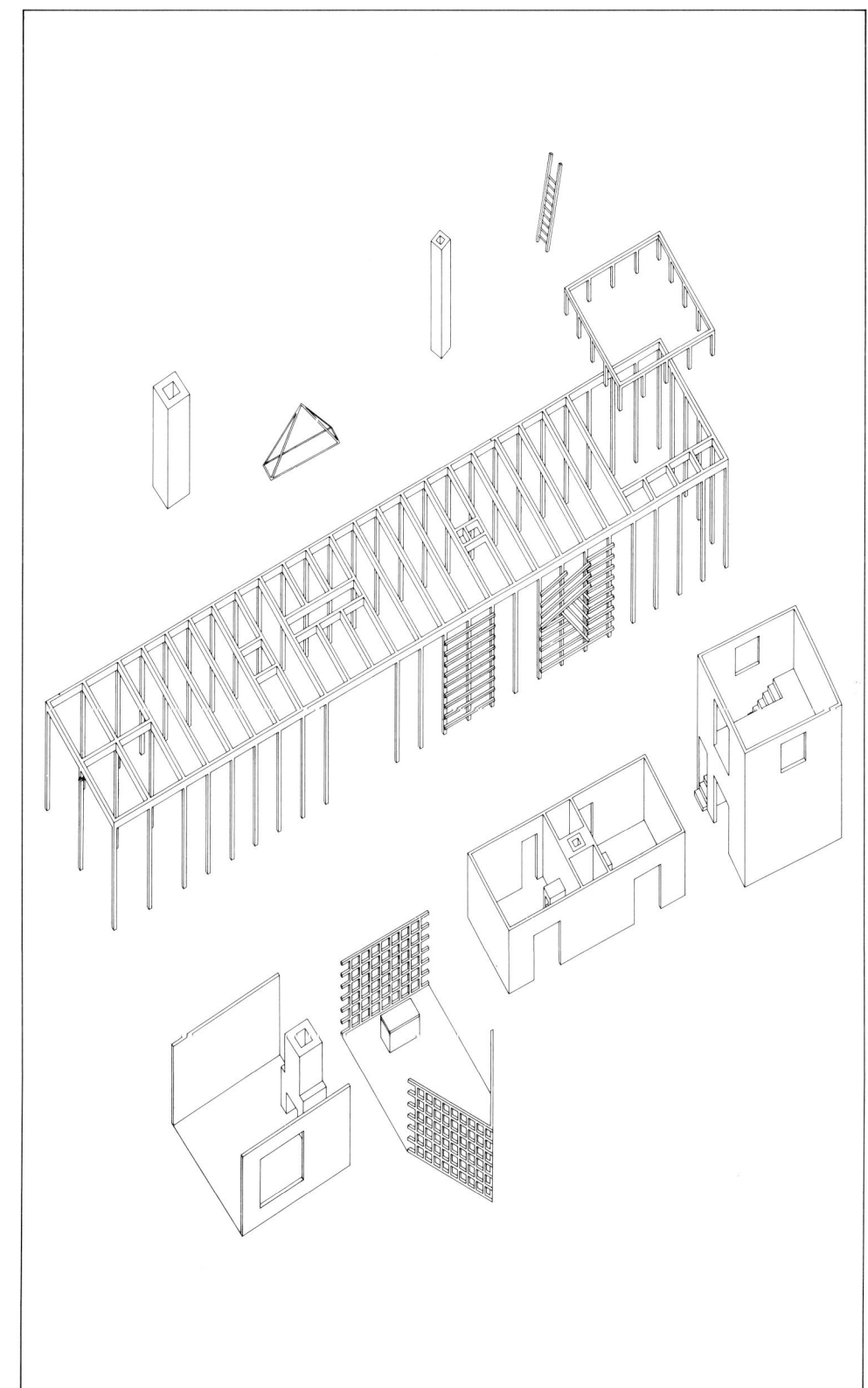

Exploded axonometric

View from approach

View from west

View from northeast

▷ *Overall view from north*

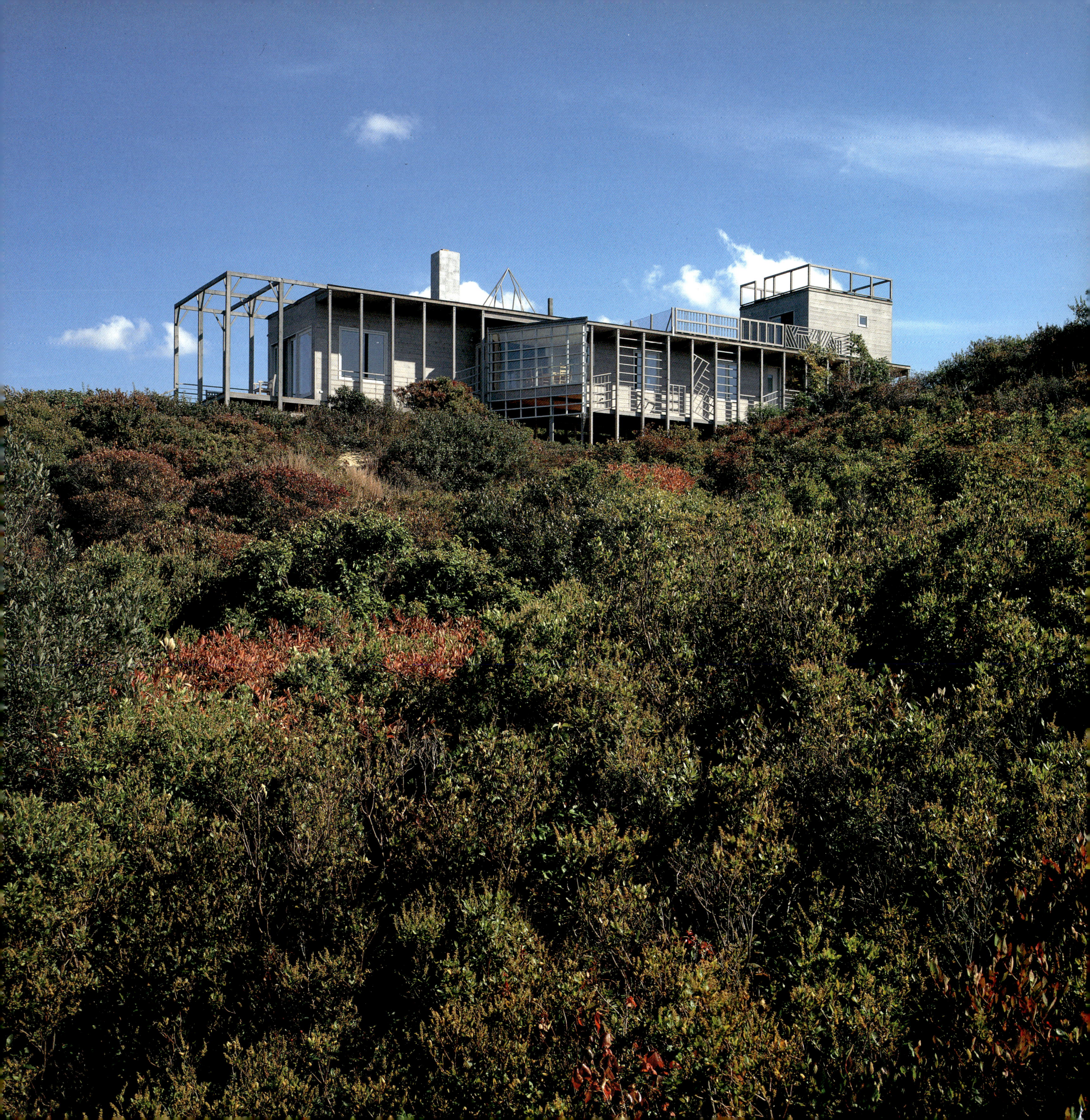

Porch

Detail

Living area

Porch

Porch

Dining area

View from living area

Kitchen

View from living area toward kitchen

Detail of east elevation

*Residence
Cleveland, Ohio
1988–90*

A thickly wooded site east of Cleveland characterized by ravines and steep grades is the site for a house for a lawyer and his wife, a painter. Large open spaces and a vertical emphasis were requested, along with a three-car garage. The house has a multilevel section shifted along a curve, which coincides with the central ravine on the site. A series of conditions erase the dialectic nature of the house's double-form:

a) The double form is displaced along the entrance plane of the house. Distinct from the other elevations, this blackened plane makes a "front" on the inside and the outside, north and south.

b) A "skywalk" suspended from the facade traverses both halves of the house, joining them in a continuous steel deck view of the trees.

c) Diagonal views of interior space, 100 feet in length, join both halves of the house.

d) Sleepwalk passage: above the "skywalk," a blind passage leads from the mezzanine to a roof terrace. This passage was inspired by C. Brockden Brown's novel, *Memoirs of a Sleep Walker,* published in 1779. The novel is based on his unpublished work *Sky Walk* (a corruption of "skiwakkee," the name given to the Delaware Indians, who were later driven into Ohio). Sleepwalking and a cave are metaphors Brown uses for subconsciousness. The novel revolves on dualities, coupling, intertwining, etc. Here the psycho-symbolic program of sleep-walking finds an architectural equivalent.

Cleveland's steel industries are employed in the steel construction. Varying automotive channel sections are rolled straight and spaced at eight feet on center along the "skywalk." The remaining structure is plywood reinforced metal studs, steel-suspended walks, and steel windows.

Interior perspectives

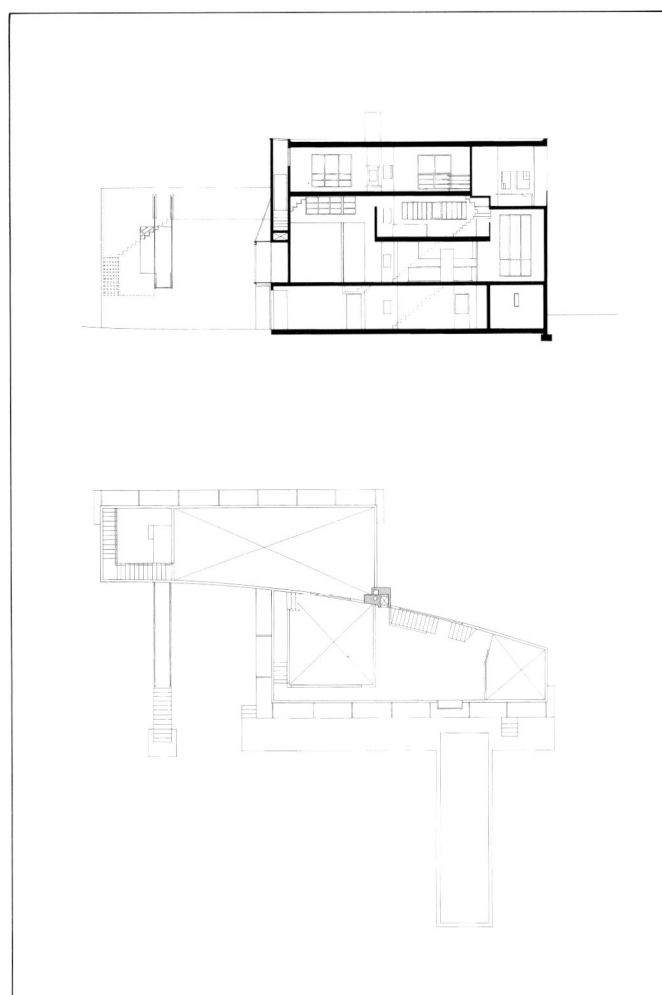

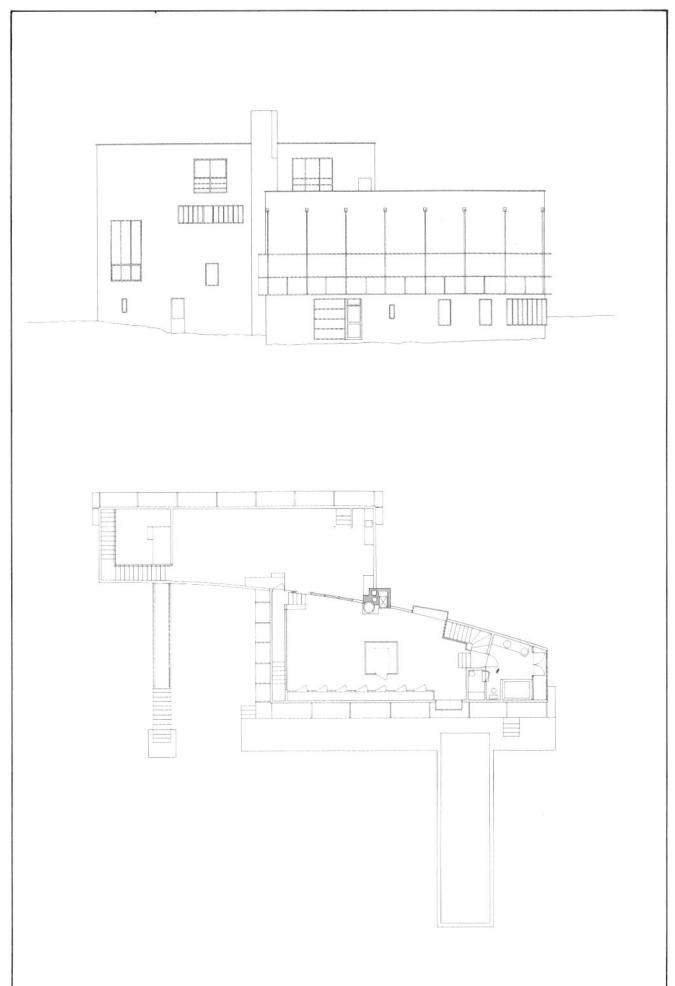

Site plan

Mezzanine level / east-west section

Upper level / north elevation

Concept diagram

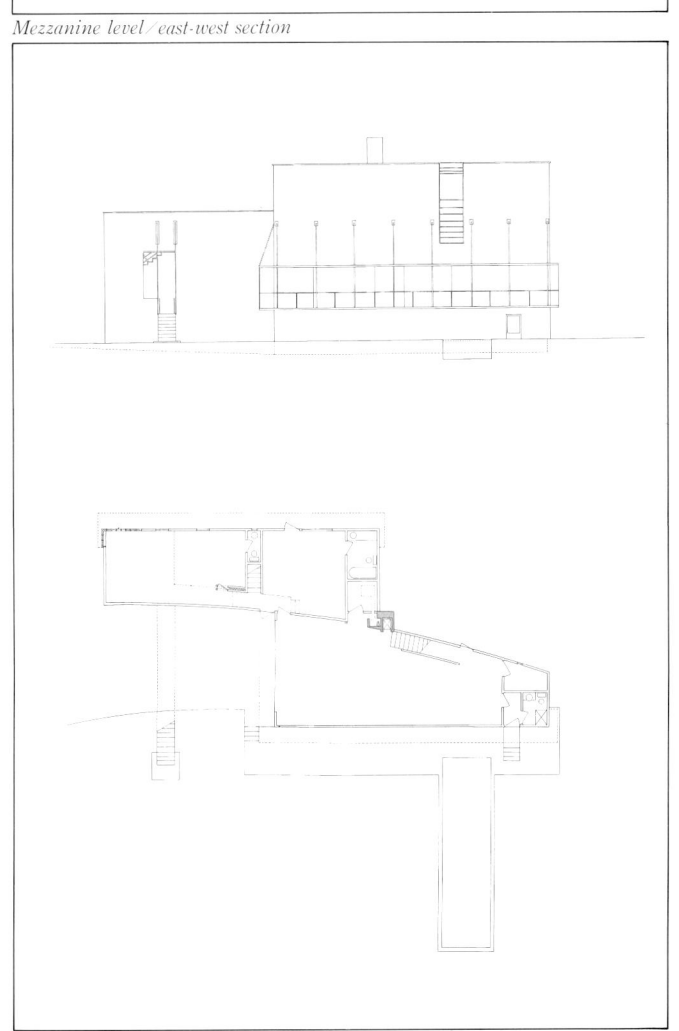

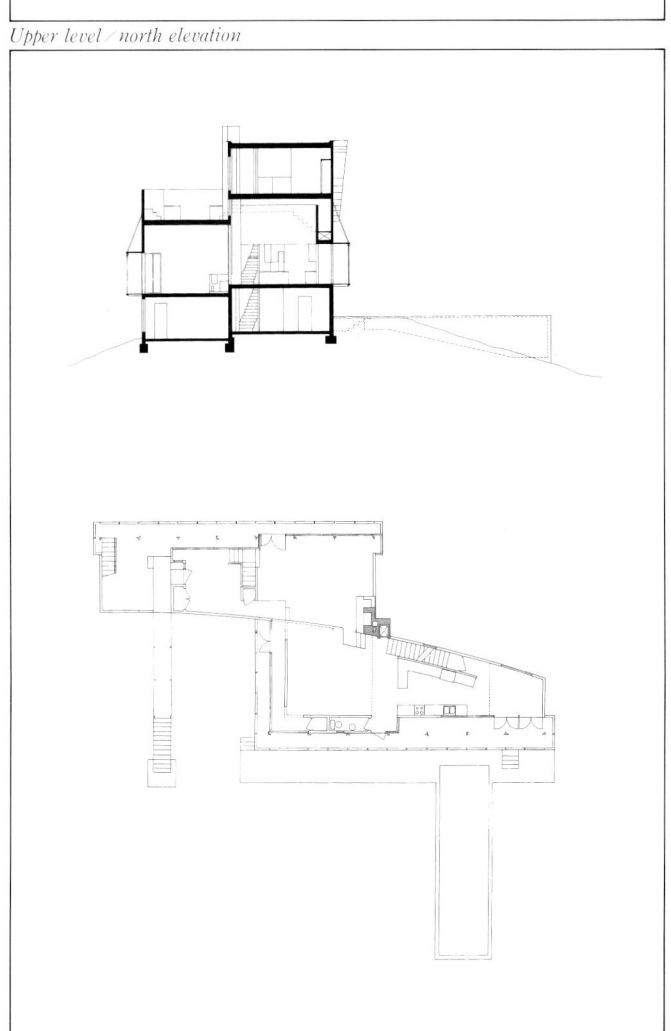

Basement level / south elevation

Ground level / north-south section

Model

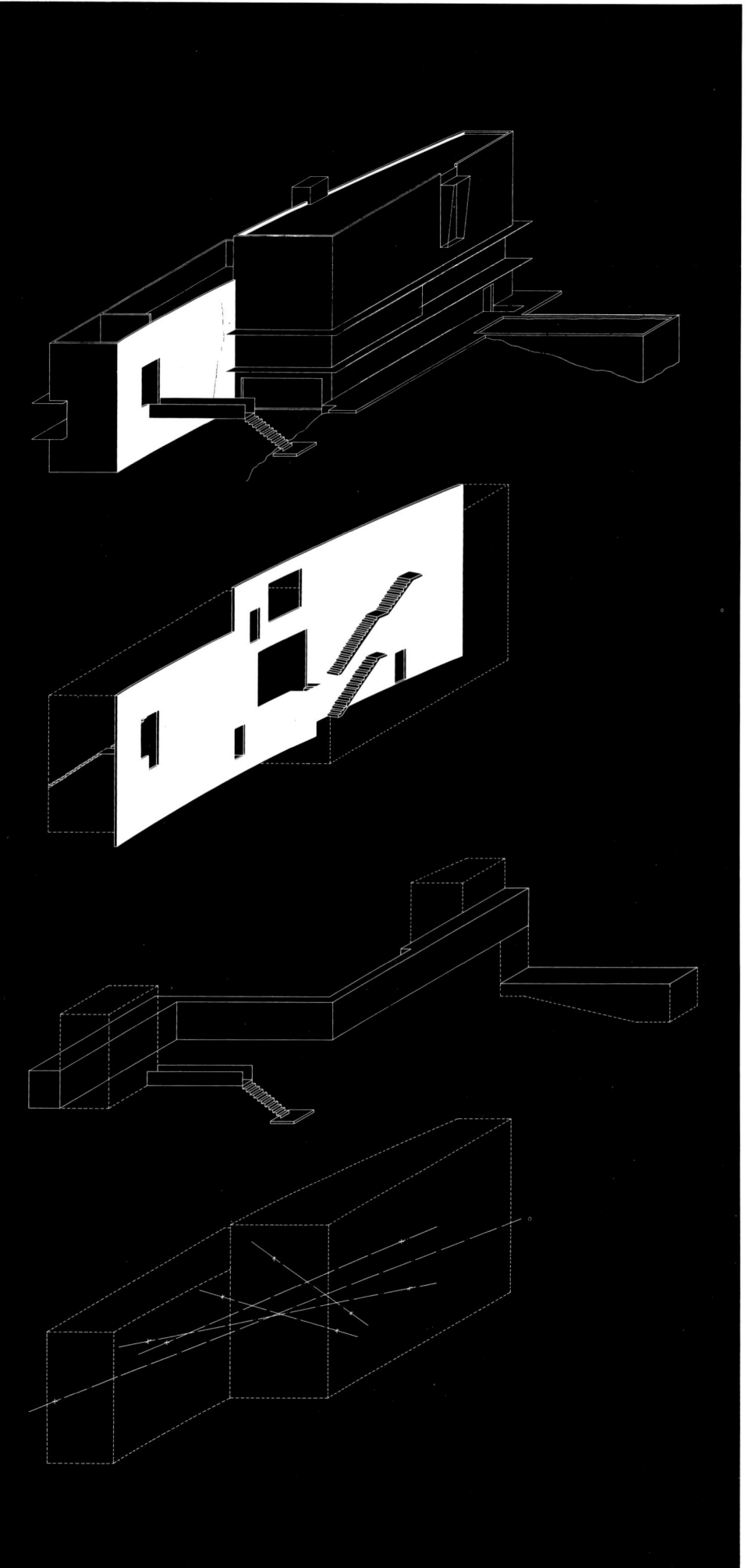

Axonometric diagrams

クリーヴランドの住宅

幾筋もの沢と急傾斜が特徴的な，クリーヴランドの東部に位置する樹影の濃い敷地には，弁護士である夫と画家の夫人というカップルのための住宅が建てられる。広々としたオープンスペースを持ち垂直性を強調した空間であること，3台の車のガレージを備えることが要望された。この住宅は，曲線に沿ってレベルを変化させ，その曲線は敷地の中心にある沢に合わせたものである。一連の状況を設定することによって，この住宅のもつダブル・フォームという論証的側面を消去する。

a) ダブル・フォームは，この住宅の玄関側の壁面に沿って退去させられている。他の立面とははっきり区別されたこの黒い壁面は，内に外に，北に南に一枚の正面ファサードを構成する。

b) ファサードに吊る「スカイウォーク」は，2つに分けられた住宅の両方を横断するようにして，どちらからも森の景色をスティールのデッキから楽しめるようにしている。

c) 内部空間を対角方向に見ると100フィートに及ぶ奥行きを持ち，2分割されたこの住宅の双方にまたがっている。

d) 夢中歩行者の通路——「スカイウォーク」の上の窓のない通路は，中2階からルーフテラスへ結ぶ。この通路はC・ブロックデン・ブラウンの『夢遊病者の記憶』という1779年に出版された小説をもとにした。この小説は，未刊行の作品『スカイウォーク』を発展させたものである（後にオハイオに移住させられたデラウェア・インディアンに与えられた名である「スキワキー」の堕落が描かれている）。夢中歩行と洞窟を，無意識に対するメタファーとして用いた。この小説は2重性を中心にして循環する。ときには2つが結び合い，ときにはそれがもつれ合う。これは，夢中歩行の精神状態を建築によって象徴的に表現したものである。

鉄骨工事には，クリーヴランドの鉄工会社が使われた。種々の量産のチャンネル鋼を「スカイウォーク」の中央に8フィートおきに巻付けた。その他の構造は合板で補強したメタルスタッドと，スティールで吊った通路，それにスティールの窓である。

Model

Stretto House
Dallas, Texas
1989–92

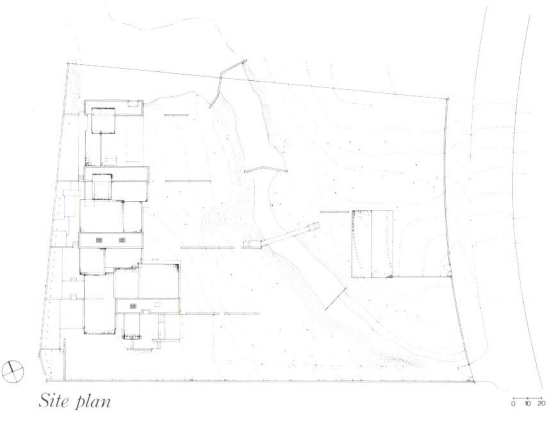

Site plan

View from south approach

Sited adjacent to three spring-fed ponds with existing concrete dams, the house projects the character of the site in a series of concrete block "spatial dams" with metal-framed "aqueous space" flowing through them. Coursing over the dams, like the overlapping stretto in music, water is an overlapping reflection of the space of the landscape outside as well as the virtual overlapping of the space inside.

A particular music with this "stretto," Bartok's *Music for Strings, Percussion and Celeste,* was a parallel on which the house form was made. In four movements, the piece has a distinct division between heavy (percussion) and light (strings). Where music has a materiality in instrumentation and sound, this architecture attempts an analogue in light and space, that is

$$\frac{material \times sound}{time} = \frac{material \times light}{space} .$$

The building is formed in four sections, each consisting of two modes: heavy orthogonal masonry and light, curvilinear metal (the concrete block and metal of Texas vernacular). The plan is purely orthogonal; the section, curvilinear. The guest house is an inversion with the plan curvilinear and section orthogonal, similar to the inversions of the subject in the first movement of the Bartok score. In the main house aqueous space is developed by several means: floor plans pull the level of one space through to the next, roof planes pull space over walls, and an arched wall pulls light down from a skylight. Materials and details continue the spatial concepts in poured concrete, glass cast in fluid shapes, slumped glass, and liquid terrazzo.

Arriving at the space via a driveway bridging over the stream, a visitor passes through overlapping spaces of the house, glimpsing the flanking gardens, arriving at an empty room flooded by the existing pond. The room, doubling its space in reflection, opening both to the site and the house, becomes the asymmetrical center of two sequences of aqueous space.

Entrance terrace

Entry

First level

Second level

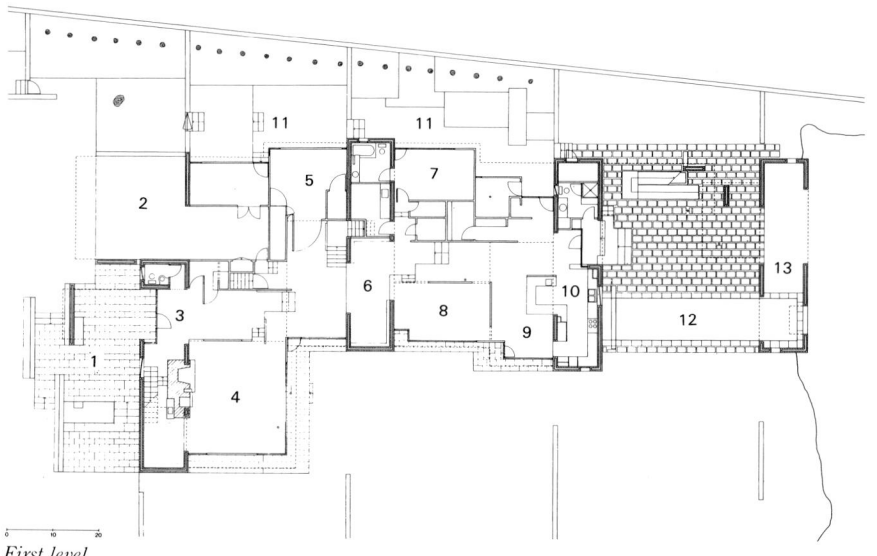

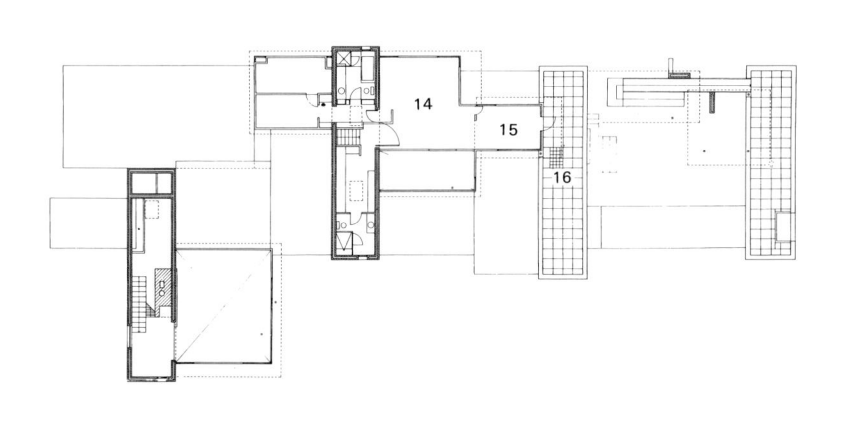

1 TERRACE
2 GARAGE
3 ENTRY
4 LIVING ROOM
5 ART STORAGE ROOM
6 LIBRARY
7 STUDY
8 DINING ROOM
9 BREAKFAST AREA
10 KITCHEN
11 WALLED GARDEN
12 POOL
13 FLOODED ROOM
14 BEDROOM
15 SITTING ROOM
16 ROOF TERRACE

View from east

ストレット・ハウス

湧水の流れ込む3つの池にはコンクリートの堰がある。その池のほとりの家は、そうした敷地の性格を反映して、コンクリートブロックの「空間を貯えるダム」が並び、金属の構造体が支える「水のような空間」が、その上を乗り越えて流れてゆくという構成である。音楽のストレットが重なるように、ダムを乗り越える水は、外の景観の様子と重なり、内部空間では同じようにして文字通り、空間が重なり合う。

バルトークの「弦楽器と打楽器とチェレスタのための音楽」という、この「ストレット」の手法を使った曲を下敷に、この住宅の形態は作られた。4つの楽章から成るこの曲は、重さ(打楽器)と軽さ(弦楽器)にはっきりと分けられている。音楽の場合の楽器編成と音における物質の位置をこの建築では光と空間におきかえてアナロジーを試みた。つまり次のような関係である。

$$\frac{物質 \times 音}{時間} = \frac{物質 \times 光}{空間}$$

この建築は4つの部分から構成されるが、それらがまた各々2つに分節される。直角で形成される重い組積造と、曲線を描く軽い金属(テキサスでよく見かけるコンクリートブロックと金属の組み合わせ)である。平面形は純粋な曲線で構成されるが、断面は直角をなす。逆にゲストハウスでは、平面に曲線をとりいれ断面を直角にするという転倒を行った。これはバルトークの楽譜の第一楽章での主題の転回のようだ。母屋では、水のような空間が種々の方法で展開される。プランは、隣より空間のレベルを持ち上げ、屋根の面は、空間を壁の上まで引き上げるし、アーチを描く壁は、スカイライトから落ちる光を下に呼びこむ。材質とディテールは空間コンセプトを連続させながら、現場打コンクリート、液体のような形にしたガラス、前傾したガラス、流し込みのテラゾーと続く。

小川をまたぐ車道を経て建物に着き、この家の重なり合う空間を通りながら横の庭を視界にとらえつつ進むと、池から水を引いたプールのある、吹放しの部屋に至る。水面に姿を映して、2倍の大きさを感じさせるこの空間は庭と家の両方をむすび、2つの水の空間の、非対称な中心という位置を占めることになる。

View toward living room

East elevation

View toward Flooded Room

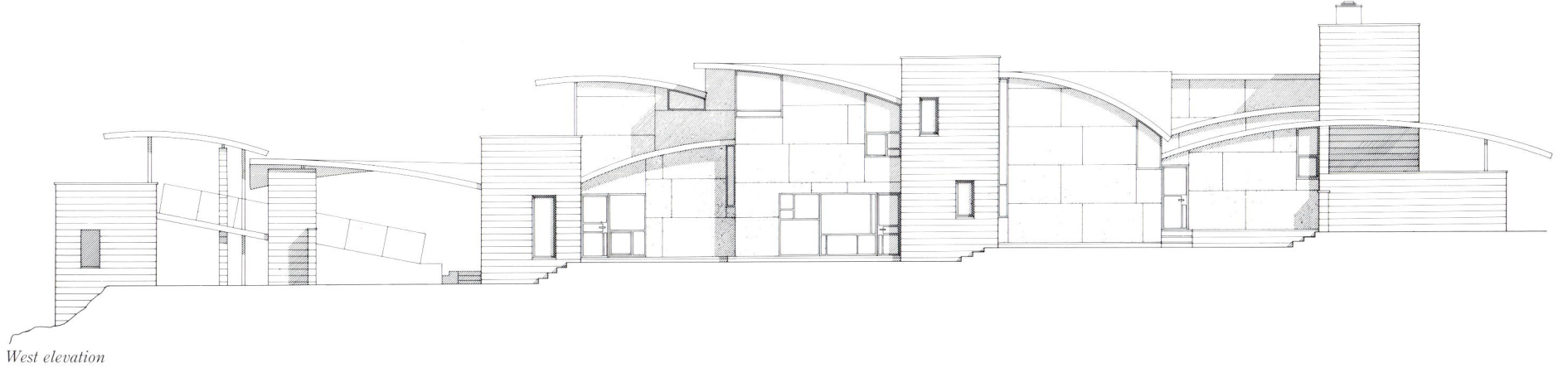

West elevation

83

△▽ *Flooded Room*

View through library toward entrance hall

View toward entrance hall

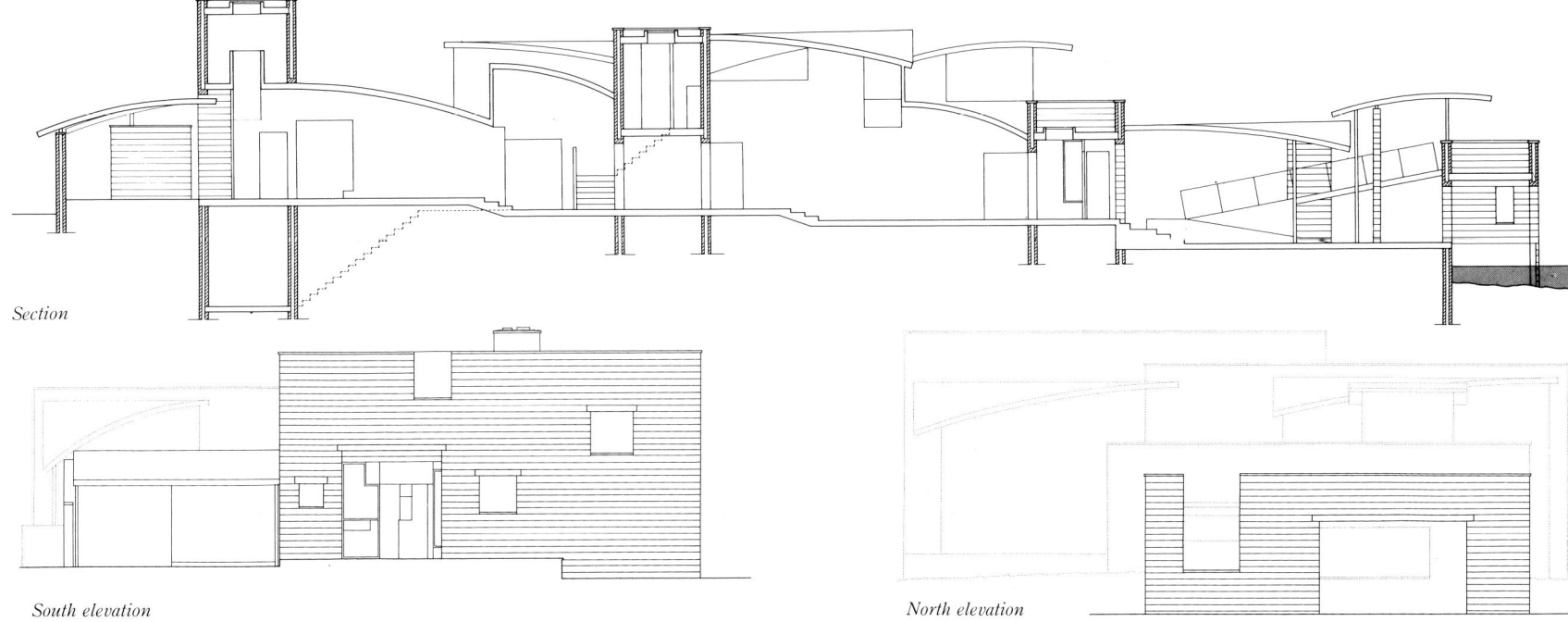

Section

South elevation

North elevation

Living room

Living room

View toward art storage room

Dining room (right)

View from living room

Exploded axonometric

3 Housing and Hybrid Buildings
ハウジングとハイブリッド・ビルディング

The concentration of many social activities within an architectural form distends and warps a pure building type. Previously neglected forms of association are wrenched together in the modern city generating buildings which might stand as an "anti-typology." Building functions are mixed, and disparate uses are combined, forming "Hybrid Buildings."

There are examples of combined-function buildings throughout history, for example, the house over the shop is prevalent in many ages and cultures. However, hybrid buildings have appeared predominantly within the past century. The modern city has acted as a fertilizer for the growth of architecture, from the homogeneous to the heterogeneous in regard to use. Urban densities and evolving building techniques have effected the mixing of functions, piling one atop another, defying those who contend that a building should "look like what it is."

The 1977 project for a gymnasium-bridge in the Bronx, New York, fused diverse programs and typological characteristics forming a hybrid building. In 1985 we began construction of the Hybrid Building in Seaside, Florida, which formed the edge of a new town square in a condensation of five diverse shops, offices and eight residences based on a mytho-poetic division between boisterous types and melancholic types. Exploration of the formation of urban space and the edges of the public space of the street, with a hybrid building of several functions, is continued with the Void Space/Hinged Space housing of Fukuoka, Japan, completed in 1991.

A hybrid combination of functions in buildings can be more than a mute mixture of uses. These juxtapositions may be "social condensers" creating primary interactions of vitality within the city, increasing the role of architecture as a catalyst for change. *(S.H.)*

数多くの社会活動をまとめて，一つの建築形態の中におさめると，建築のタイプは純粋なものではなく，膨張したりねじれたりしたものになって来る。それまでは省みられることのなかった集合形態が現代都市の中にねじり合わされ，「反類型的」な建築が生れてくる。建築の機能が混在し，共通するもののない用途が組み合わされると，「ハイブリッド・ビルディング」が形成される。

さまざまな機能を組み合わせた建築の例は，歴史を通じていつの時代にも存在してきた。たとえば，商店の上に住宅を重ねる形式は，多くの時代多くの文化を通じてよく見られる。複合ビルは，前世紀になって目につくようになってきたタイプである。単一の機能から複合機能へと建築が成長するにあたっては，現代都市が肥料の役割を果たしたのである。都市の密度が上昇し建築技術が進化したことが影響を及ぼして，機能が混ざり合い，次々と重ねられてゆくようになり，その結果，建築は「それらしく見える」ものでなければならないと考える人達を無視するようになった。

1977年の，ニューヨーク，ブロンクスのジムナジウム・ブリッジのプロジェクトでは種々のプログラムと類型を融合させて複合ビルをつくった。1985年には，フロリダ州シーサイドのハイブリッド・ビルの建設にかかった。新しくつくられた広場の一辺を形成して5つの業種からなる独立した店舗とオフィス，8戸の住宅を集合させた。住宅は想定した住人に神話詩的な分類をほどこし，躁タイプとメランコリータイプに分けて考えた。都市空間の組立て方と街路に面するパブリック・スペースの境界のありかたを探り，複数の機能をもつ複合ビルを配するという方法は，1991年に完成した福岡のハウジング，〈ヴォイド・スペース／ヒンジド・スペース〉に引きつがれる。

建築に異質の機能を盛り込むことは，ただ用途を混合させるというだけのものではない。これはいわば「ソーシャル・コンデンサー」の働きをして，都市に生き生きとした活力を引きおこし，建築が変化のための触媒としての役割を増すことになるだろう。 *(S.H.)*

Hybrid Building, Seaside ▷

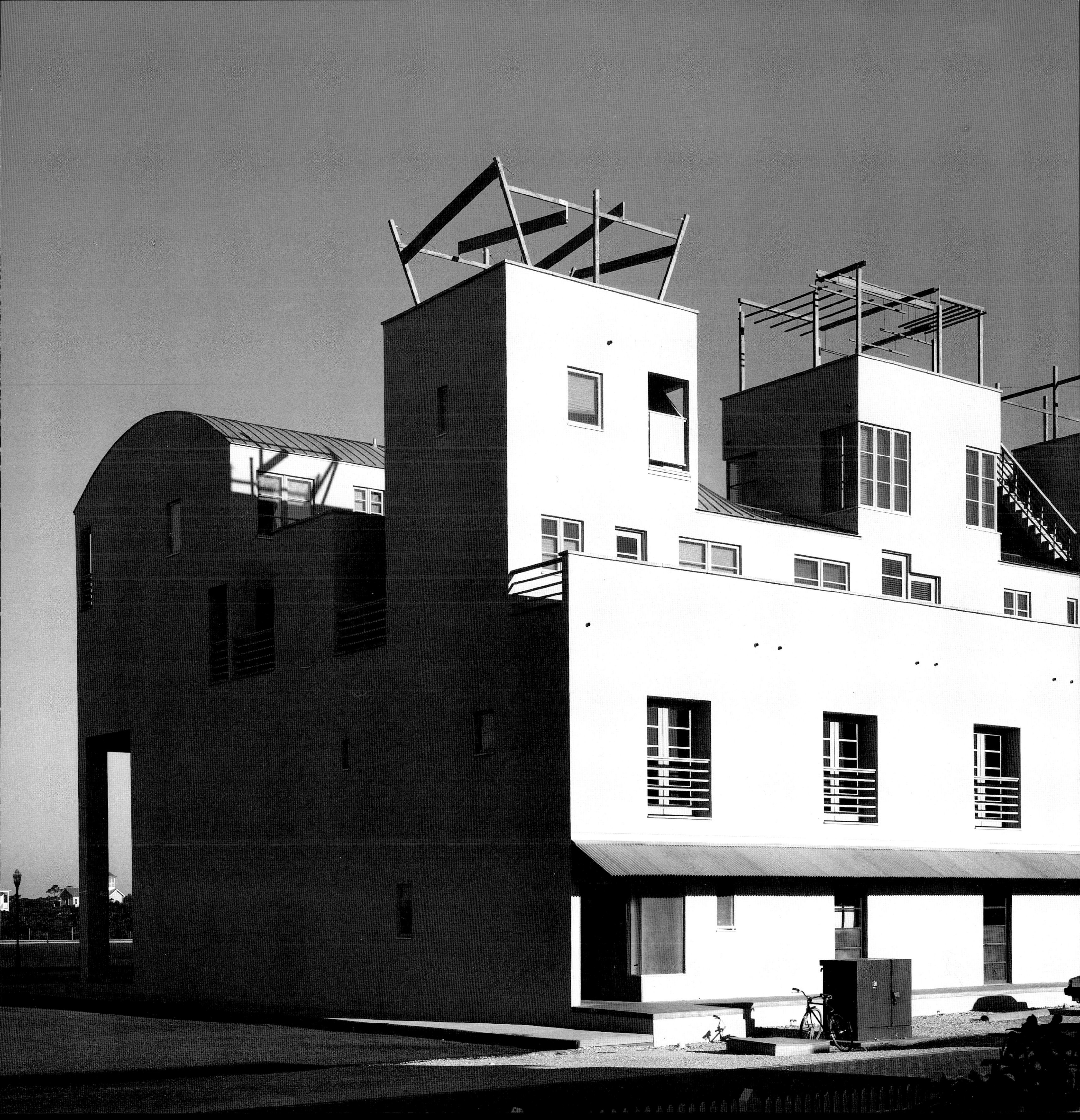

Gymnasium Bridge
South Bronx, New York
1977–78

Penn Central's South Bronx railroad yards have fallen into disuse. The site is boxed in by bridges and elevated highways with a ceiling formed by the flight patterns of planes landing and taking off from La Guardia Airport. The program called for "ideas or strategies that would yield incremental benefits for the immediate neighborhood." The only explicit requirement is a pedestrian bridge from the South Bronx to the park on Randall's Island. The bridge "must not assume a form that would jeopardize the future development of the site for commercial or industrial purposes, including deep water ship movement in the canal." The immediate neighborhood of the South Bronx with a population of approximately 400,000 has unemployment of 45 to 50 percent.

The Gymnasium-Bridge is a hybrid building synthesized as a special strategy for generating positive economic and physical effects. The Gymnasium-Bridge condenses the activities of meeting, physical recreation, and work into one structure that simultaneously forms a bridge from the community to the park on Randall's Island.

Along the bridge, community members participate in competitive sports and physical activities organized according to a normal work day with wages provided by a branch of the Urban Jobs Corp or a reconstituted WPA. While earning enough money to become economically stable, community members gain physical and moral strength and develop a sense of community spirit. The bridge becomes a vehicle from which destitute persons can reenter society, become accustomed to a normal work day, and help gain the strength to develop their full individual potential.

The form of the architecture is a series of bridges over bridges. The small entrance bridges at each end of the main span preserve the view down Brook Street to the canal, and from Randall's Island up Brook Street. The main span is aligned with this axis and is crossed by a fourth and highest bridge. In water rather than over water, this bridge acts as a structural pivot from which the turn-bridge portion of the main span rotates to allow future ship passage in the waterway. At its base are floats for competition rowboats, which are an extension of the activities and payroll of the Gymnasium.

The structure is a two-story steel truss covered in translucent white insulated panels. The panels at eye-level may be opened outward forming awnings over their sills. At night the interior lighting produces a glowing effect, lighting the axis and pathway below the bridge.

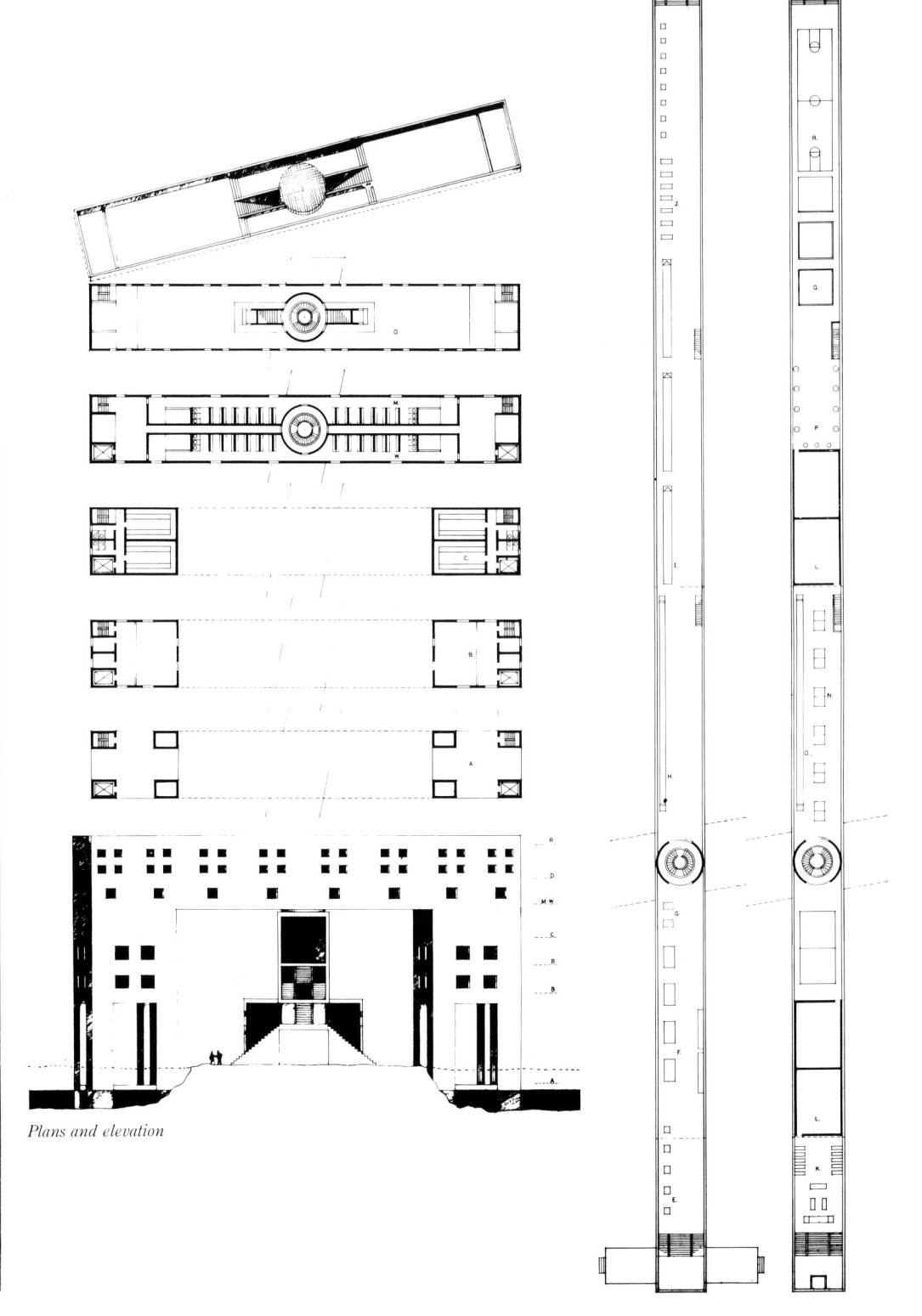

Perspective

Plans and elevation

ジムナジウム・ブリッジ

ペン・セントラルの，サウス・ブロンクス鉄道の用地はすっかりさびれてしまい，使用されることもなくなった。この敷地は橋と高速道路に四方を囲まれ，ラガーディア空港に離着陸する飛行機の航路が，さながらそこに架けられた天井のようである。これは「隣接地域の利益を増進する戦略」と呼ばれる計画である。ただひとつの明快な要望は，サウス・ブロンクスからランドール島の公園にゆく歩行者用の橋を作ることであった。この橋は「この地域の将来の商工業の発展や，河を航行する船の活動を阻害するようなものであってはならない」という。サウス・ブロンクスの隣接地域は，およそ40万の人口をかかえ，失業者がその45％から50％を占めていた。

ジムナジウム・ブリッジは，経済的にも体育の上でも積極的な効果の期待される，特別な戦略を統合するための複合的な建物なのだ。集会，スポーツやトレーニングなどの活動を凝縮して，それを建築物という形にしたもので，同時に，この地域からランドール島の公園へ渡る橋でもある。

この橋を渡って，地域の住民たちは競技スポーツや体育活動に参加する。これらはウィークデーに行われ，都市職業協会の出張所や再建されたWPA（事業企画庁）によって賃金が支払われる。経済的安定を得るだけの金を手に入れるかたわら，地域住民は肉体的にもモラルの上でも強化されて，コミュニティ意識を育てられてゆくことになる。この橋は人を乗せる乗物のようなものかもしれない。これを降りる時には，貧しい人々が社会に戻って，労働に日々を送り，ひとりひとりの能力を充分に発揮できるような力を得るための手助けをするのだ。建築の形態は，橋の上に橋を載せるという形を繰返したものである。主要部の両端にある，エントランスとなる小さなブリッジからは，ブルック通りの側から運河を望み，ランドール島側からはブルック通りを見通すことができる。主要部はこれを結ぶ軸に沿って渡り，それと交差する形で4つ目の，一番高いブリッジがある。水の上というより，水の中に建つこのブリッジを中心にして，主要部分の一部が回転し，将来，運河で船の航行が行われれば回転橋になる。橋の足許には競技用のボートの浮桟橋がある。このボートはジムナジウムの活動と報酬支払事業の一部として運営される。

構造は，2層のトラスを透光性の白いパネルで包んだものだ。その一部，目の高さのパネルは，突出し窓として開けることができる。夜になると，内部の明りがにじみだし，ブリッジそのものが発光体となってその下の通路も照らし出される。

Perspective

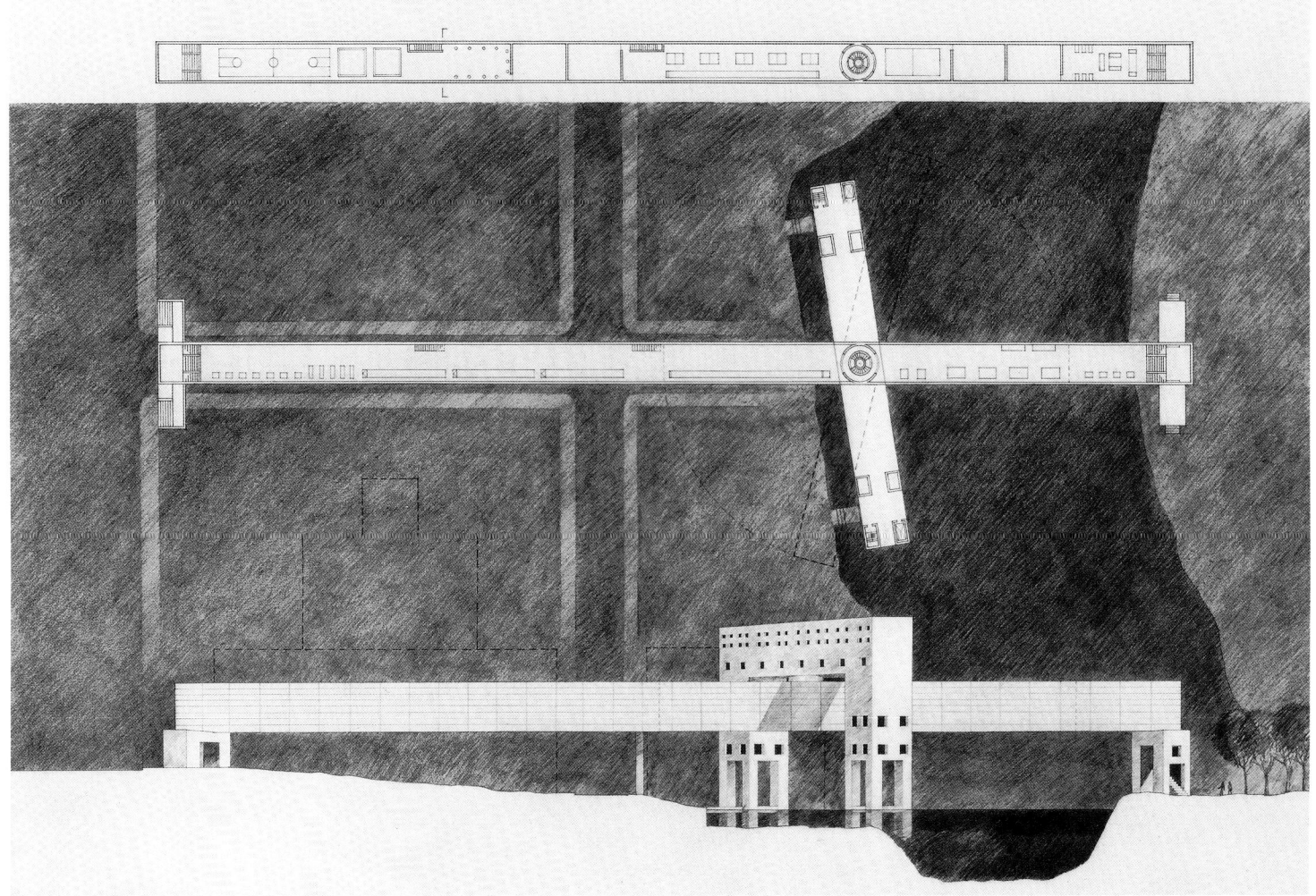

Site plan and perspective

Model

Model

95

Bridge of Houses
New York, New York
1979–82

Perspective

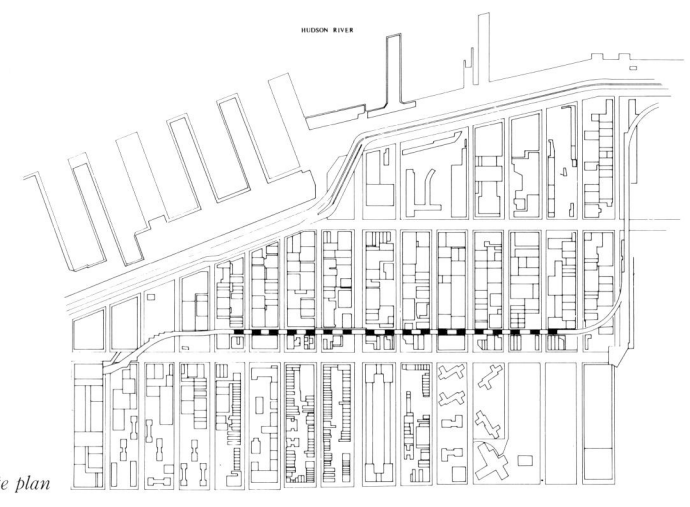

Site plan

The site and structural foundation of the Bridge of Houses is the existing superstructure of an abandoned elevated rail link in the Chelsea area of New York City. This steel structure is utilized in its straight leg from West 19th Street to West 29th Street parallel to the Hudson River.

West Chelsea is changing from a warehouse district to a residential area. With the decline of shipping activity on the pierfront, many vacant warehouses are being converted to residential lofts. The Bridge of Houses reflects the new character of the area as a place of habitation. Re-use rather than demolition of the existing bridge would be a permanent contribution to the character of the city.

This project offers a variety of housing types for the Chelsea area, as well as an elevated public promenade connecting with the new Convention Center on its north end. The structural capacity and width of the existing bridge determine the height and width of the houses. Four houses have been developed in detail, emphasizing the intention to provide a collection of housing blocks offering the widest possible range of social-economic coexistence. At one extreme are houses of single-room-occupancy type, offered for the city's homeless; each of these blocks contains twenty studio rooms. At the other extreme are houses of luxury apartments; each of these blocks contains three or four flats. Shops line the public promenade level below

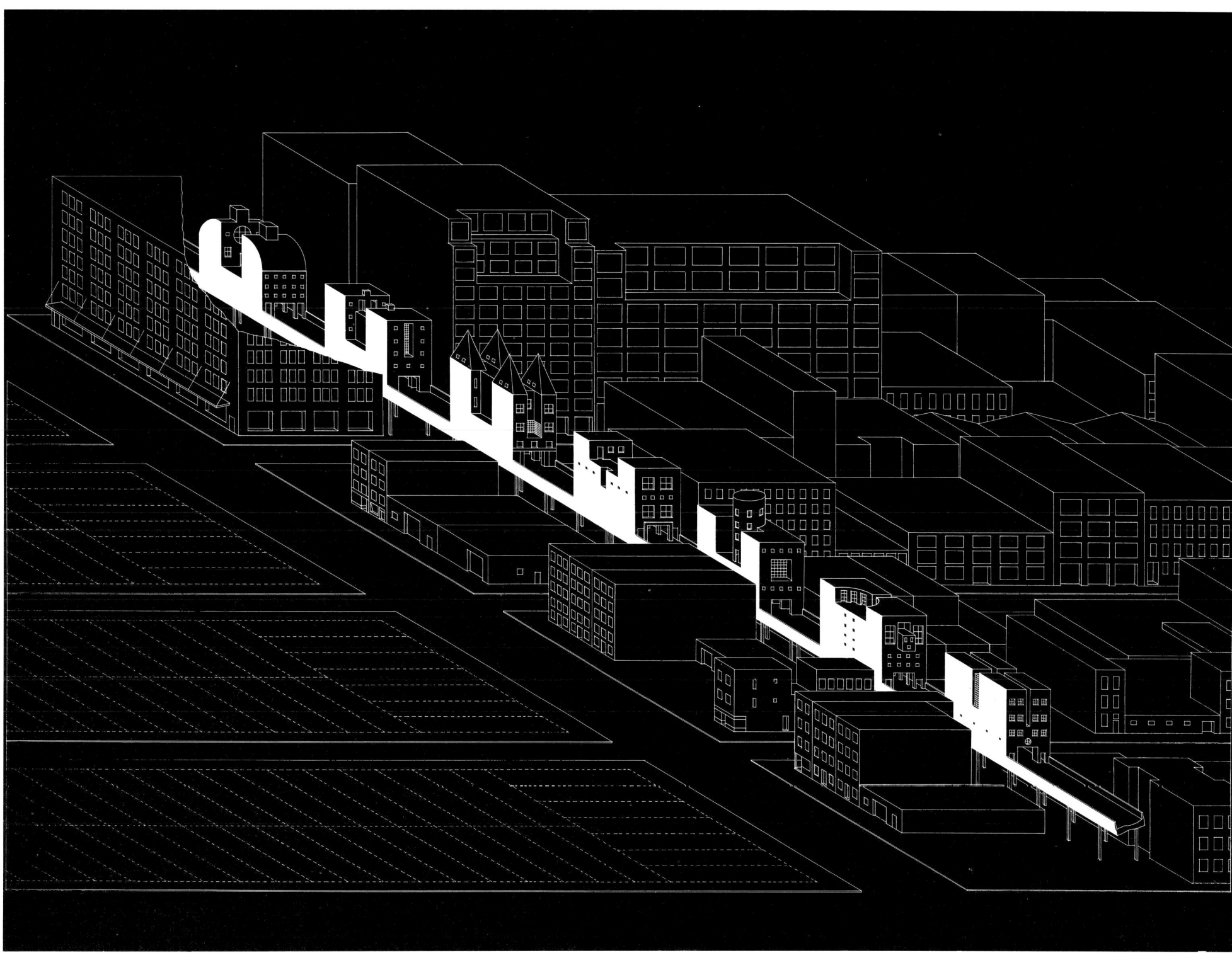

Site condition

the houses.

The new houses are built in an alternating pattern with a series of 2,000-square-foot courtyards (50% open space). All new houses align with the existing block front at the street walls, reinforcing the street pattern. The ornamental portions of the rail bridge that pass over the streets remain open.

Construction consists of a lightweight metal frame with a reinforced exterior rendering on wire lath and a painted finish. Windows have a baked enamel finish, while doors are made of solid core wood with sandblasted glass drawings on the entrances and brass lever handles.

ブリッジ・ハウス

ブリッジ・ハウスの場合には敷地というか，基礎というか，それは，ニューヨーク市のチェルシー地区にある高架鉄道の，今では使われなくなった既存の構造物なのだ。スティール製の構造物は，西19番地から西29番地まで，ハドソン河に平行に直線をなしている。

ウェスト・チェルシー地区は，倉庫街から居住地域へと変貌しつつある。埠頭がかつてのにぎわいを失うにつれて，使われなくなった倉庫の多くが住宅用のロフトに変わっているのだ。ブリッジ・ハウスは，この一帯の住居地域化という新たな性格の変化に応じたものである。もともとある高架線を取壊すよりは，再利用を図るほうが，この都市の本来の性格を守るのに役立つはずである。

この計画は，高架線上にチェルシー地区のために種々のタイプの住宅を作り，その建物の足元には空中プロムナードを通し，北の端にはコンヴェンションセンターを作るというものである。既存のブリッジの構造上の余力と寸法によって住宅の高さと幅は決定される。4つの住宅棟が詳細まで作られた。居住対象となる住民を，社会的にも経済的にも幅の広いものにしたいと私たちは考えた。一方の極には，ワンルームで，ホームレスたちのためのタイプがある。これには1棟に20戸のワンルーム・タイプが含まれる。もう一方の極には，豪華なアパートメントがある。こちらは1棟が3戸から4戸のフラットで構成される。住居の下のプロムナードのレベルには店舗が軒を連ねる。

新しい住宅は，2,000平方フィートの中庭（50%のオープンスペース）と交互に建てられる。これらは全て，街のグリッドに合わせて，通り沿いの壁と整列させ，街路のパターンを強めることになる。街路をまたぐ高架橋の装飾もそのまま残される。

構造は軽量鉄骨にワイヤラス下地で外部仕上のうえ塗装する。窓はエナメル焼付塗装，無垢の木製の玄関のドアは，ガラスにサンドブラスト仕上でドローイングを描き真鍮のレバーハンドルを取付ける。

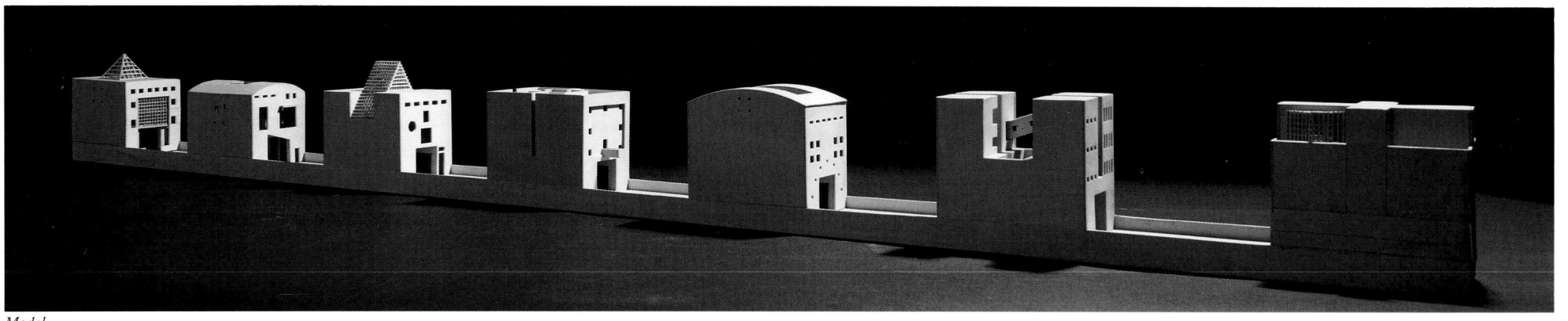

Model

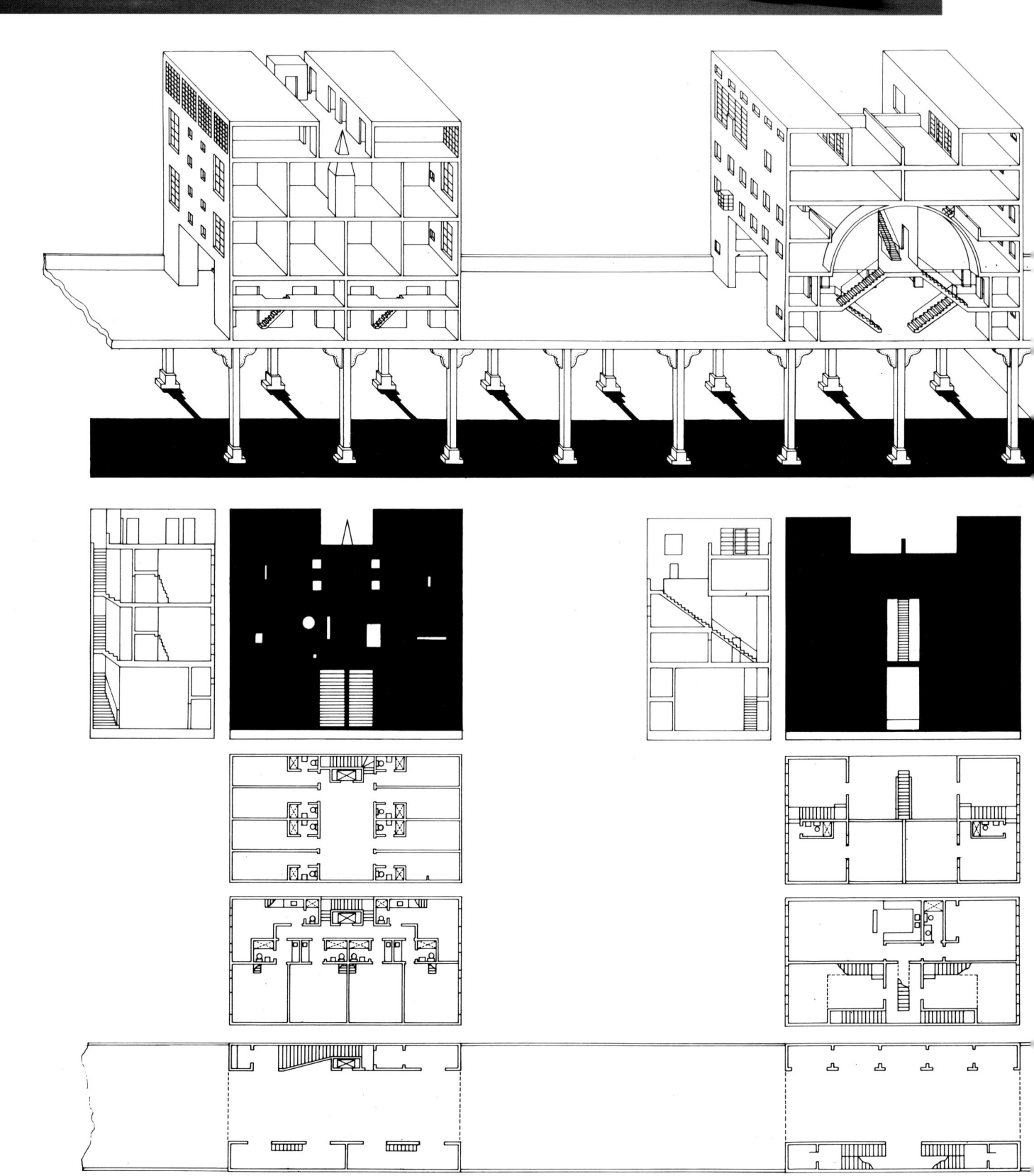

98

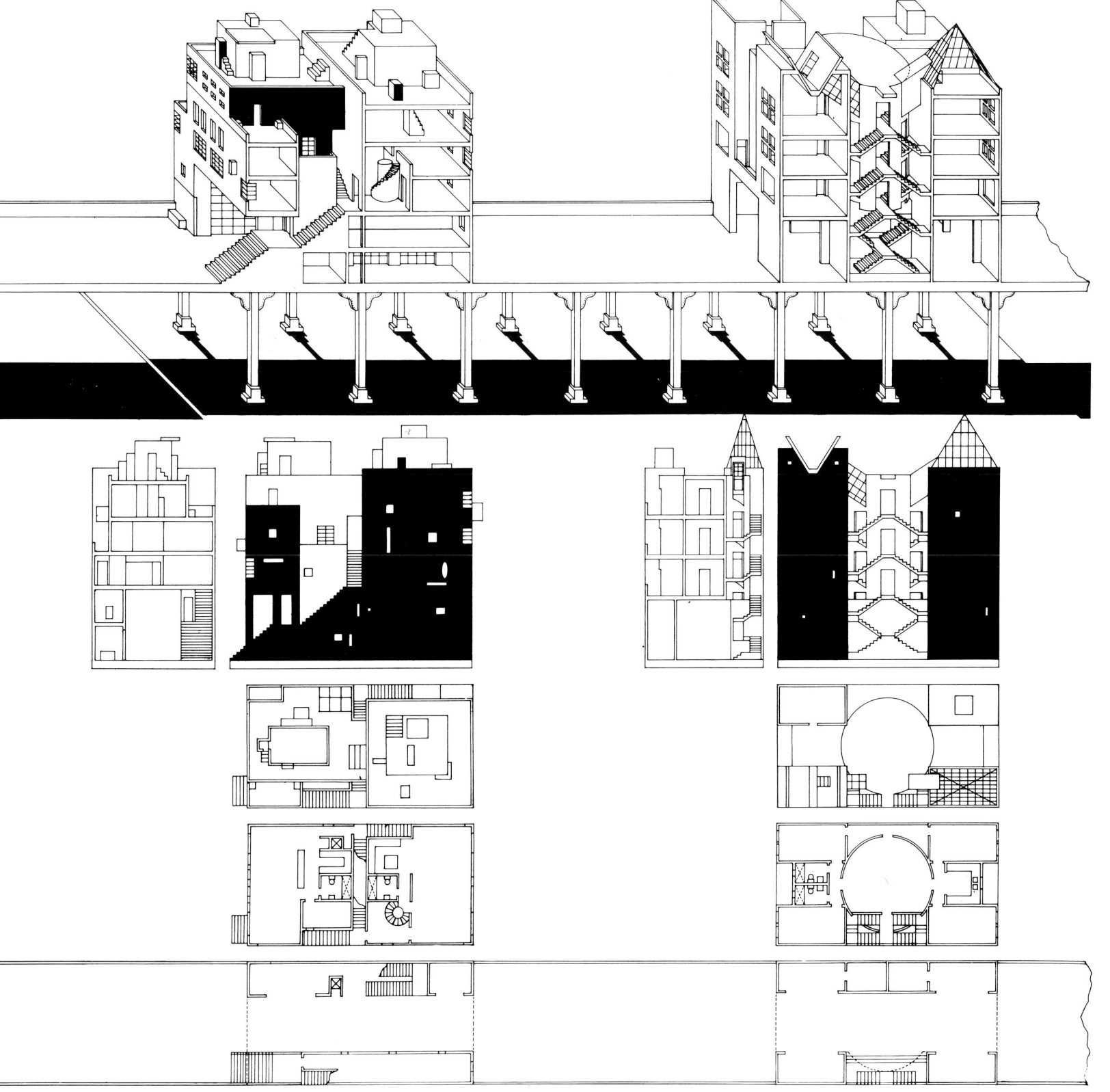

Cutaway axonometrics, sections, elevations and plans

*Autonomous Artisans' Housing
Staten Island, New York
1980–84*

Site plan

An existing warehouse is converted to work space held in common by artisans working in several disciplines. Against the warehouse wall, houses are built in a pattern allowing for private gardens between each house. The plan/section is based on the "shotgun" type.

The individual autonomous artisan's craft is expressed in the second level of each house: the paper maker's house has a roof terrace shaped specifically for drying paper; the wood worker's house displays the skills of a boat builder; the mason has a brick barrel vault roof. A roof of etched glass covers the glass etcher's entry way. Similarly, expressions of craft exist in the plasterer's and metal worker's houses.

Outdoor areas include private gardens between each of the houses, as well as roof terraces. The urban street edge is maintained with the alignment of the front walls. Construction of the foundation level of each house is insulation-filled concrete block and wood floor joists. Roofs and second level elements are in different materials according to each artisan/occupant.

自由な職人のハウジング
既存の倉庫を，それぞれ分野を異にする職人が共有する仕事場に改造し，その倉庫の壁を背にして住宅が建てられる。住棟の配置は，各戸の間に専用の庭をはさみこんでゆくというものだ。平面と断面はショットガン・タイプを基にして作られた。自由職人のひとりひとりの仕事が，各々の家の2階に表現される。たとえば紙漉き職人の家には，紙の乾燥台の形をしたルーフテラスがあるし，木工職人の住いでは船大工の腕前を見せる。石工の家の屋根にはレンガ造のヴォールトがかけられるかと思えばエッチングを施したガラスの屋根が，エッチング職人の家の入口を蔽う。そんな具合に，左官や金工職人の住いにもその腕を示すものが作られる。

屋外のスペースは，各戸の間を分かつ専用庭の他にもルーフテラスがある。道路側の面は壁の位置を揃えて並ぶ。1階レベルの構造は断熱材詰のコンクリートブロックに木造の梁だが，屋根と2階の各部は，職種に応じてそれぞれに異なった材料が使われる。

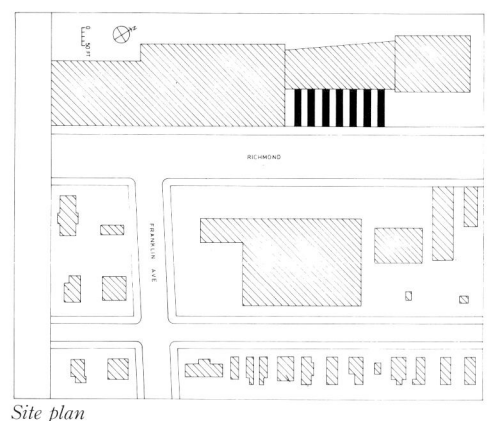

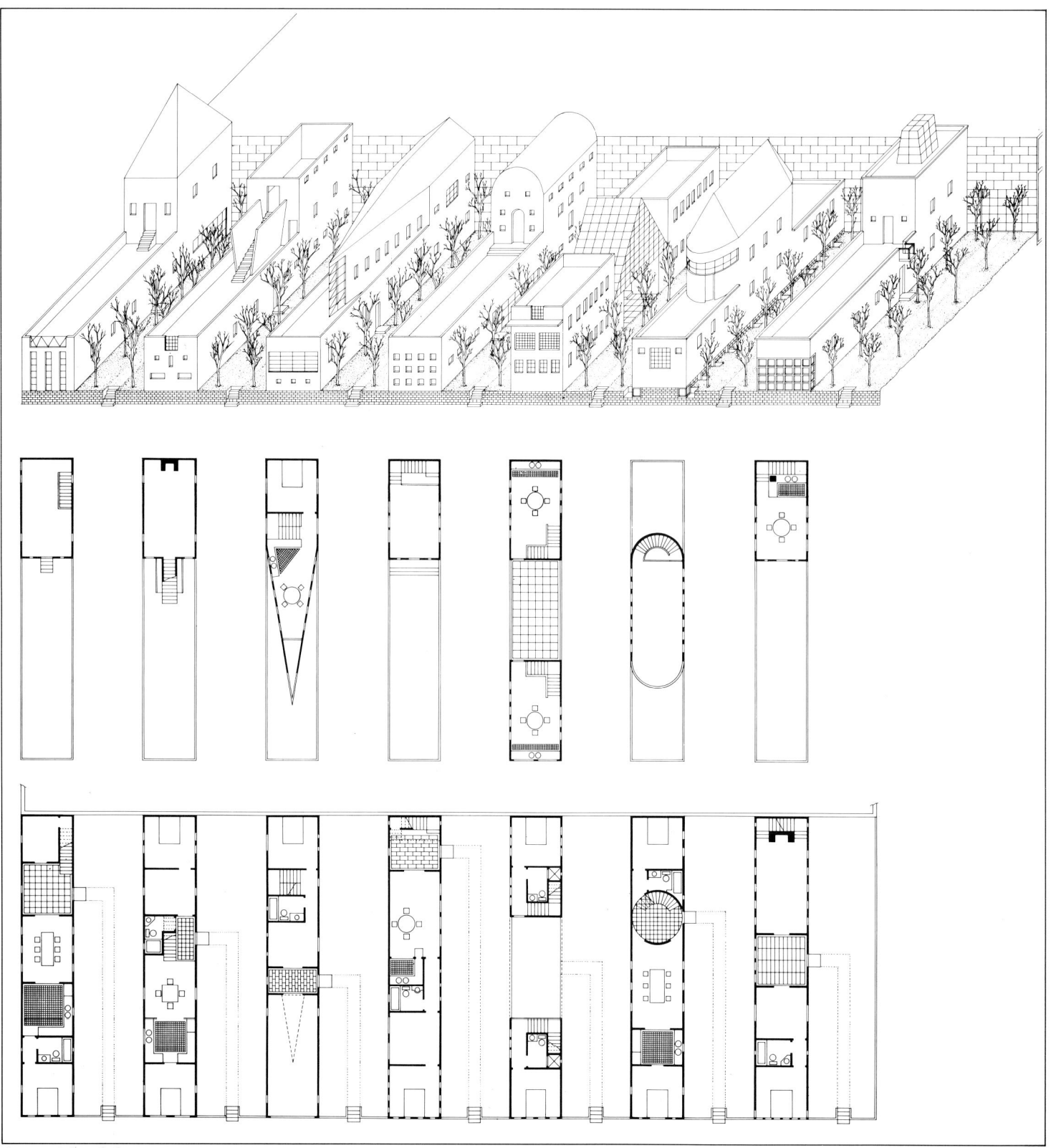

Axonometric and plans

Perspective

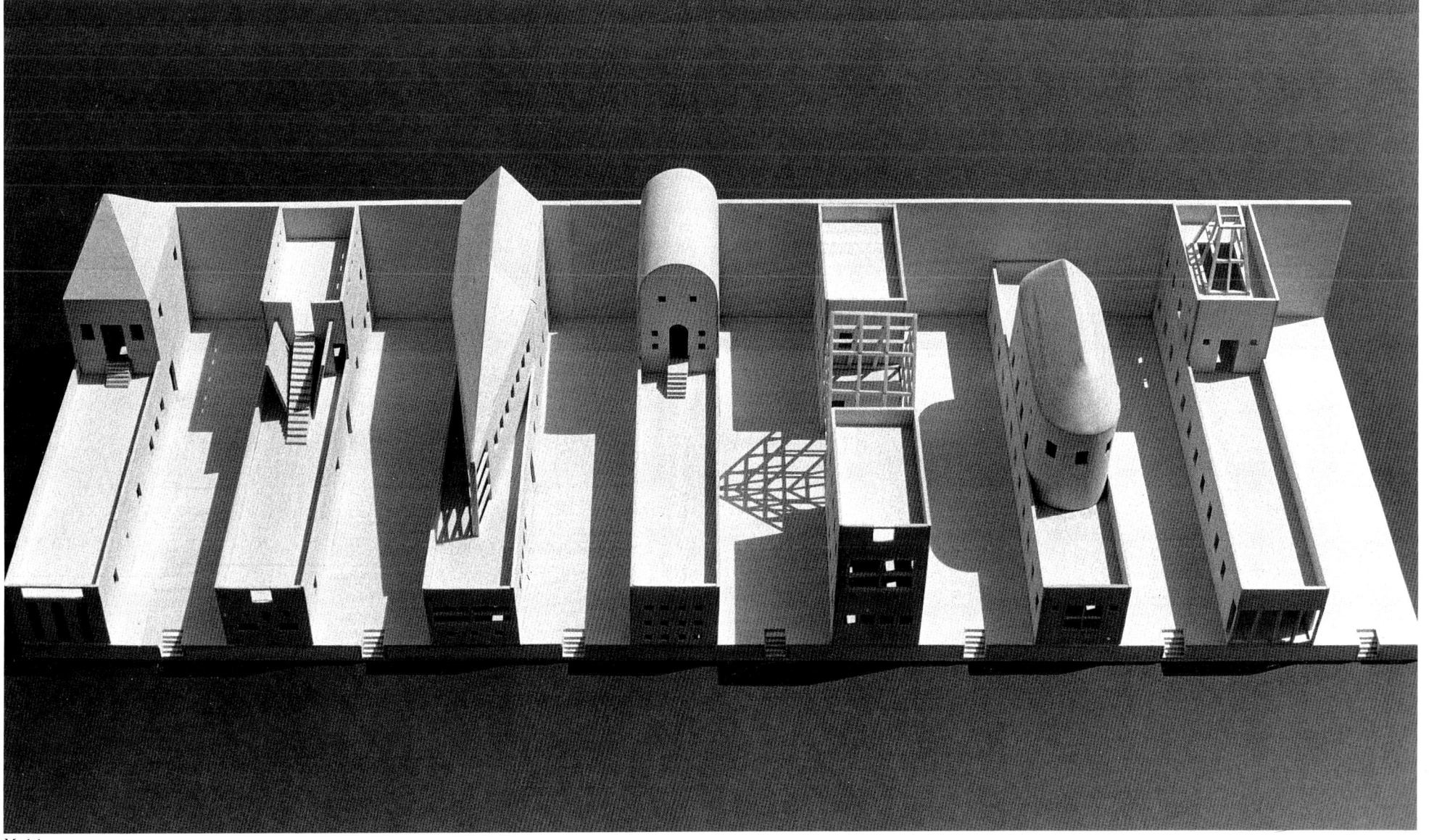

Model

Hybrid Building
Seaside, Florida
1984–88

Seaside is a new town on the Gulf of Mexico. The planners have established height restrictions, design guidelines, and easements. By their code, this project and adjoining buildings are required to form a continuous public arcade around the square.

The Hybrid Building combines retail, office, and residential uses. The concentration of disjointed programs forms an incidental urbanism. Along with intensification of an urban condition, the building expresses the idea of a "society of strangers." The building forms split at the upper levels into east and west types. Rooms facing the setting sun and central square are for boisterous types, late risers who enjoy watching the action, toasting the sunset, etc. All of their two-level flats are identical. They contain luxury bathrooms, microwave ovens, and space for parties.

Facing east to the rising sun are rooms for melancholic types. These individuals are early risers, inclined to silence and solitude. Melancholic types are imagined as: a tragic poet, a musician, and a mathematician. The plans and sections of the three rear flats are characterized accordingly. The house of the tragic poet has dim light; every window is of the same narrow and tall dimension. The awning at the roof is like a rag on a peasant's table. In the house of the musician, light is cast down from the corner windows on the upper level. A black plaster wall slips from the lower to the upper floor, enhancing the flowing nature of the space. In the house of the mathematician everything is slightly warped. The stair to the second level warps over the bathroom. The warp over the ceiling joists forms a slight doubly-curved surface. At the second level is a calculating table with a skull shelf, in homage to Johannes Kepler.

Construction is of precast concrete columns and beams, and hollow-core planks. Walls are integral-color stucco on concrete block; roofs are galvanized metal.

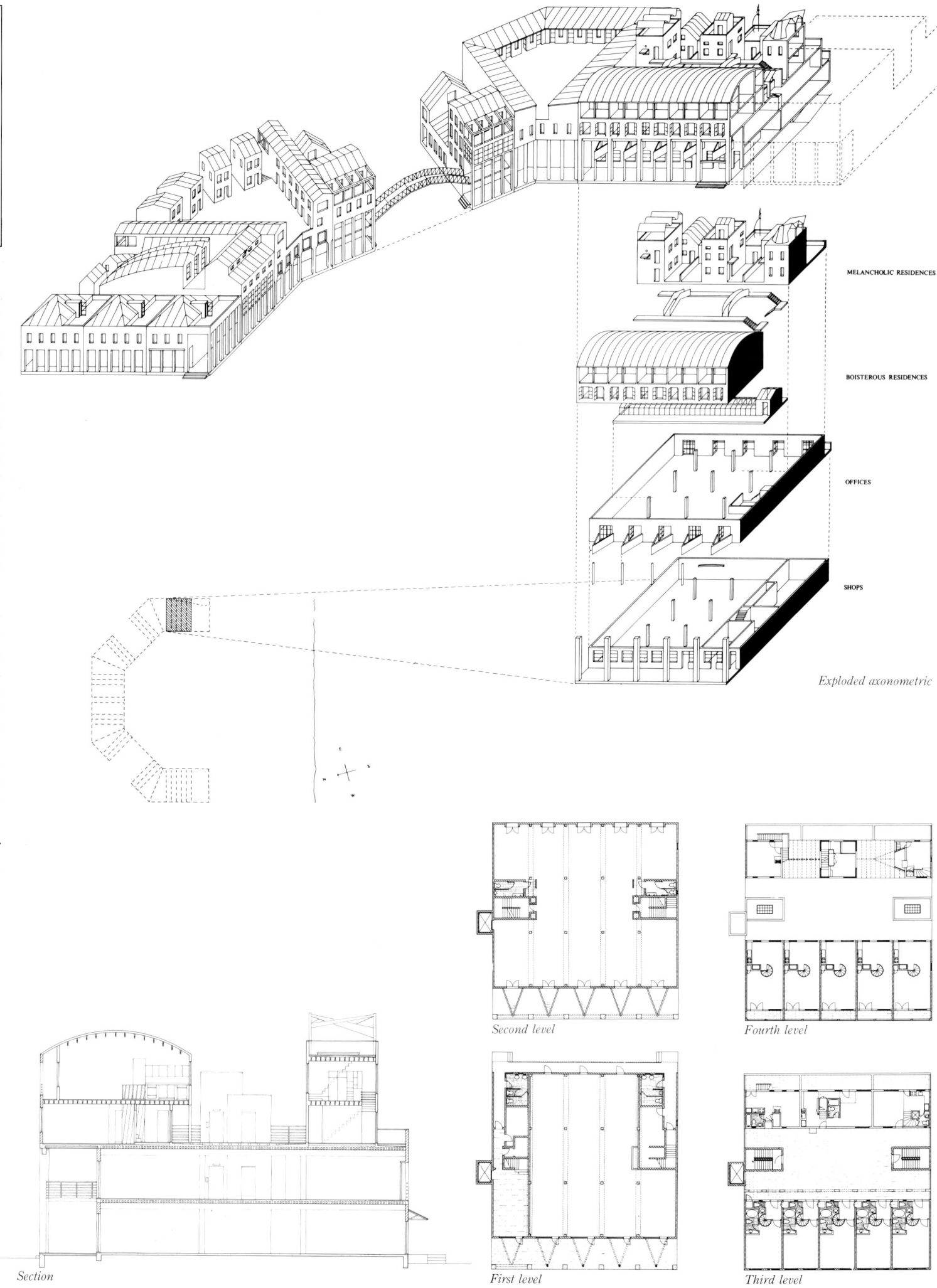

Exploded axonometric

Section

Second level

Fourth level

First level

Third level

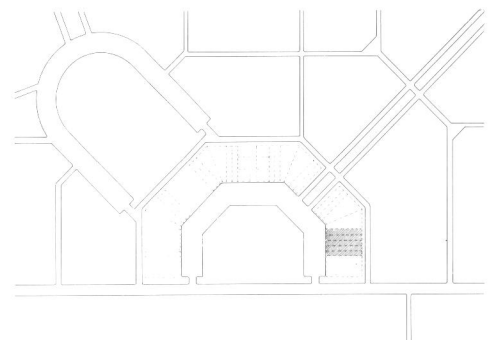

Site plan

ハイブリッド・ビルディング

シーサイドは，メキシコ湾に臨むニュータウンである。これを作るにあたって，高さ制限，デザイン・ガイドライン，地役権などの規定をプランナーは用意した。この協定によって，この建物と隣につづく建物は，広場を囲むアーケードを連続させてゆくことを求められた。

ハイブリッド・ビルは，小売り店舗，オフィス，住宅などで構成される。個々の独立を重んじる設計に集中した結果，都市的な雰囲気が生じることになった。都市的な状況を強調すると同時に，これは「見知らぬ者たちの社会」というテーマを表現する。上層の階は，東向きと西向きのタイプに分かれる。夕陽をのぞみ広場に向いた部屋は，にぎやかなのが好きなタイプ，朝はおそく起きて街のにぎわいや燃える夕陽をながめるのを楽しむ人たち向きだ。2層からなるフラットは，すべて同じ形式である。豪華なバスルームと電子レンジを備え，パーティーのためのスペースも用意される。

朝日を望む東を向いた部屋は，メランコリー気質の人の部屋だ。この人たちは早起きで静けさを好み孤独にひたる。たとえば悲劇詩人，音楽家，数学者などである。裏側の3戸のフラットは，このようにして性格付けされた。悲劇詩人の住いはうす暗い。窓は，どれも細長い。屋上の日除けは農夫のテーブルにかける布のようだ。音楽家の住いには，上の階の角の窓から光が落ちる。黒いプラスターの壁が下の階から上まで続いて空間の連続を強調する。数学者の住いでは，すべてがわずかにねじれている。上へ昇る階段はバスルームの上をねじれながら昇ってゆく。その天井は垂木をねじらせることで，2重曲面を作った。上階には，ヨハネス・ケプラーを讃えて，頭蓋骨をのせるための棚を備えた，計算用のテーブルがある。構造は，プレキャスト・コンクリートの柱梁にヴォイド・スラブ。壁はコンクリートブロックにカラースタッコ塗，屋根は亜鉛メッキ板である。

Roof terrace

View from northwest

View from east

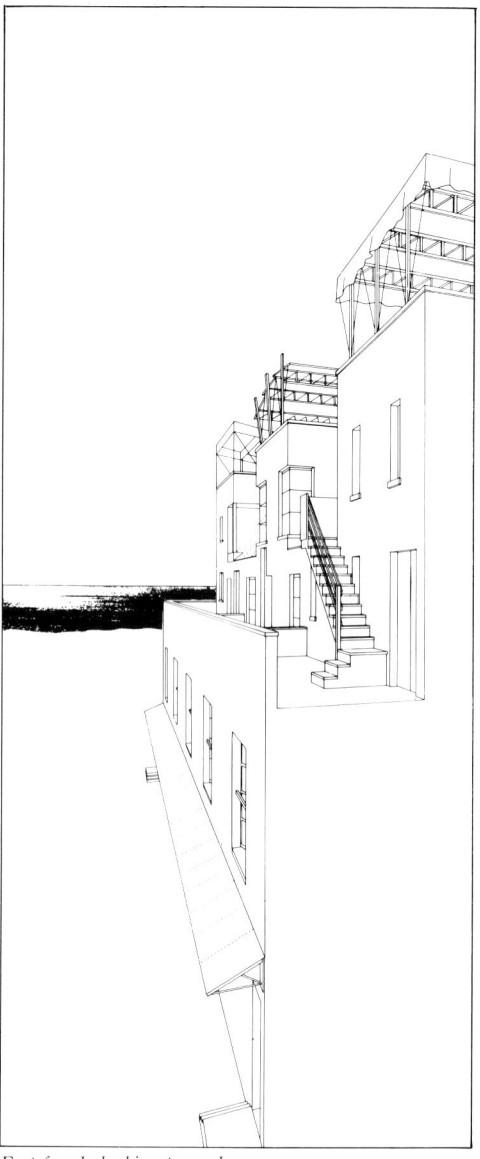

East facade looking toward ocean

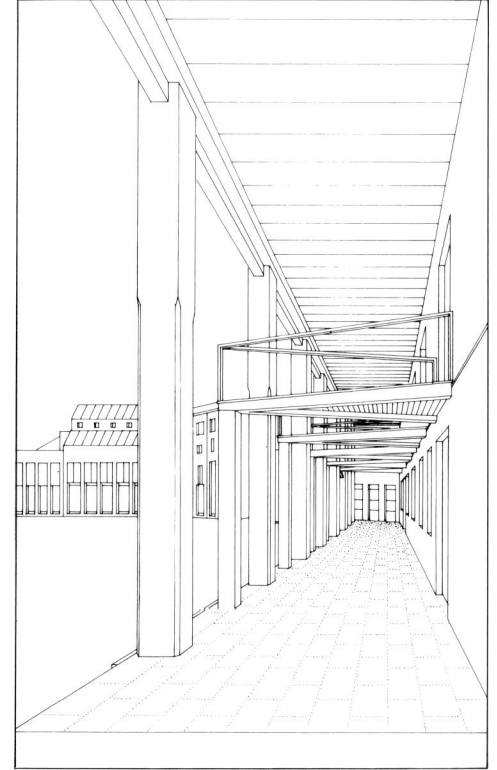

Arcade

Cutaway axonometric

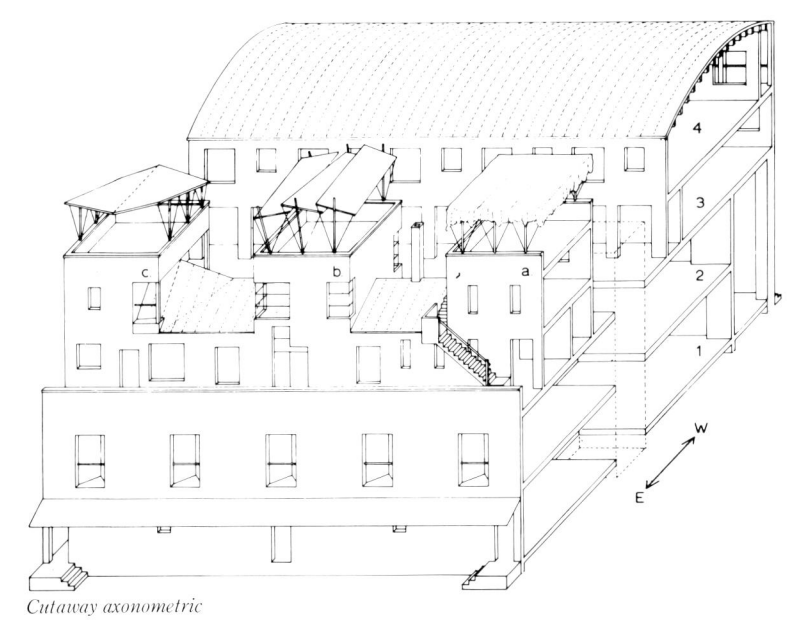

Courtyard at residential level

View from west

Boisterous residences

105

Lobby

Reception desk

Detail

Study

Concept drawing

View from stairs of House of the Tragic Poet ▷

106

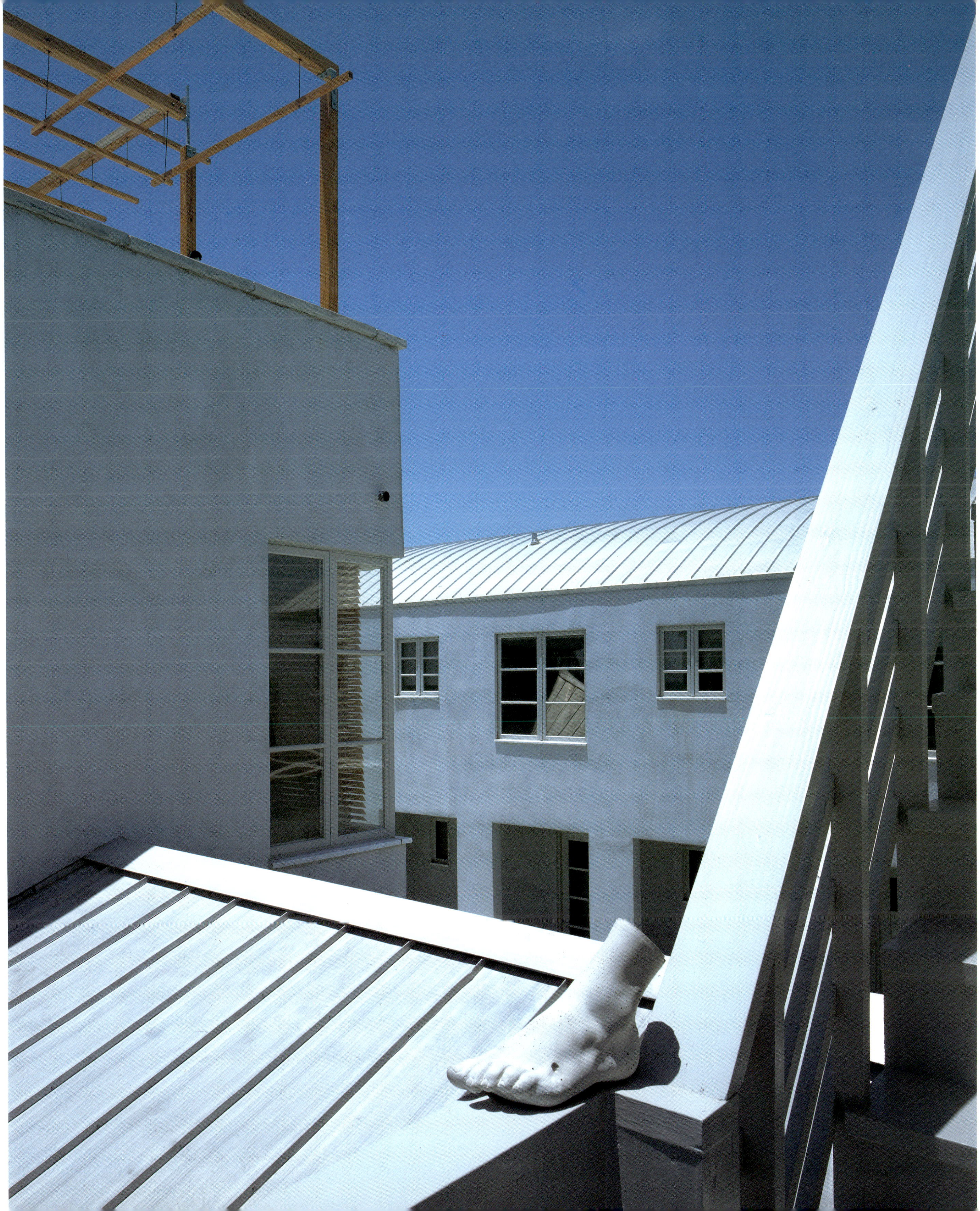

Boisterous unit

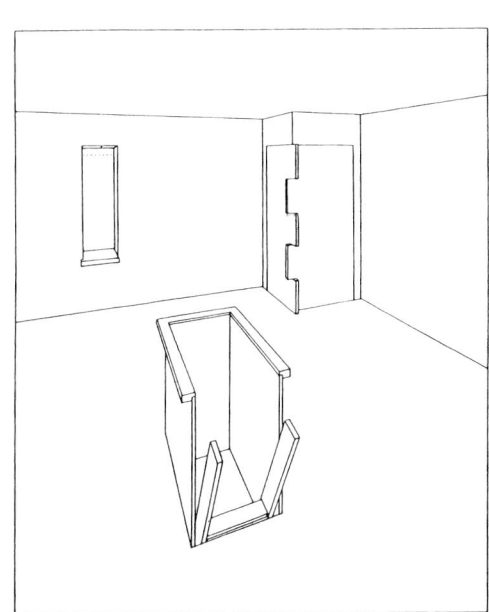

House of the Tragic Poet

109

House of the Mathematician

House of the Musician

Town Square
Four Houses and Chapel
Port Ludlow, Washington
1991–92

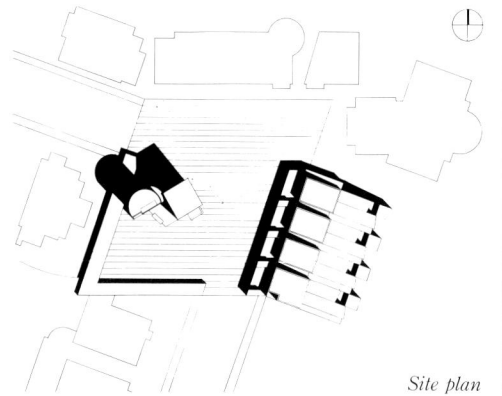

Site plan

Port Ludlow is a new community being built on the site of a former saw mill, on a small, deep-water bay in Washington State. Different architects are at work on various parts of the town. The town square by Steven Holl and Don Carlson, is a parallelogram with its acute angles oriented to Admiralty Bay to the north and the Cascade Mountains to the south-west.

One side of the town square is formed by four houses which are a four part "Ode to the Pacific Northwest": 1) "A walk through the forest," 2) "Melancholia," 3) "Free spirit," and 4) "A gaze at the mountains."

The exteriors reinforce a collective space while the interiors are individually developed.

The Chapel is programmed as a duality. As a place of silence and reflection, it accommodates sacred events, such as small weddings, vigils or last rights. As a meeting house it accommodates receptions, and concerts, etc.

The dual form of the building, curved and square, recalls the transformation of timber from the cylindrical trunks of the big Douglas firs to their final milled form, rectangular in section. The round tower is also inspired by the old saw mill burners, such as the one that existed in Port Ludlow.

The curved space recalls the mythical time of the ancient trees and the first inhabitants of the site. The square section embodies the profane: on-going historical time. The curved wall of the round tower is washed by sunlight from the tall south-facing window. The square tower is lit by the morning light from the east, which filters through a window of clear and cast colored glass, playing onto interior walls and the stained concrete floor. A light wooden stair, passing inside the curved wall, leads to the upper roof.

From the observation point at the top, one can see the whole bay of Port Ludlow and beyond to the mountains. The steel structure, with scratch-coat stucco interior, will be skinned in lead-coated copper; weathered to a silvery blue gray.

タウン・スクエア／4つの住宅と礼拝堂

ポートラドロウは、かつて製材加工場のあった土地で、ワシントン州の、小さな奥まった湾に面する小ぢんまりとしたコミュニティである。町の各所にはそれぞれ別の建築家が仕事をしている。スティーヴン・ホールとドン・カールソンによるタウン・スクエアは平行四辺形をなし、その鋭角のひとつは北のアドミラルティ湾を指し、他のひとつは南西のカスケード山を向いている。

広場の一辺は、4部構成の「北西太平洋沿岸州の頌歌」と呼ぶ4つの住宅で構成され、それぞれ、1）森を歩く、2）メランコリア、3）自由の精神、4）山々を凝視める、と名づけられた。

住宅の外形は広場の公共の性格を強めるものでありながら、内部はそれぞれに個性的である。

チャペルは2重の性格を持つよう計画された。静寂と思索の場として使われる時には、小規模な結婚式、徹夜の祈り、葬式などの宗教的な儀式が行われるが、にぎやかな集会場としては、レセプションやコンサートが開かれる。

曲線と四角で構成されるこの建築のもつ2重の形態は、ダグラスファーの巨木の円筒形が製材されて直角の断面に形を変える様を思わせるところがある。円筒形の塔は、ポートラドロウにあった製材工場の焼却炉をもとにしたものである。

曲線で作られた空間は、太古の樹々とともにこの地の先住者が暮らした神話時代を思わせる。正方形の断面は世俗の世界、現代を含めて歴史に記された時代をあらわす。円筒形の塔の曲面が南向きの高い窓から降り注ぐ陽の光に照らされるなら、四角い塔は、東からの朝の光に洗われて、透明ガラスと色ガラスの窓に濾された光が内壁とステイン塗のコンクリートの床に戯れる。その中を軽やかな木の階段が内壁の曲面に沿って上の屋根へ昇ってゆく。

頂上の物見台に立てば、ポートラドロウの湾とその向こうの山並みを一望に納める。鉄骨の構造体にスタッコのかき落しで内壁を仕上げ、銀色を帯びたブルーグレーに腐蝕させた鉛を張った銅板で外壁を包む。

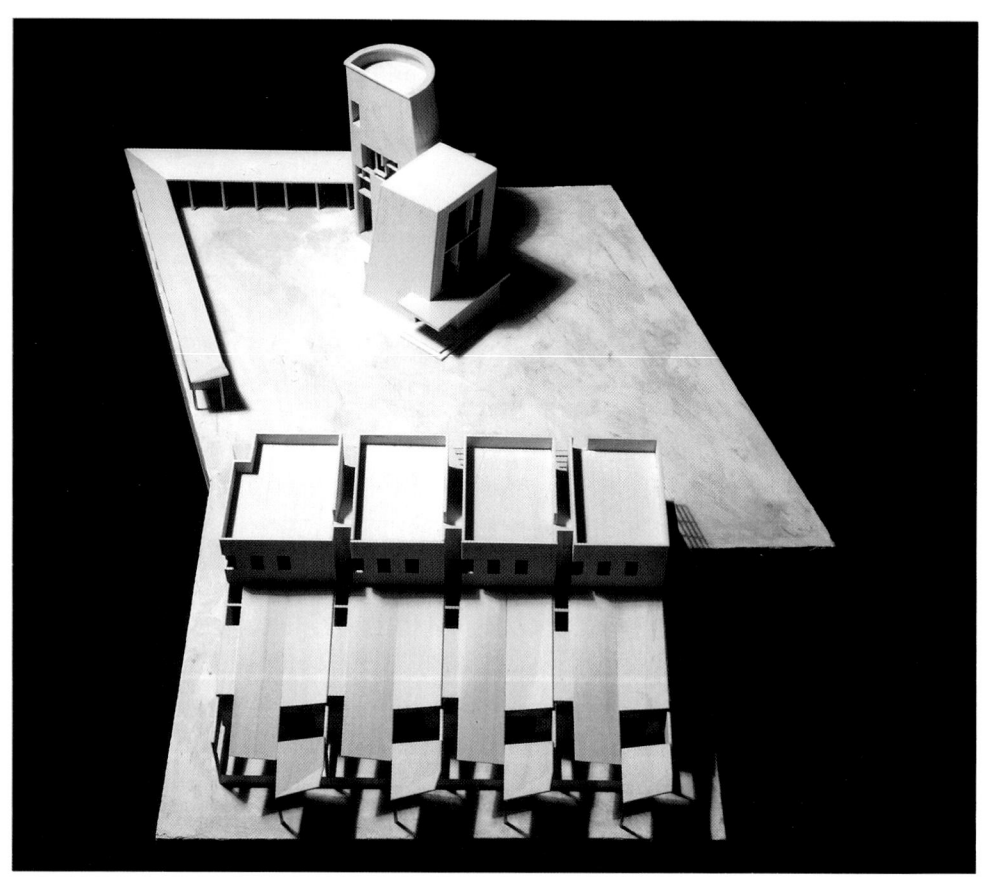

Model

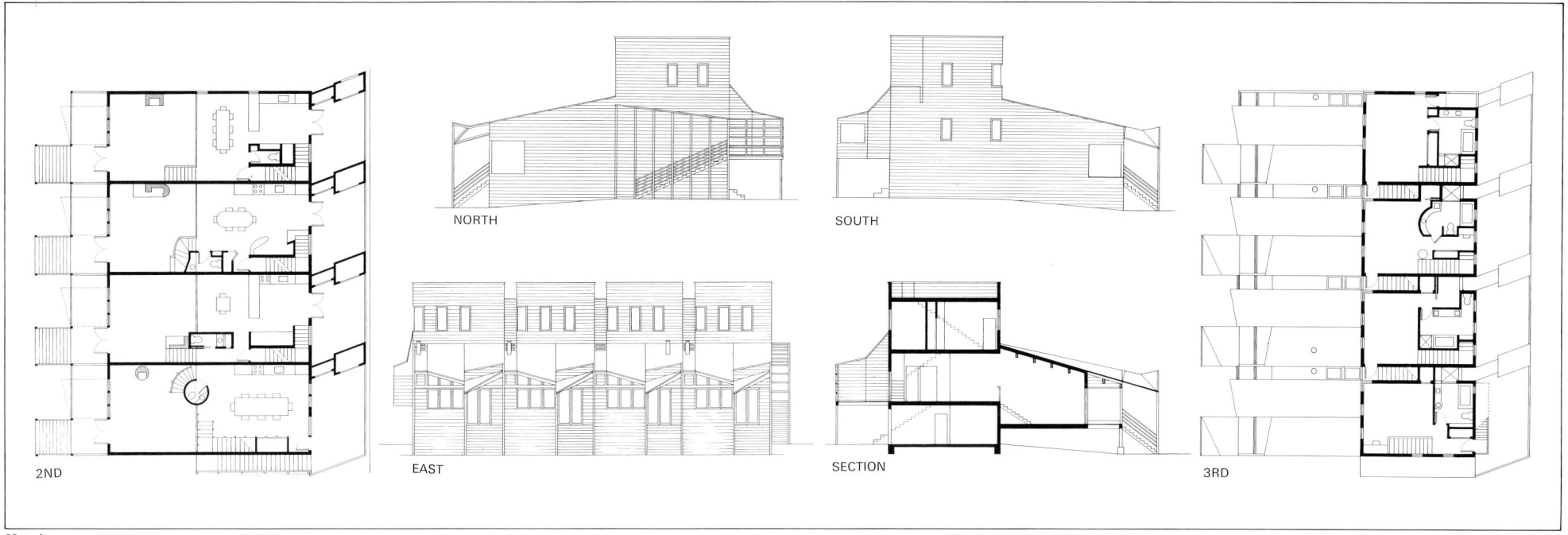

Housing

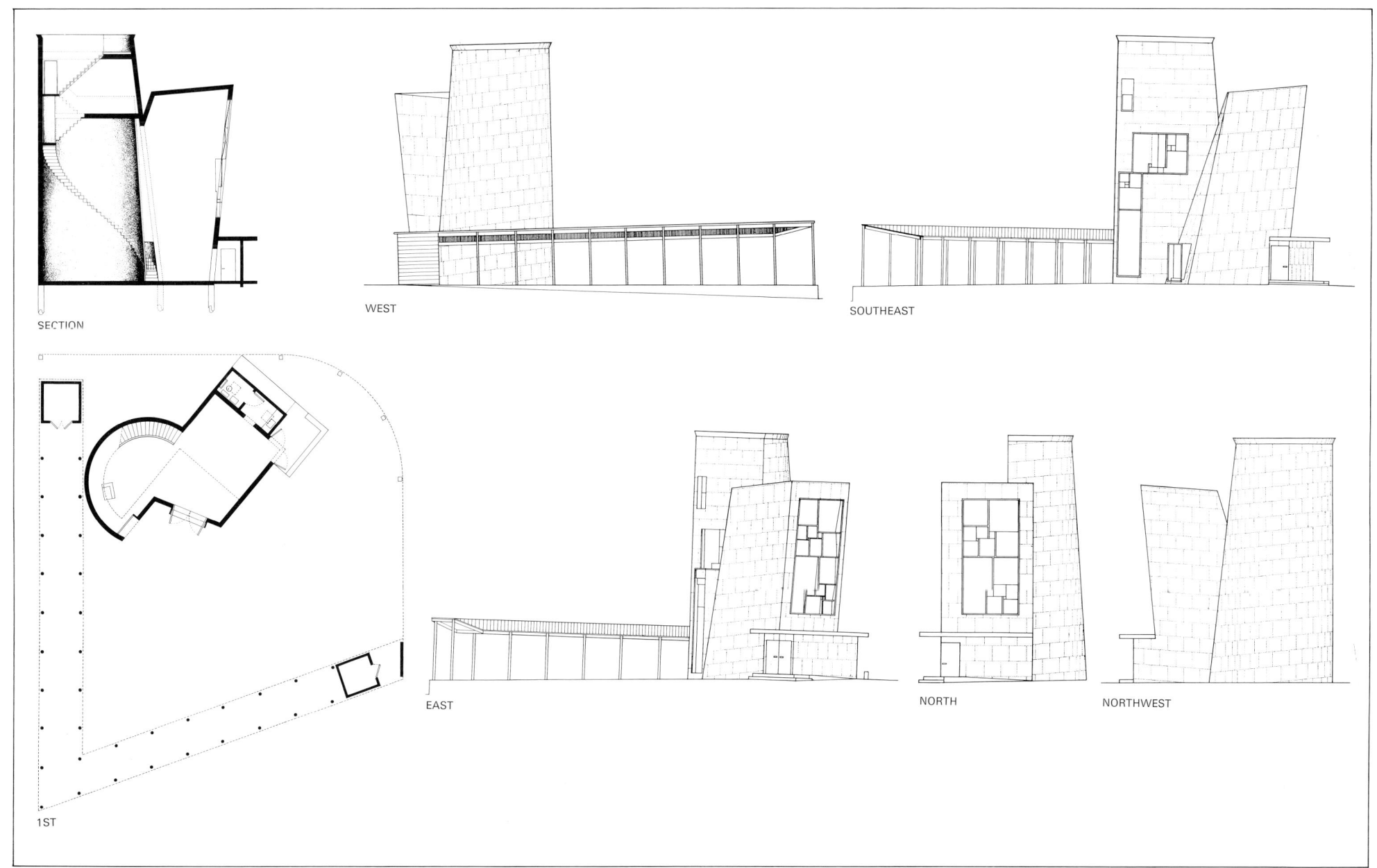

Meeting House

113

*Void Space/Hinged Space
Housing
Fukuoka, Japan
1989–91*

Concept: From hinged space to the silence of void space.

Four active north-facing voids interlock with four quiet south-facing voids to bring a sense of the sacred into direct contact with everyday, domestic life. To ensure emptiness, the south voids are flooded with water; the sun makes flickering reflections across the ceilings of the north courts and apartment interiors.

Interiors of the 28 apartments revolve around the concept of "hinged space," a development of the multi-use concepts of traditional Fusuma taken into an entirely modern dimension. One type of hinging—diurnal—allows an expansion of the living area during the day, reclaimed for bedrooms at night. Another type—episodic—reflects the change in a family over time; rooms can be added or subtracted to accommodate grown children leaving the family or elderly parents moving in.

An experiential sense of passage through space is heightened in the three types of access, which allow apartments to have exterior front doors. On the lower passage, views across the water court and through the north voids activate the walk spatially from side to side. Along the north passage one has a sense of suspension with the park in the distance. The top passage has a sky view under direct sunlight.

The apartments interlock in section like a complex Chinese box. Individuation from the standpoint of the individual inhabitant has an aim in making all 28 apartments different. Due to the voids and interlocking section, each apartment has many exposures: north, south, east and west.

The structure of exposed bearing concrete is stained in some places. A lightweight aluminum curtain wall allows a reading of the building section while walking from east to west along the street; an entirely different facade of solids is exposed walking from west to east.

The building, with its street-aligned shops and intentionally simple facades, is seen as part of a city in its effort to form space rather than become an architecture of object. Space is its medium, from urban to private, hinged space.

Water court

Overall view from south

View from south

115

5TH FLOOR

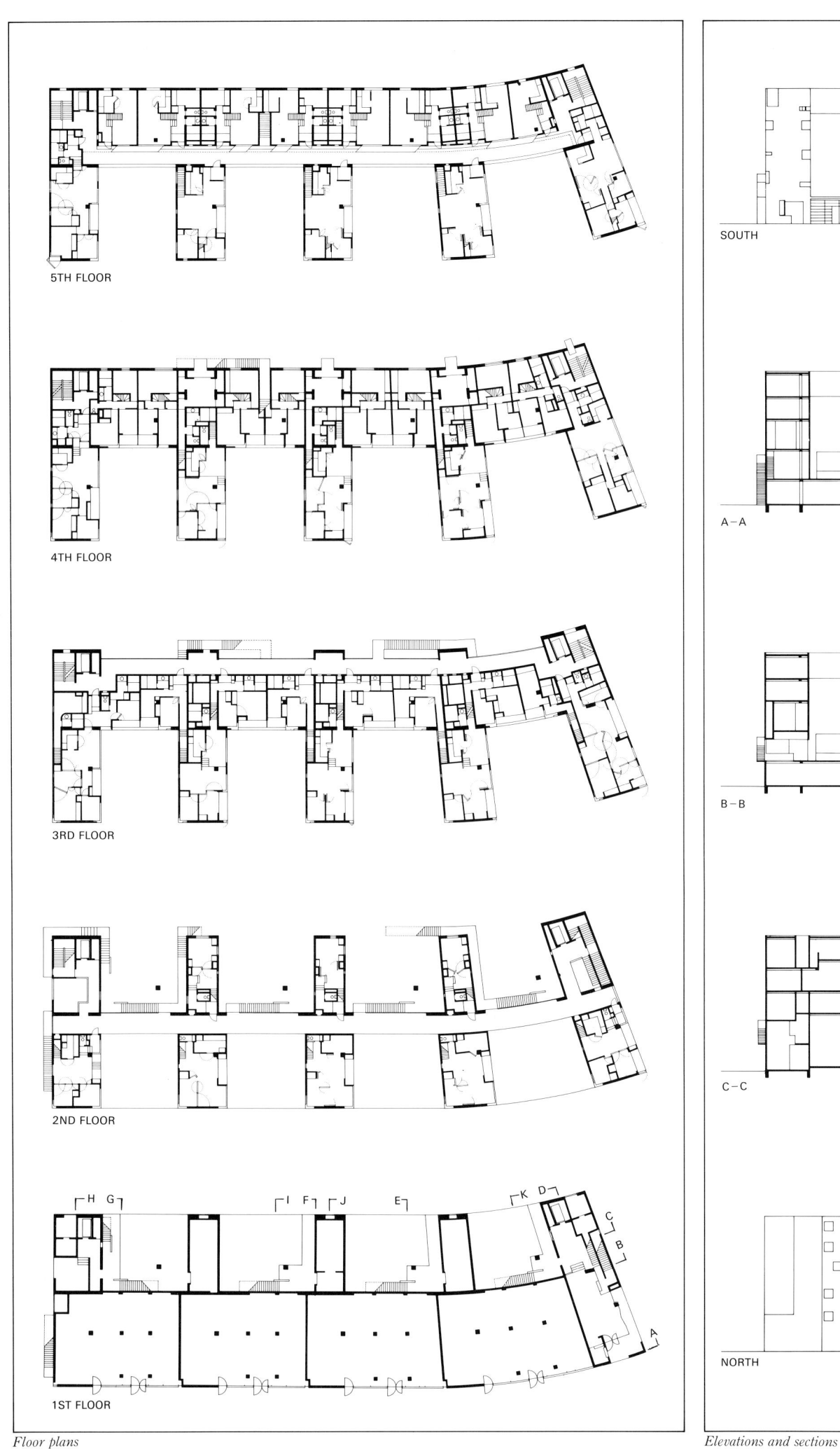

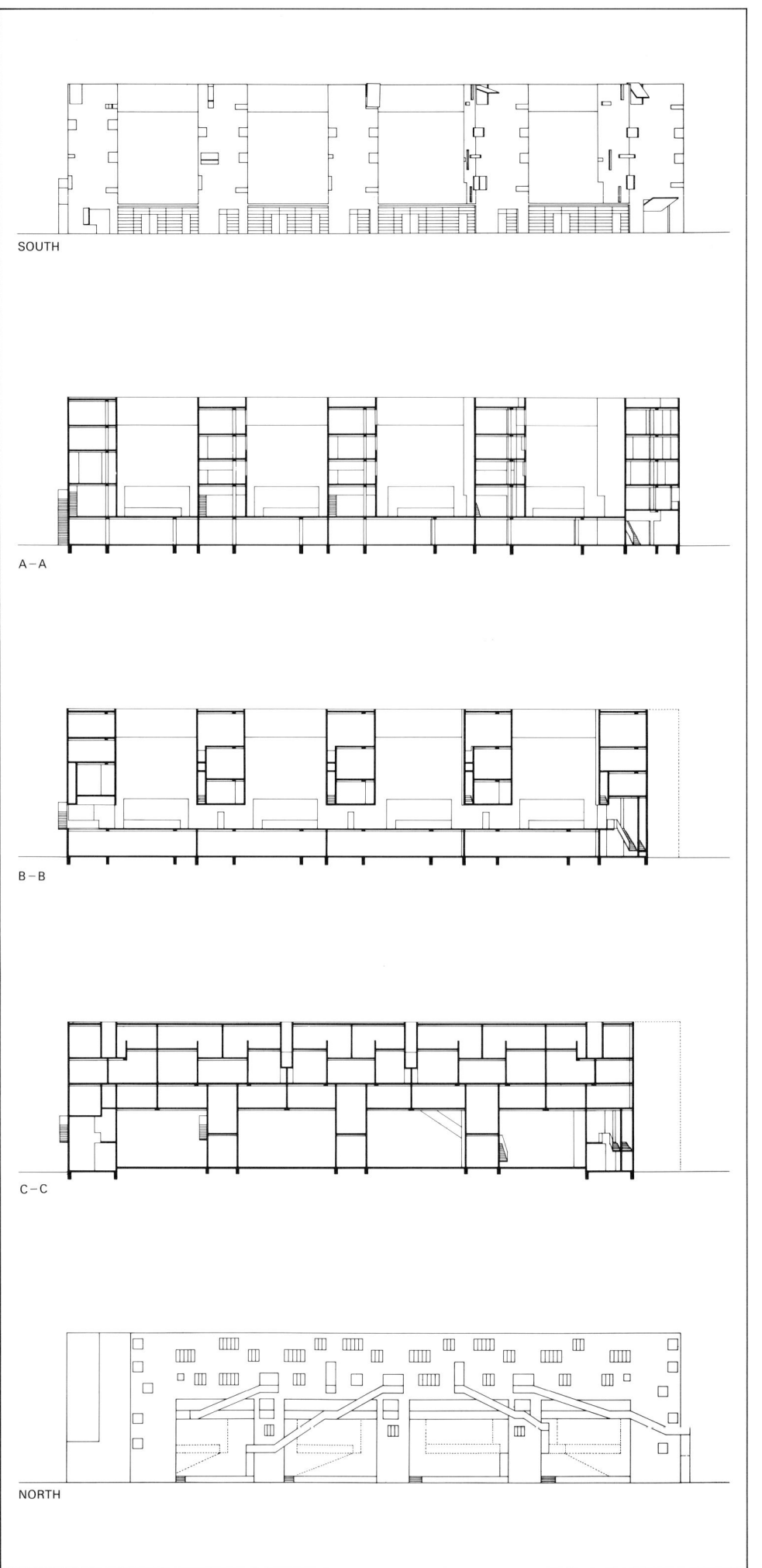

4TH FLOOR

3RD FLOOR

2ND FLOOR

1ST FLOOR

Floor plans

SOUTH

A–A

B–B

C–C

NORTH

Elevations and sections

EAST	WEST
D-D	H-H
E-E	I-I
F-F	J-J
G-G	K-K

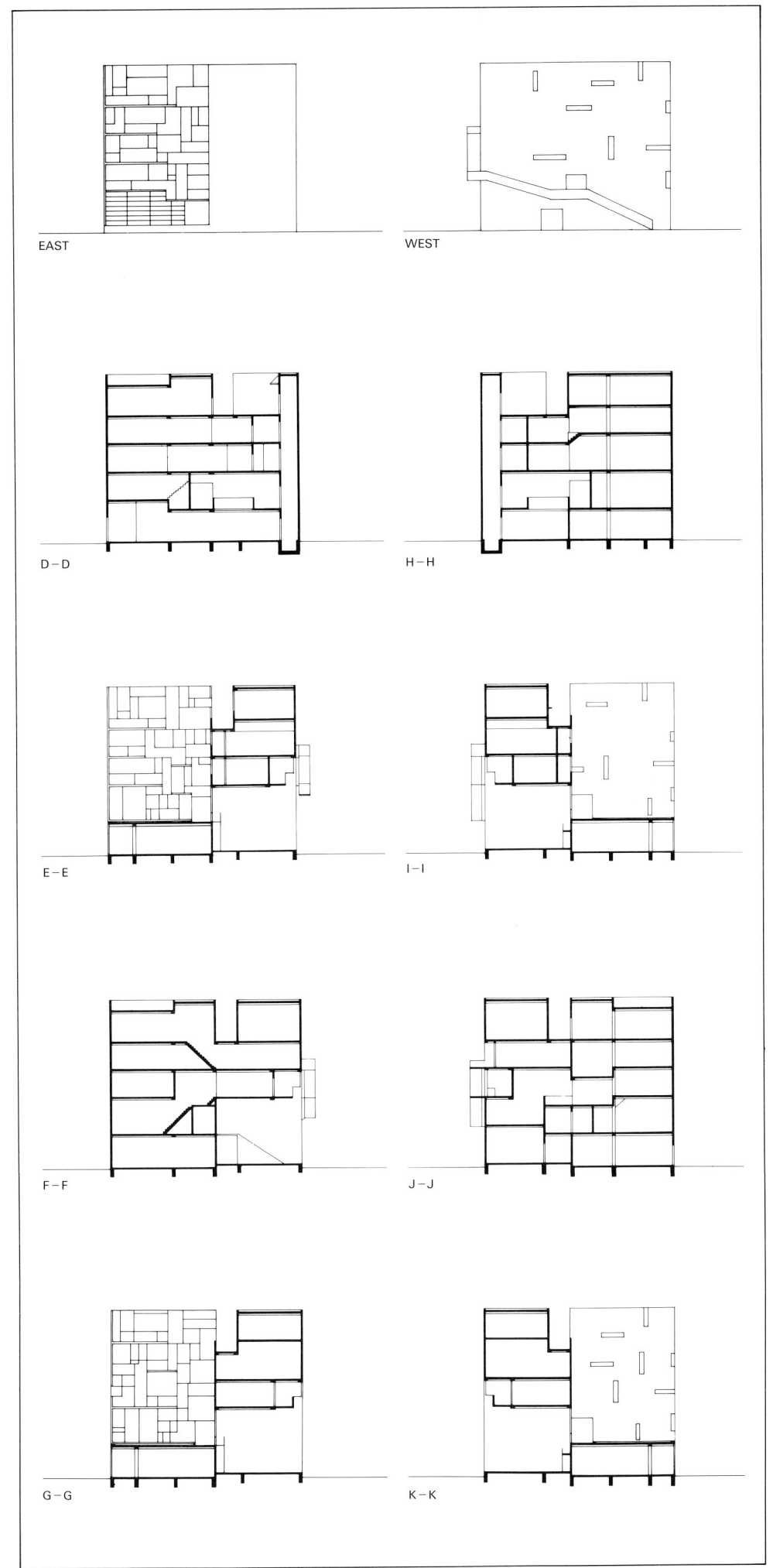

Elevations and sections

ヴォイド・スペース／ヒンジド・スペース・ハウジング
コンセプト：ヒンジの作る空間から吹抜の静寂まで。

　北側に向いた，4つの活動的な吹抜と南向きのやはり4つではあるが静かな吹抜をかみ合わせることで，日々の家庭生活と神聖な感覚を直接に結びつけようとした。空間が何もないままに護られるよう，南側の吹抜の下のスラブには水を張る。ここに反射したきらめく光は，北の吹抜の天井やアパートメントの室内の天井にまで届く。

　28戸のアパートメントは，「転換する空間」というコンセプトを軸に展開する。これは，日本の伝統的な襖の多用途のコンセプトを現代的な次元に高めたものである。転換の第1の形式――日ごとの――は，日中には生活空間を広くして，夜には一部を寝室に改めるというものだ。次の形式――時々起こる――は，家族の変化への対応である。成人した子供たちが家を出たり，逆に年老いた親などがやって来たりするのに応じて，部屋数を増やしたり減らしたりすることができる。

　3つのタイプが設けられたアクセスルートを通ってゆくと，空間の中をめぐってきたという実感が高められるし，このルートのおかげで，各戸には直接外に面した玄関がつけられる。下の廊下を歩けば，水の中庭ごしの景観と吹抜を間にした北の景色が眺められるので，空間は生き生きとしたものになる。北側沿いの廊下を歩くと，かなたの公園と一緒に宙に浮かぶような思いにとらわれるし，最上階の廊下に立てば，陽を浴びながら空を眺められるのだ。住戸はさながら複雑なパズルのように断面が嚙み合う。それぞれの住人の立場に立って個性を守るために28戸のアパート全てを違うものにしようという目的があった。吹抜と組み合わせる断面のおかげで，どのアパートメントにも数多くの開口が可能になった。北にも南にも，そして東も西も。

　打放しコンクリートの構造体は，ところどころステインを塗ってある。道を東から西へ歩いて建築を見ると，軽量のアルミのカーテンウォールによって構造体の断面の形を読みとることができる。逆に，西から東に向って歩くと，それぞれに全く違ったファサードが見えてくる。

　道路に面して店舗を並べ，ファサードをあえて単純なものにしたことで，建築が都市の一部として感じられる。それは，オブジェとしての建築ではなく，空間を作るものとしての建築を意図したからにほかならない。空間とは，都市とひとりの人間の間にあって両者を結ぶヒンジのような転換のしかけなのだ。

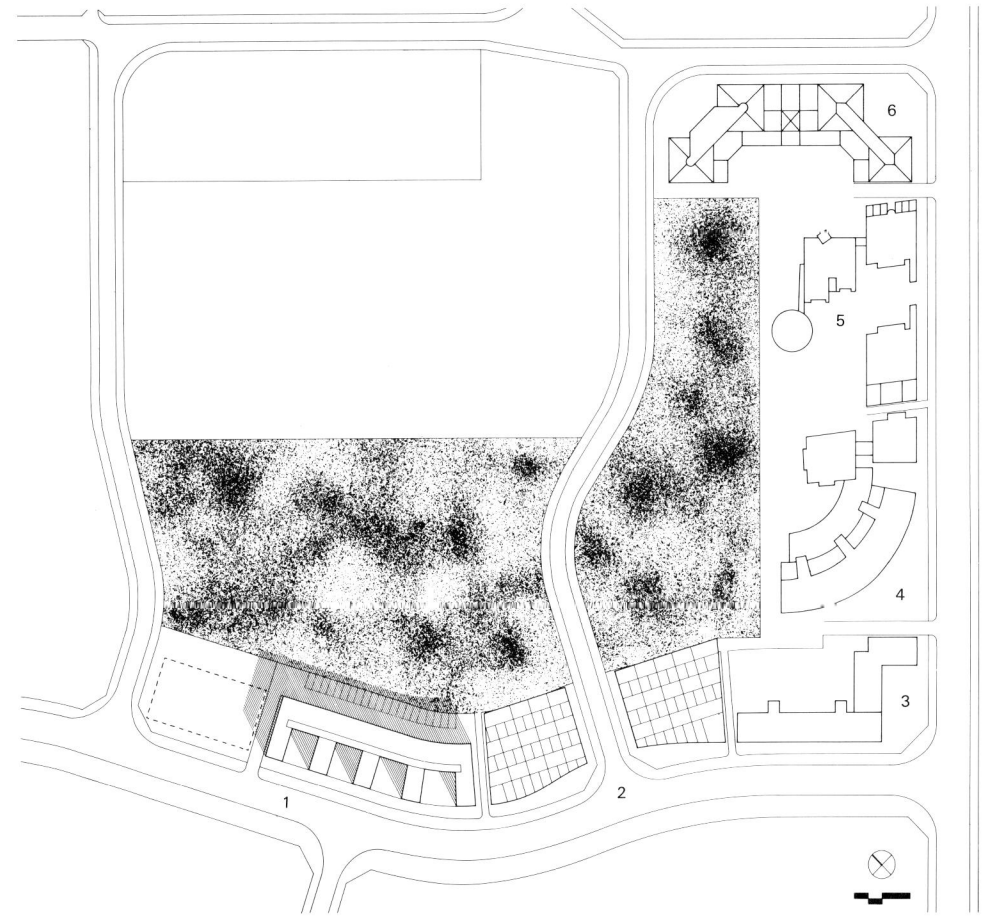

NEXUS WORLD KASHII HOUSING
1 STEVEN HOLL
2 REM KOOLHAAS
3 MARK MACK
4 OSAMU ISHIYAMA
5 CHRISTIAN DE PORTZAMPARC
6 OSCAR TUSQUETS

Site plan: Nexus World

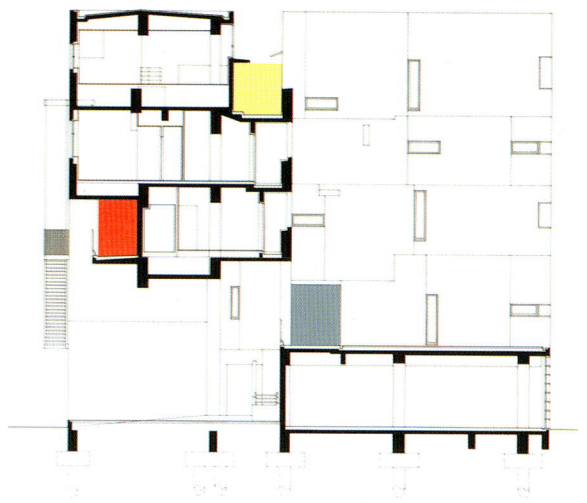

Section

Entrance hall

Entrance

Entrance hall

Entrance hall

View from living room

View from dining room

Living room

View from entrance

Living room

Hall

Cabinet

4 Ontology of Institutions
組織の存在論

In a tentative search for expression, an architecture of public institutions seeks to open barriers between the individual and the institution, between the teacher and the child, between the reader and the book. This openness exists in steps between the micro and macro scales, moving from the intimacy of fingers touching a handrail to the cultural connections of a city, to the green landscape of a campus, to the connection between earth and sky.

Monumental architecture of institutions of the past have expressed the philosophical preoccupations of their time. A belief in reason and the perfectibility of man in relation to an exalted view of past civilizations provoked monumental classical architecture. Bourgeoisie cultural desires for "ennobling edifices" placed institutions on a higher plane, apart from the vulgar day-to-day. Gradually this symmetrical stone monumentality has given way to desires for openness and public accessibility. Compared to the civilizations of the past, (for example, Athens, at its cultural apex, had a population of a mere two hundred and fifty thousand) ours is a society larger in numbers, more open in spirit and fostering freedom of passage and access. Along with this general opening-up, which is political as well as physical, society is questioning the environmental degradation of our times, which has occurred due to our disregard of the interrelation of all things.

Today, questioning past habits and exploring new ways of thinking and making is fundamental. The nature of being, the order of our cultural reality and the nature of our institutions is open to inquiry. This questioning at all scales should involve the individual as well as the institution. An ontology of institutions as a fundamental reconsideration is being written by our society in the dreams and proposals for new public programs and an open architectural expression of those programs. As yet unformulated, new ideas and new technologies may lead to new institutions. The self-assured certainty of monumental classical expression is giving way to tentative expressions of openness, uncertainty and new freedoms.

(S.H.)

表現を実験的に追求する過程で、公共建築の分野では、個人と組織や施設、教師と子供の間、読者と本の間をさえぎるようなものを取り払おうとしはじめている。このような開放化は小さなスケールから大きなものまで何段階も存在している。手摺と触れあう指の親密なかかわりから都市の文化的なつながり、キャンパスの緑のランドスケープ、大地と空の間のつながりにまでおよぶ。

かつては、公の建築は時流に乗った思想を表現するものだった。ある時は、理性と人間の完全性に対する信仰が、過ぎ去った数々の文明への賛美を伴ってモニュメンタルな古典建築をつくらせた。ブルジョワ文化は「高貴な殿堂」を望むあまり、公を高い位置にすえ、庶民の日常からかけはなれたものにしようとしてしまった。こうした対称性を重んじたかつての石造の記念碑は、開放的で誰もが近づけるものを求める趨勢に道をゆずることになった。過去の文明と比較すると（たとえば、アテネはその文化が頂点を極めた頃で、25万の人口にすぎない）私たちの社会は、はるかに人口も多く、精神も開放的で、通行自由な形を育ててきた。分野を問わず、政治的にも物理的にも開放化が進められるにつれて、我々の時代になって環境の悪化が社会的に問われるようになった。世の中のあらゆるものが互いの関わり合いを持ちながら存在するという事実を我々が無視してきたことがその原因となっていたのである。

これまで続けてきたことを問い直しながら、考えること、作ることの新たな方式を探ることは、今日の基本的な課題である。存在の本質、私たちの文化的現実、時代をつらぬくものの本質が問われている。規模を問わず、このような問い直しには、個人から組織に至るまでを巻き込む必要がある。根源的な再検討を必要とする公共組織の存在論は、新たな公共計画の夢や提案、それを実現するための開放的な建築という形で描かれだしている。未だ確立されるには至らないが、新たな思想と技術が新しい公共建築を導きだすことになるのかもしれない。モニュメンタルな古典的表現の自己過信的なまでの普遍性を求める姿勢は、今や、開放的で、不確かさを許容しながら、新たな自由を目指す実験的な表現に道をゆずろうとしている。

(S.H.)

Parthenon, Athens ▷

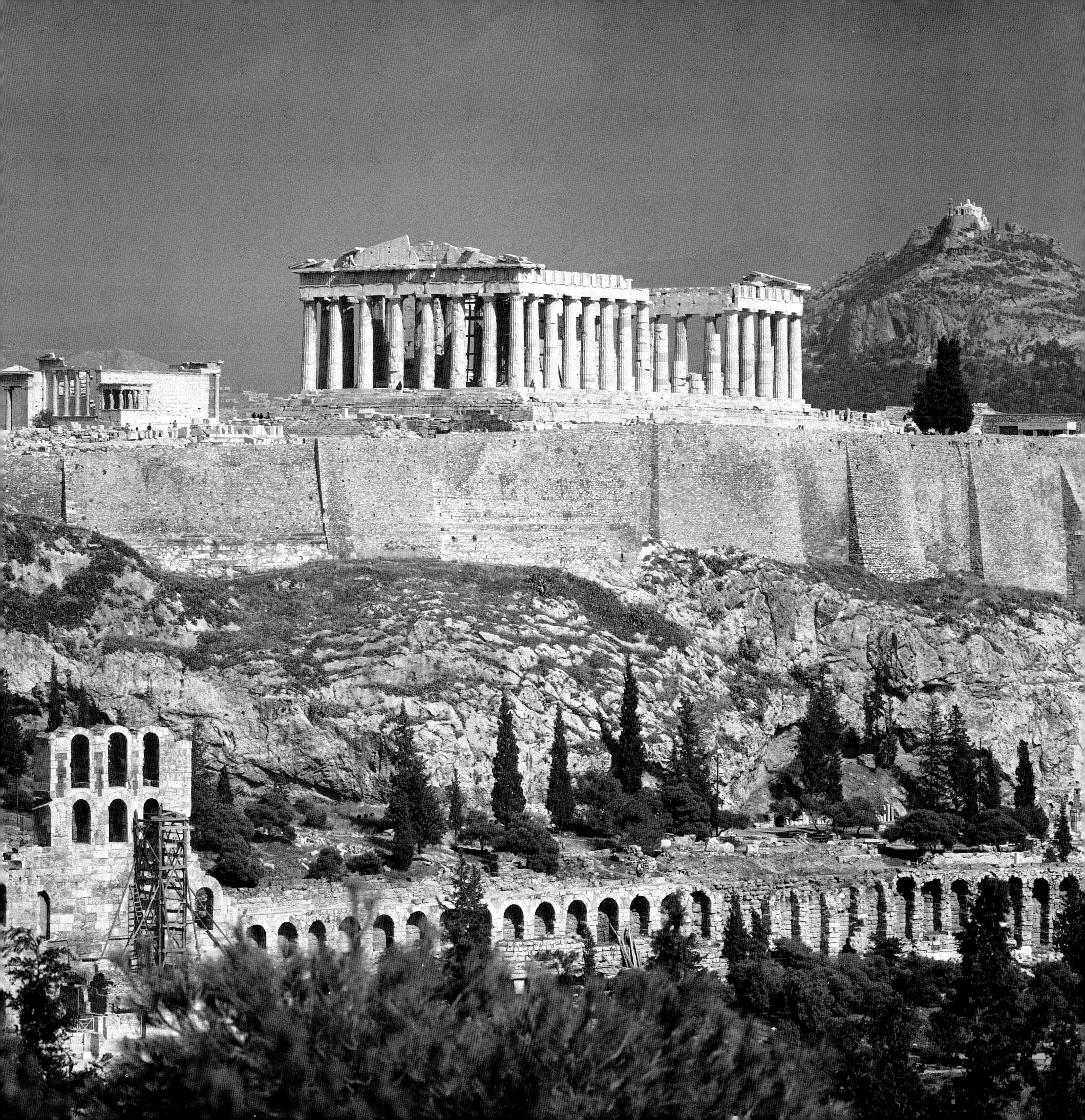

Berlin AGB Library
Competition
Berlin, Germany
1988

This project is a competition entry for an addition to the Amerika Gedenk Bibliothek in Berlin and surrounding area.

The design extends the philosophical position of the open stack—the unobstructed meeting of the reader and the book—by organizing the offerings along a browsing circuit. The circuit is a public path looping the building, presenting the collection of the entire library. The library stacks are developed as furniture, giving different characteristics to areas of the open plan. The concept of a browsing circuit is given memorable variety by these different stack arrangements.

The circuit forms a slipped ring bracketing the original building. The extension holds the original building in space without overpowering or deferring to it. Proportions of all major architectural elements, including interior and exterior spaces and structural grid, are determined by a single series (1:1.618) based on the height of the existing building.

The importance of the site within the city plan is expressed by making the library a major urban element, analogous to a city gate. The north face of the library addition defines the south edge of the new Blücherplatz. Additional buildings to the east and west, containing public programs, complete the definition of space. A clearly defined park to the east and west strengthens the connection to the Holy Cross Church. The tower offers a public observation point—a lens focused on the city— and supports the children's library. Suspended over the original building, the library elevates children to caretakers of the city. It has sloped floors for reading while lying down. The structure is a lattice truss sheathed in sandblasted glass with vision panels.

The main structure is an exposed concrete frame with glass curtain walls of sandblasted white, amber, and blue glass set off by areas of lead or stainless-steel covered panels. Under the gray skies of Berlin, the effects of east and west light in the library will be highly varied according to the sandblasted lines and mullion patterns in the curtain walls. For the interior, careful attention has been given to acoustics to assure silence, while natural materials and subdued colors have been selected for their contributions to a serene and reflective mood.

ベルリン・アメリカ記念図書館

ベルリンのアメリカ記念図書館の増築とその周辺部のコンペの応募案である。

読者と本が直接出会うことのできる開架式の考えを発展させ，本を眺めながら全体を一巡りできるよう書架を配した。このルートは，図書館全体の蔵書を提示するとともに，建物を一周するための出入り自由な通路でもある。書架は家具として扱い，連続する空間プランの中でそれぞれのエリアに相応しい性格を与える。このようにして，それぞれ独自の本棚を設けることによってブラウジング・サーキットにはそれぞれの場所が心に留まりやすくなるような多様な性格が与えられる。

このサーキットは，現在の建物の上をまたいで，ややねじれた環状をなす。増築は旧館の建物を圧倒することもなく，異質に見せることもなく，旧館をとりこんでいる。建築の主要な要素は，内部空間，外部空間にかかわりなく，構造体のグリッドに至るまで，そのプロポーションは旧館の建物の高さをもとにした一貫した比率（1：1.618）で構成される。ベルリンの都市計画に占めるこの敷地の重要性を示すために，この図書館を都市の門になぞらえることでその主要な要素の地位に引き上げようとした。図書館の新しい北側ファサードは，新しくつくられるブリュッヒャー広場の南端を形成する。公開の催し物も行われる東西の増築部でこの空間が完結する。東西に広がる公園によって聖十字教会との結びつきは強められる。塔状の部分は，展望台——レンズはベルリンに焦点を合わせる——であると同時に，子供図書館の部分を支持する構造体でもある。旧館をまたぐ子供図書館は，子供たちをこの都市の守護神に押し上げる。横になって本を読めるよう，床は傾斜している。ラチストラスの構造体をサンドブラストのガラスで包み，ところどころに外を見るためのガラスがはめこまれる。

打放しのコンクリートを主要な構造体として，そこに白やアンバーあるいはサンドブラスト処理されたブルーのガラスのカーテンウォールが，鉛やステンレスのパネルより表面を下げて取付けられる。ベルリンの灰色の空の下では，図書館の照明を滲み出させる東西面は，サンドブラストで刻まれる線やカーテンウォールの方立のパターンによって変化に富んだものになる。内部については，静けさを保つための音響上の配慮が注意深くなされ，同時に自然の素材やくすんだ色彩を選んで静寂と内省的な雰囲気づくりに役立てられる。

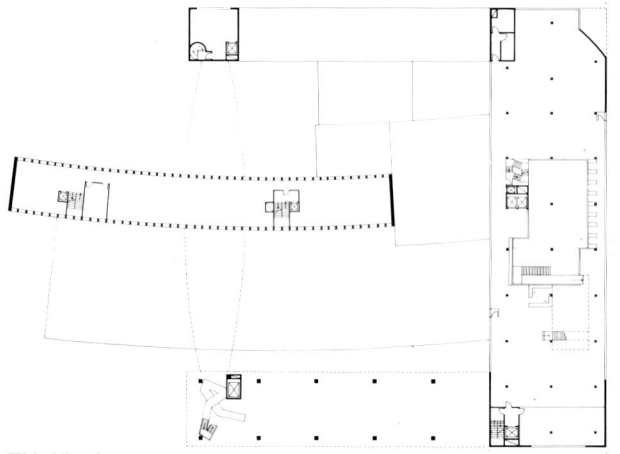

Third level

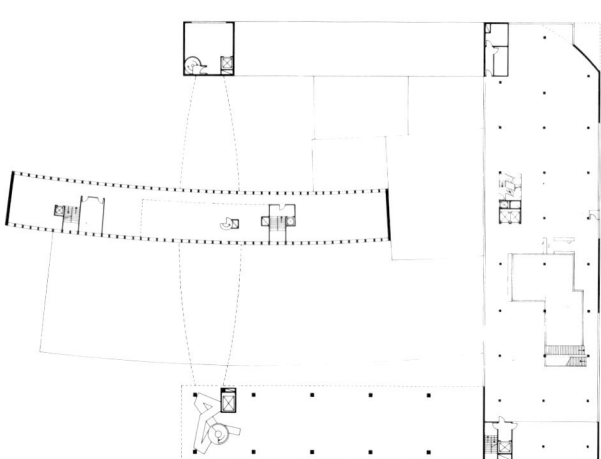

Fourth level

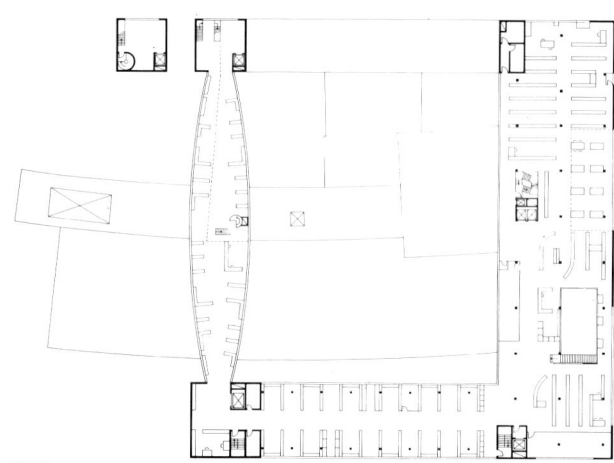

Fifth level

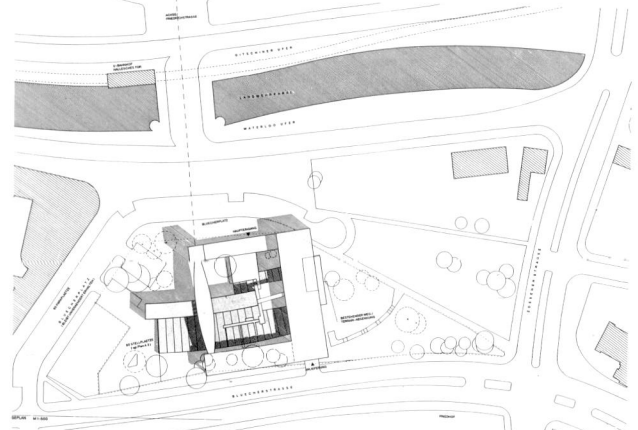

Site plan

Basement level

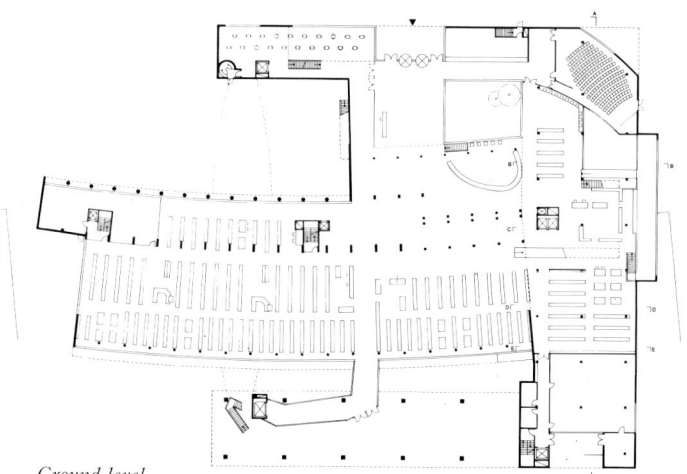

Ground level

Model

Model

Model

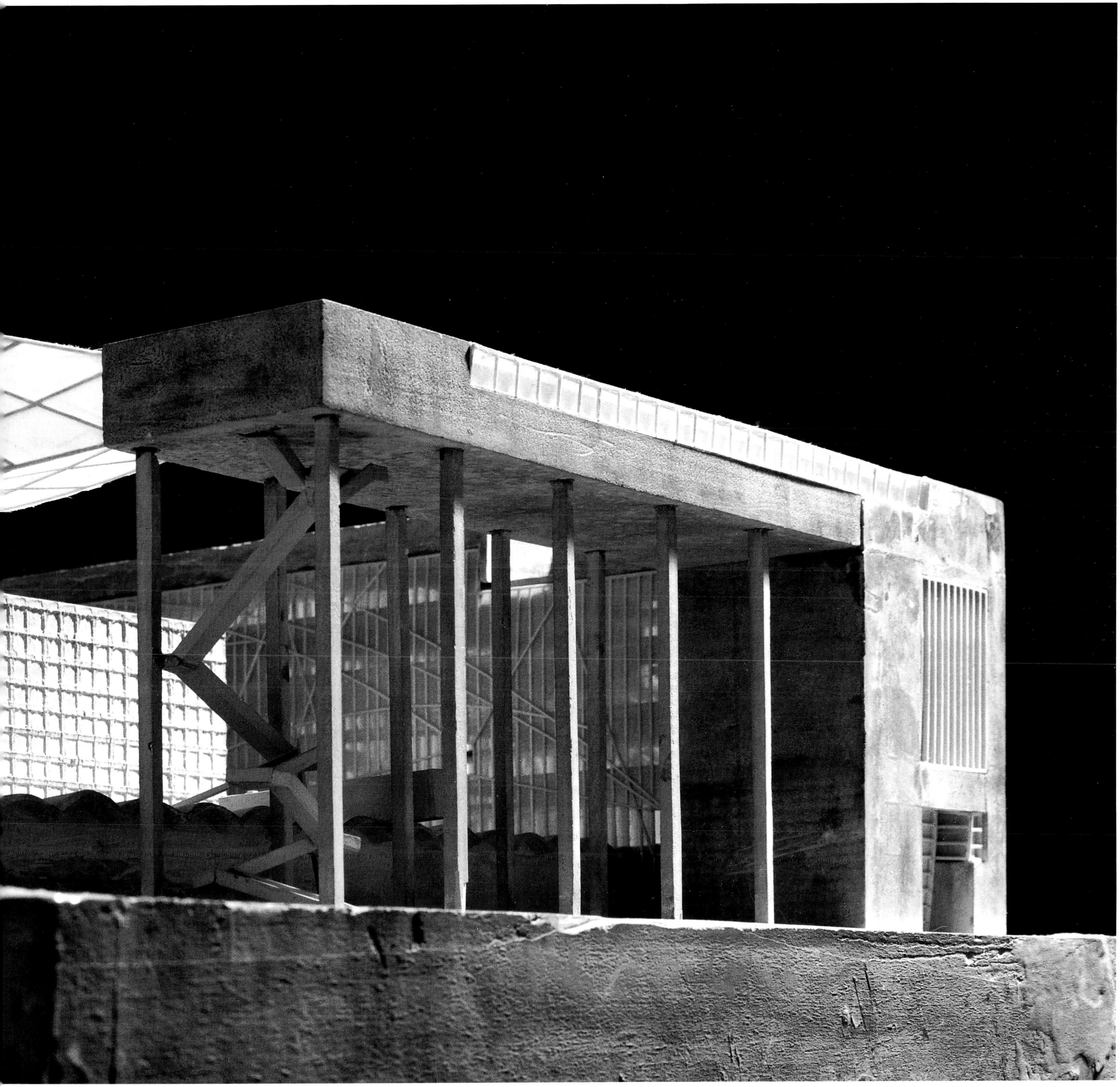

BROWSING CIRCUIT

BERLIN

URBAN LOCUS

VARIETY OF STACK TYPES

PROGRAM DISTRIBUTION

- MUSIC
- CHILDREN'S LIBRARY
- OBSERVATION
- WORKROOMS
- OFFICES (EXISTING SLAB)
- HUMANITIES (EXISTING READING ROOM)
- ART
- SOCIAL SCIENCES
- NATURAL SCIENCES
- PERIODICALS
- REFERENCE
- BERLIN ARCHIVES
- MAIN ENTRY   CAFE

Site plan

West elevation

Section

Section

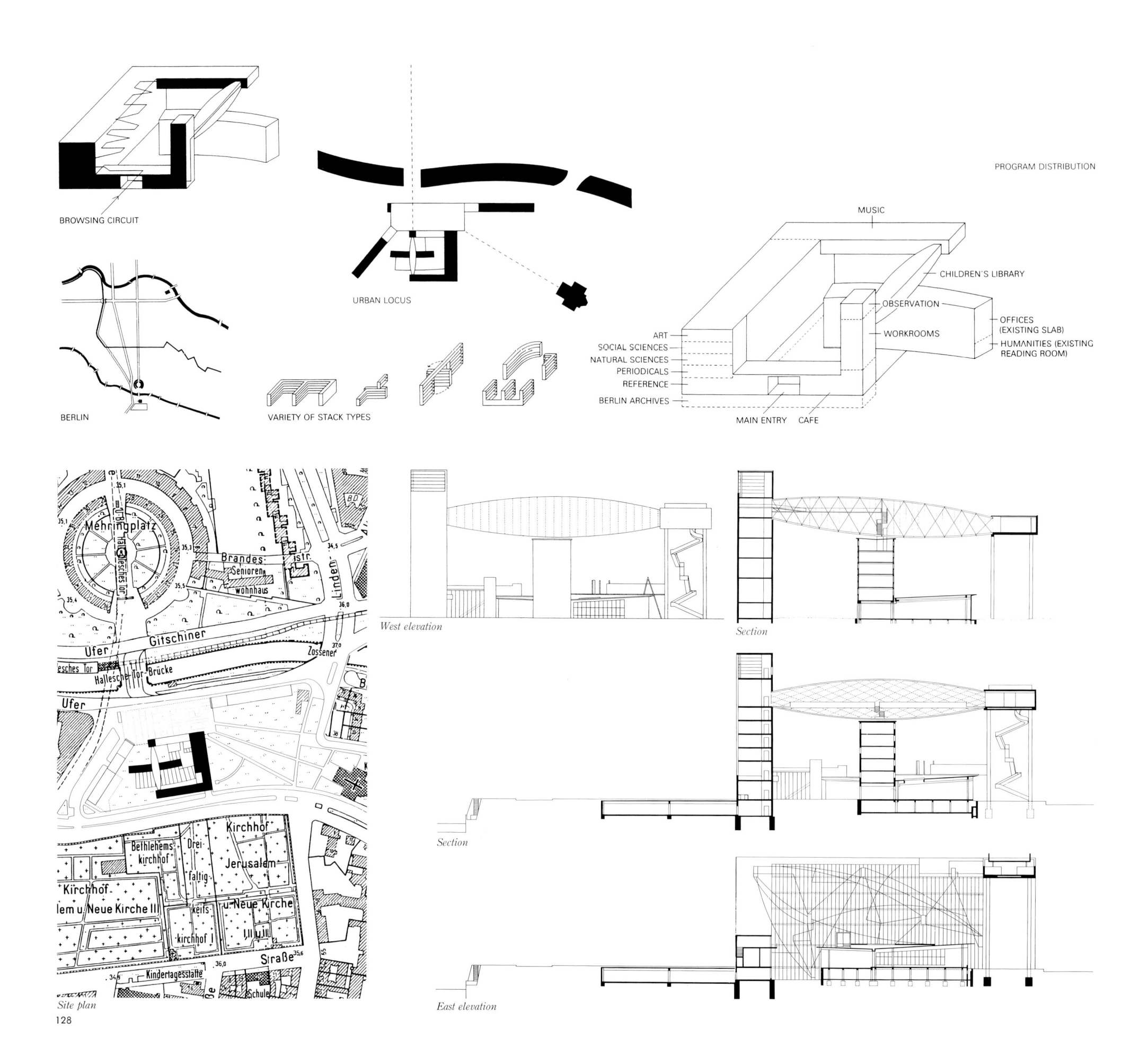

East elevation

Children's library

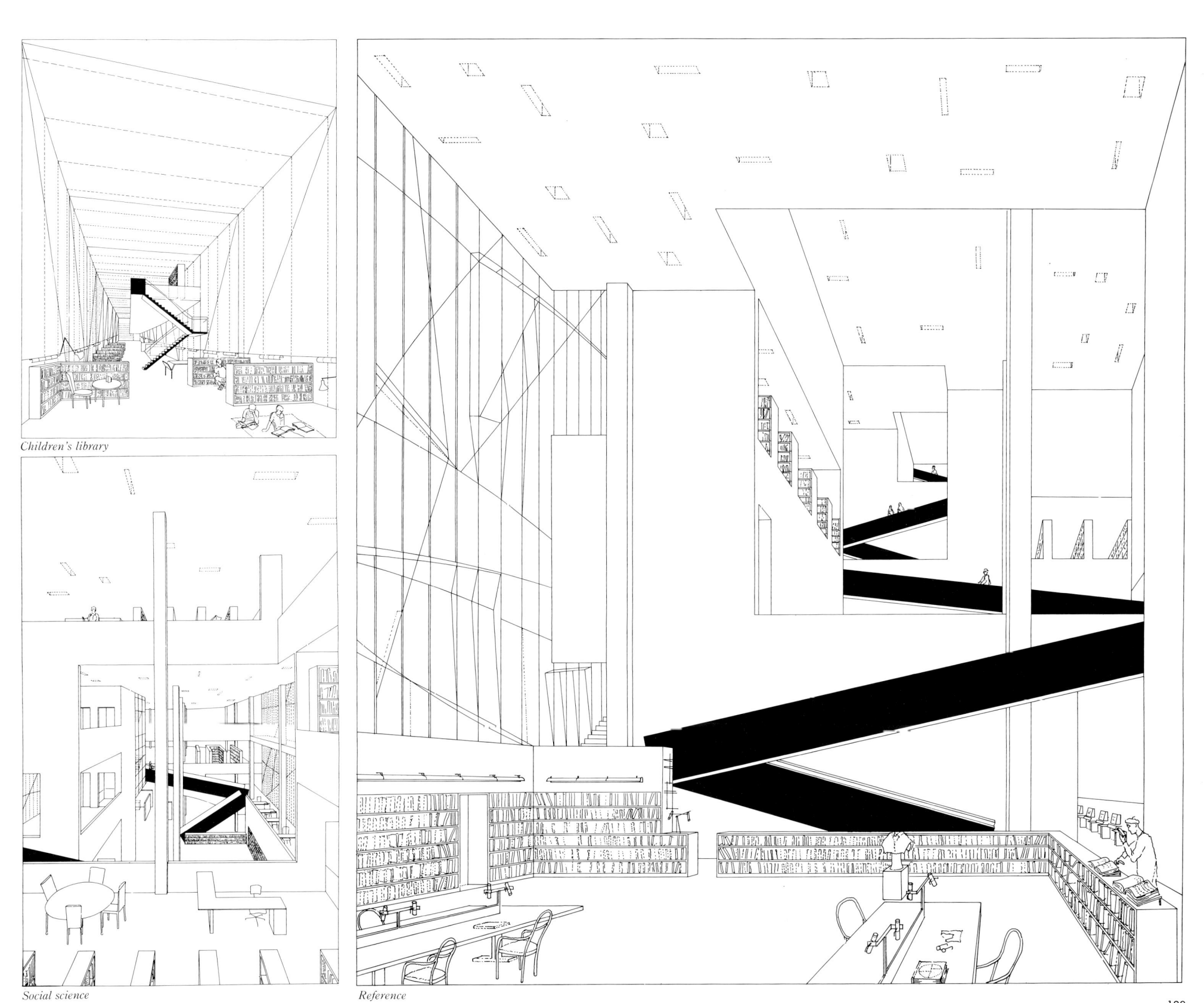

Social science

Reference

129

Model

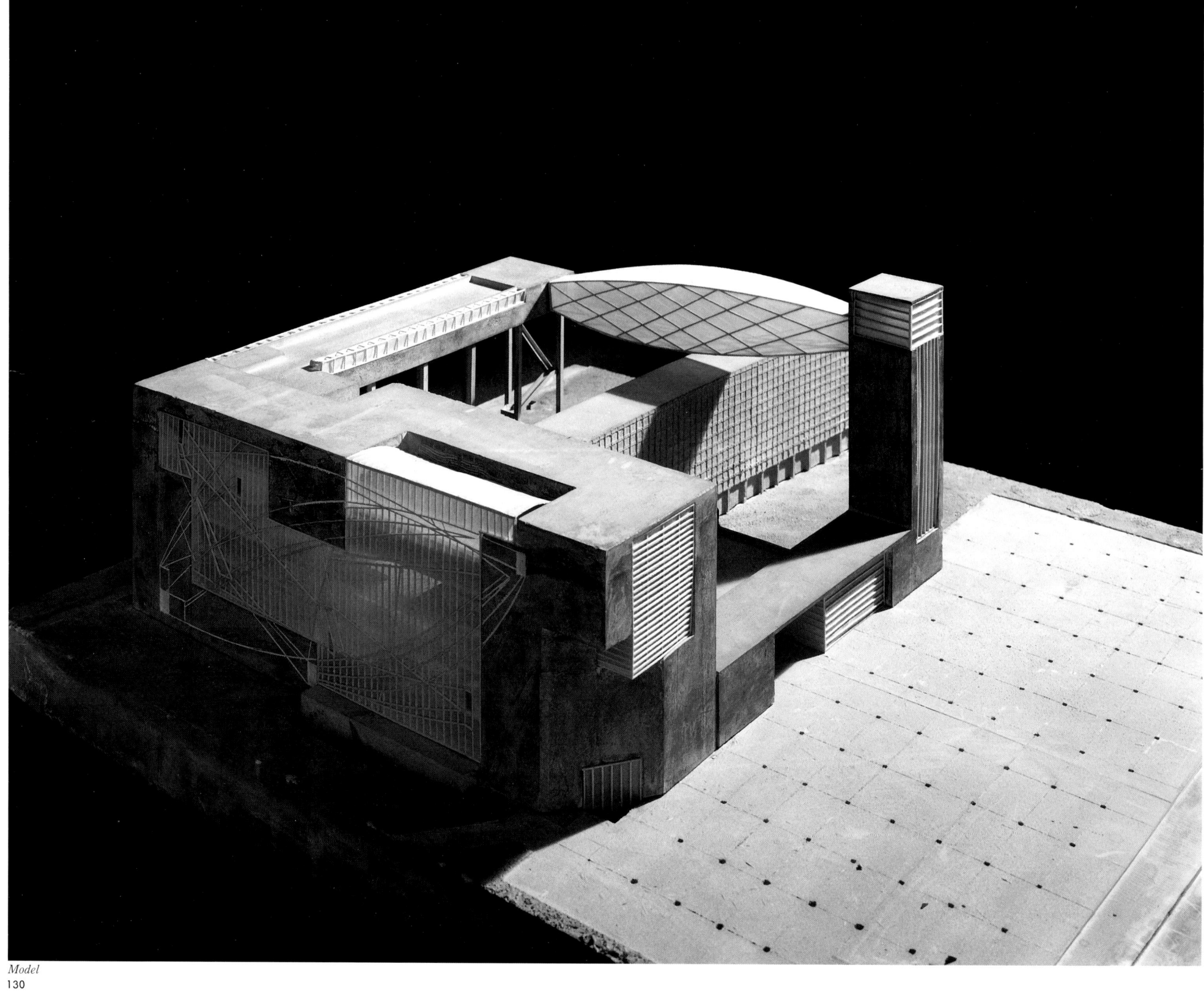

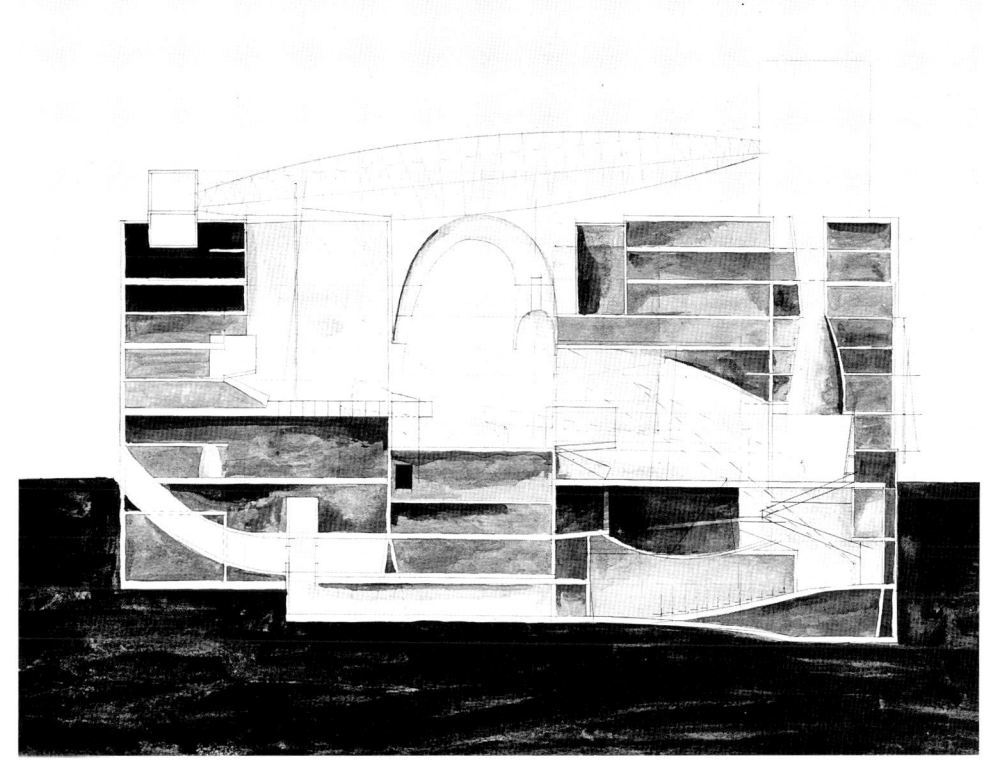

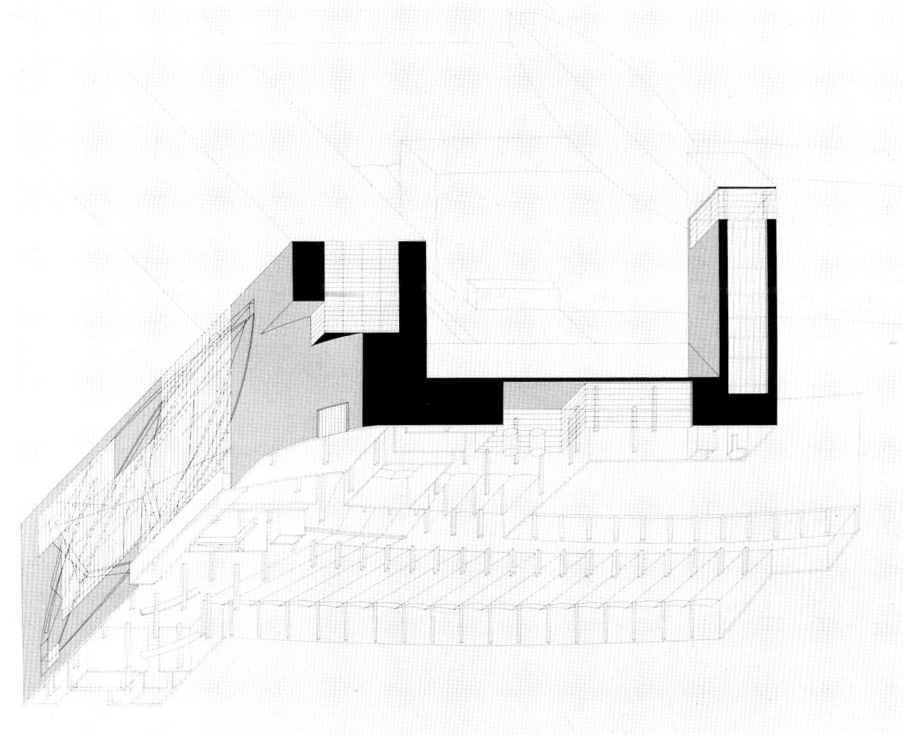

Studies

*College of Architecture &
Landscape Architecture
University of Minnesota
Minneapolis, Minnesota
1988-91*

The site on the University of Minnesota campus is to the north and west of the existing School of Architecture. The existing building (1958, Thorshov and Cemy) is 200 feet square and 29 feet high, with a 100-foot-square central atrium.

The program calls for a 90,000-square-foot addition of studio space, offices, a library, and an auditorium, allowing the Schools of Landscape Architecture and Architecture to be housed in one building.

Two Centers
Analogous to the joining of the architecture and the landscape architecture programs, the new building is formed around two centers: the existing center is a static interior space of hard surfaces; the new center is an elastic exterior space of complex surfaces.

Towers of Light
Shafts of campus space are marked by four masonry towers. Placed at the conjunction of campus routes, these towers mark new entrances to the building. The towers are laboratories of daylight; each captures a different light condition. North, east, west, and south light are variously screened and projected into the upper studios in the towers.

"Figure 8" Promenade
A ramp rising from the north entry through the east wing to the second level of the existing building begins a "figure 8" promenade through the building. This promenade links all major spaces of school, joining the studios on the top with offices, jury rooms, and the library below. The last passages of the promenade take the form of catwalks over the roof of the existing building.

The construction of the addition has a didactic intention, expressing the heavy construction of the towers and lightweight construction of the curving wings. The towers are concrete frame with a concrete-block cavity

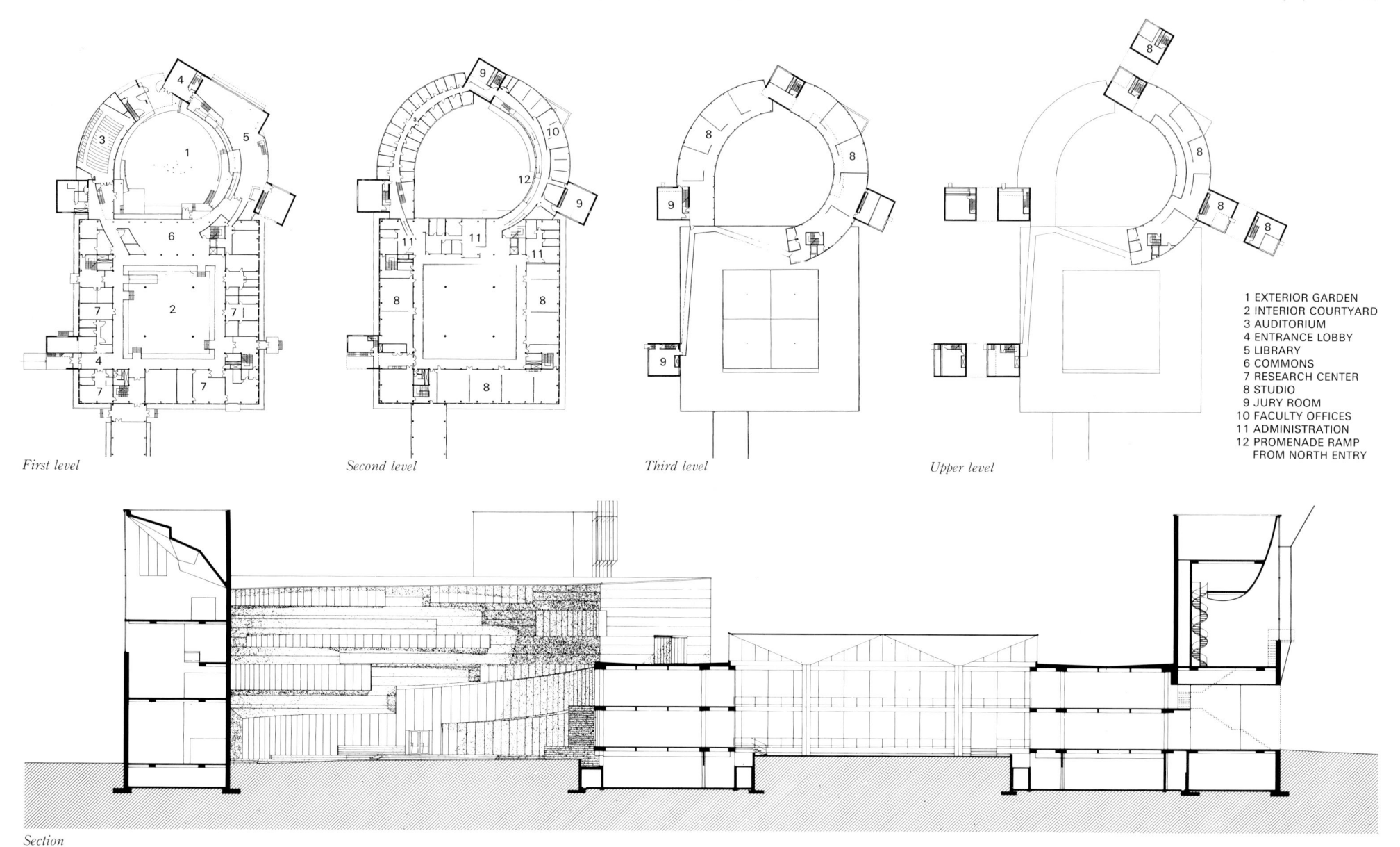

First level *Second level* *Third level* *Upper level*

1 EXTERIOR GARDEN
2 INTERIOR COURTYARD
3 AUDITORIUM
4 ENTRANCE LOBBY
5 LIBRARY
6 COMMONS
7 RESEARCH CENTER
8 STUDIO
9 JURY ROOM
10 FACULTY OFFICES
11 ADMINISTRATION
12 PROMENADE RAMP FROM NORTH ENTRY

Section

ミネソタ大学建築／ランドスケープ・アーキテクチュア学部

ミネソタ大学のキャンパス内にある敷地は，現在の建築学部の北と西にあたる。既存の建物(1958年ソーショフとシーミーの設計)は200フィート角で高さ29フィート，中央に100フィート角のアトリウムがある。

計画では，90,000平方フィートの増築によって，スタジオ，オフィス，図書館，オーディトリアムを含み，ランドスケープ・アーキテクチュア学部と建築学部を1つの建物に納めるというものである。

2つの中心――ちょうど，建築とランドスケープ・アーキテクチュアが一緒になるのと同じように，新しい建物は2つの中心の周りに作られる。既存の中心は固い表面をもつ静的な内部空間，新しい中心はいろいろな表面を持つ自在な外部空間である。

光の塔――キャンパスの空間全体を支える柱のような，組積造の4つの塔がある。キャンパス内の動線の節目に位置するこれらの塔は，建物への新しい入口の印でもある。塔は日射の実験室で，それぞれが異なった日射条件にある。北，東，西，南の光をいろいろな形で遮ったり，塔の上部のスタジオに光を当てたりする。

「8の字型」のプロムナード――北の入口から入り東棟を抜けて既存部の2階に達するルートは，建物を巡る8の字型のスロープとなる。このプロムナードは，主要なスペースを結び，最上階のスタジオやオフィス，評議員室，下にある図書館までをつなぎ，最後には，既存建物の上にかかるキャットウォークになる。

増築部の構造は，あえて教育的な意図を表に出した。塔の重い構造と曲線部分の軽い構造を対比的に表現したのである。塔はコンクリートの柱梁にコンクリートブロックの壁。円形の棟は鉄骨を露出して，スティールのサッシにアルミの壁である。

wall. The curving wings are exposed lightweight steel frame, with steel windows and an aluminum skin.

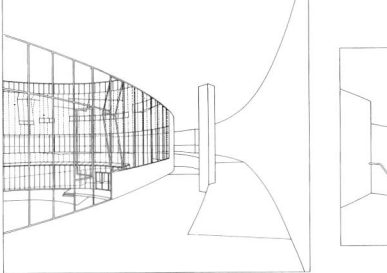

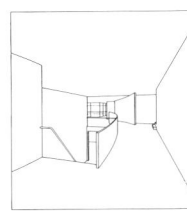

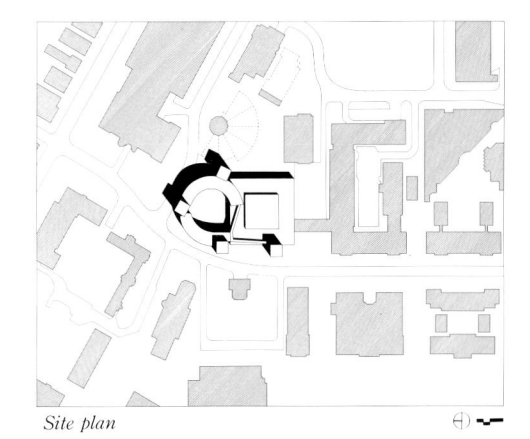

Site plan

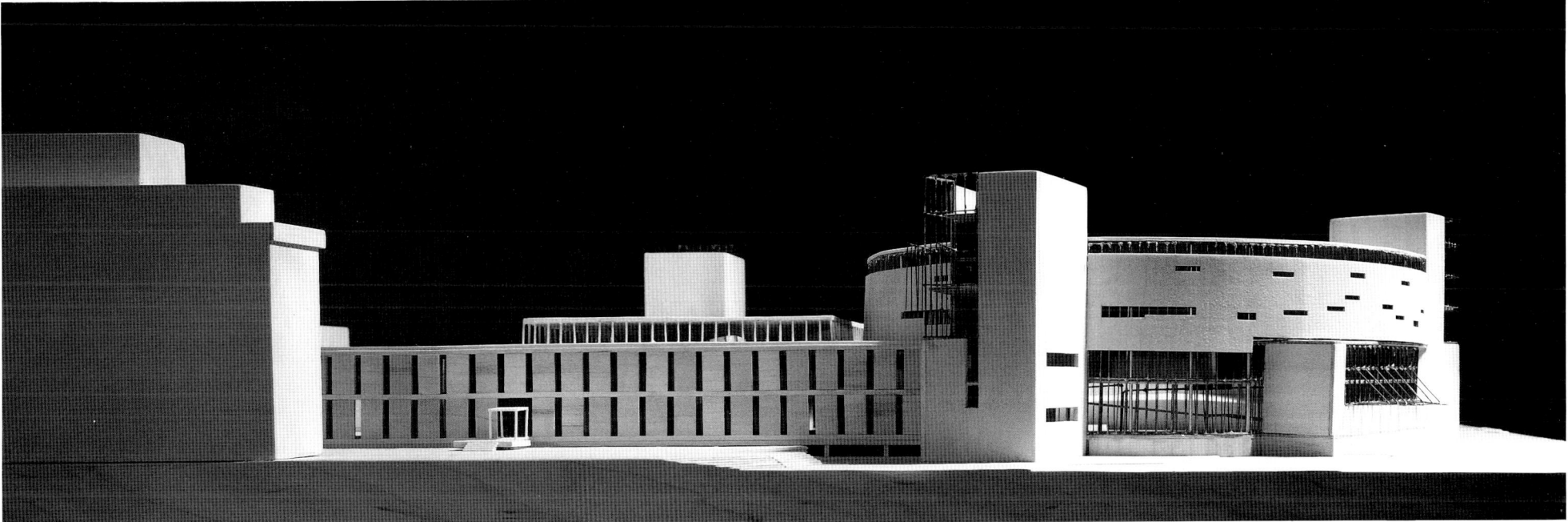

Model

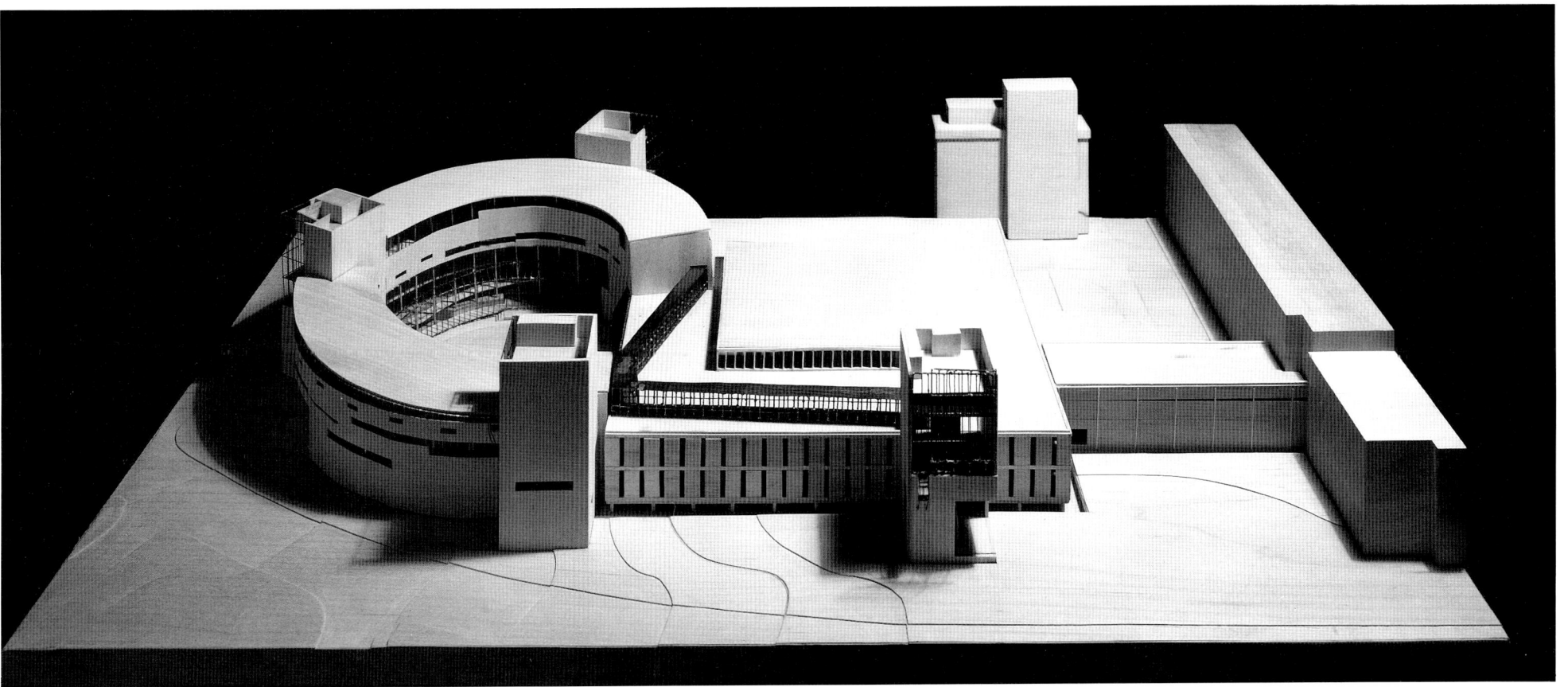

Model

Auditorium study

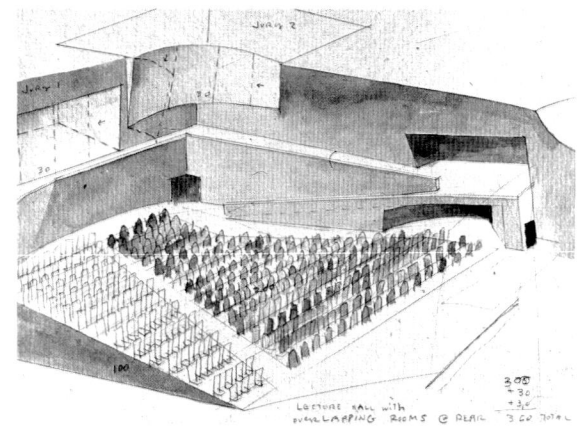

Auditorium study

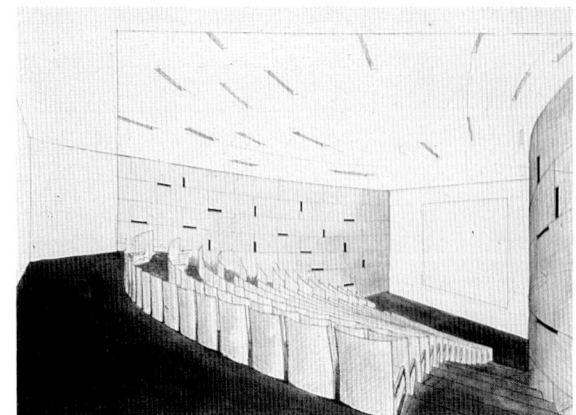

Ramp

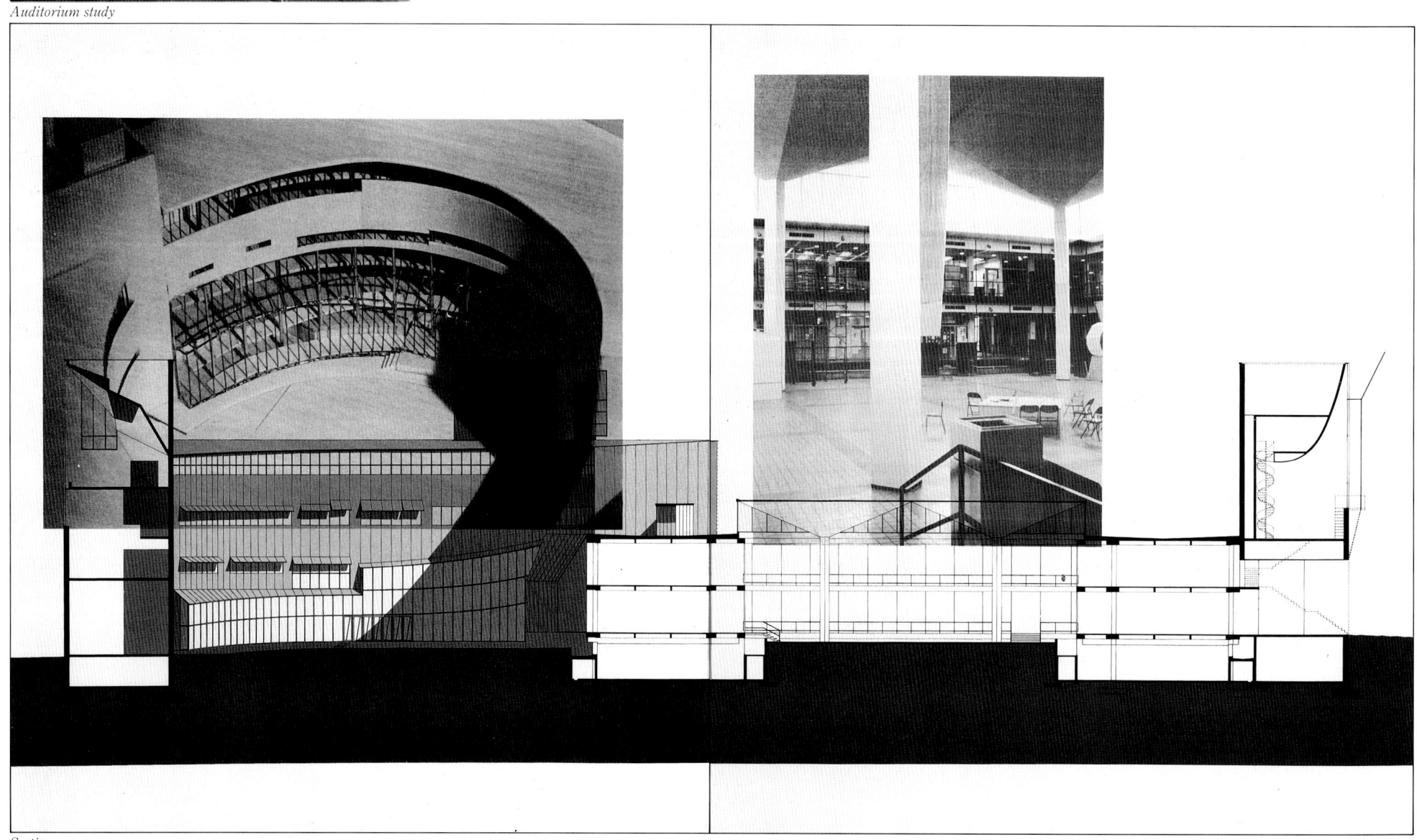

Interior study

Section

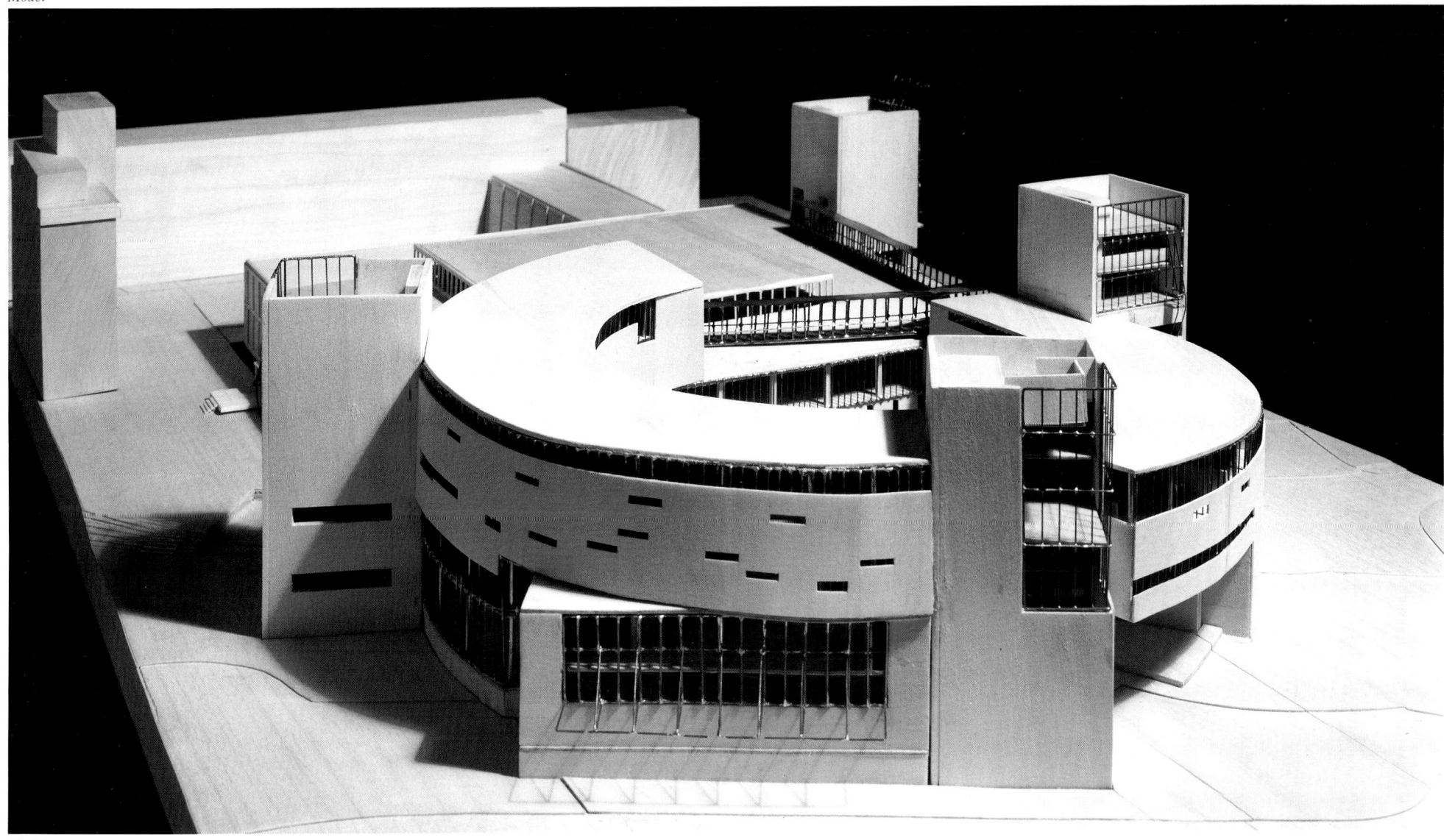

Model

Model

*Palazzo del Cinema
Competition
Venice, Italy
1990-91*

An invited competition for the rebuilding of the Venice Film Festival building on the Lido in Venice. Among the ten invited architects were: Aldo Rossi, Italy; Rafael Moneo, Spain; Sverre Fehn, Norway; James Stirling, U.K., and Jean Nouvel, France. Steven Holl represented the United States.

The connection of the Lido site to Venice by water is emphasized by a grand arrival of space on the lagoon. Filled with diaphanous light from gaps between the cinemas above, this space—a homage to Venice—would also be a place for the Lido community. During the months when there is no cinema festival, this public grotto might have shops along the arcade or marina functions coexisting with the Palazzo del Cinema.

Time in its various abstractions links architecture and cinema. The project involves three interpretations of time and light in space:

1) Collapsed and extended time within cinema is expressed in the warp and extended weave of the building, analogous to cinema's ability to compress (20 years into 1 minute) or extend (4 seconds into 20 minutes) time.

2) Diaphanous time is reflected in sunlight dropping through fissure space between the cinemas into the lagoon basin below. Ripples of water and reflected sunlight animate the grand public grotto.

3) Absolute time is measured in a projected beam of sunlight that moves across the "cubic pantheon" in the lobby.

The projection of light in space, light in reflection, and light in shade and shadow are seen as programs to be achieved parallel to solving functional aspects.

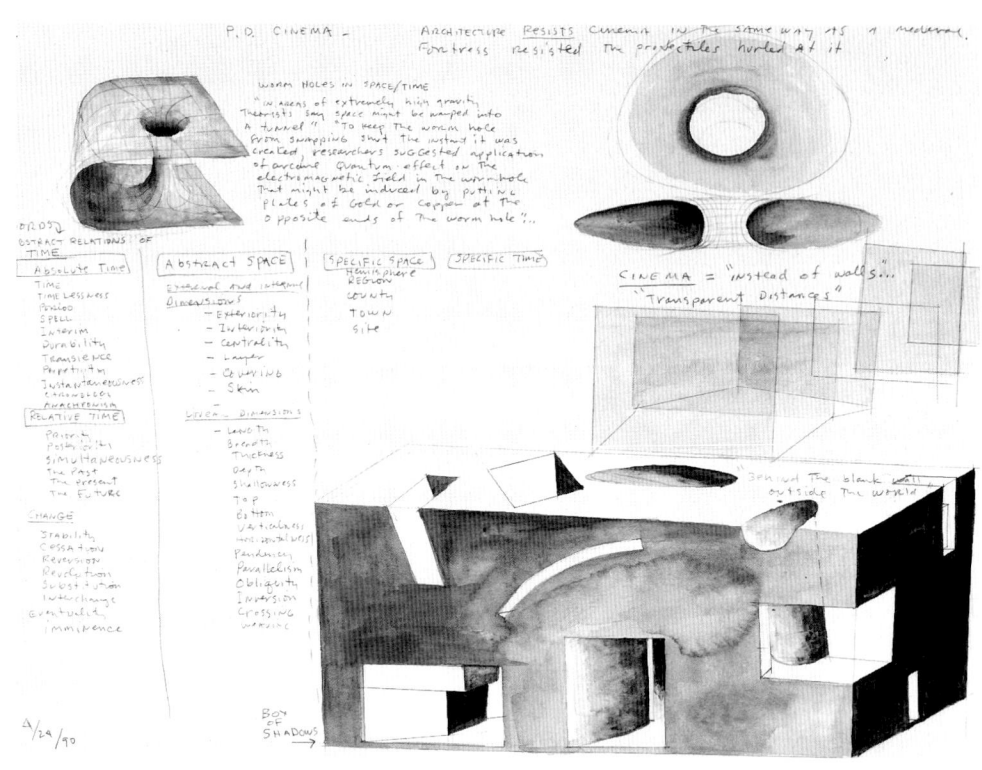

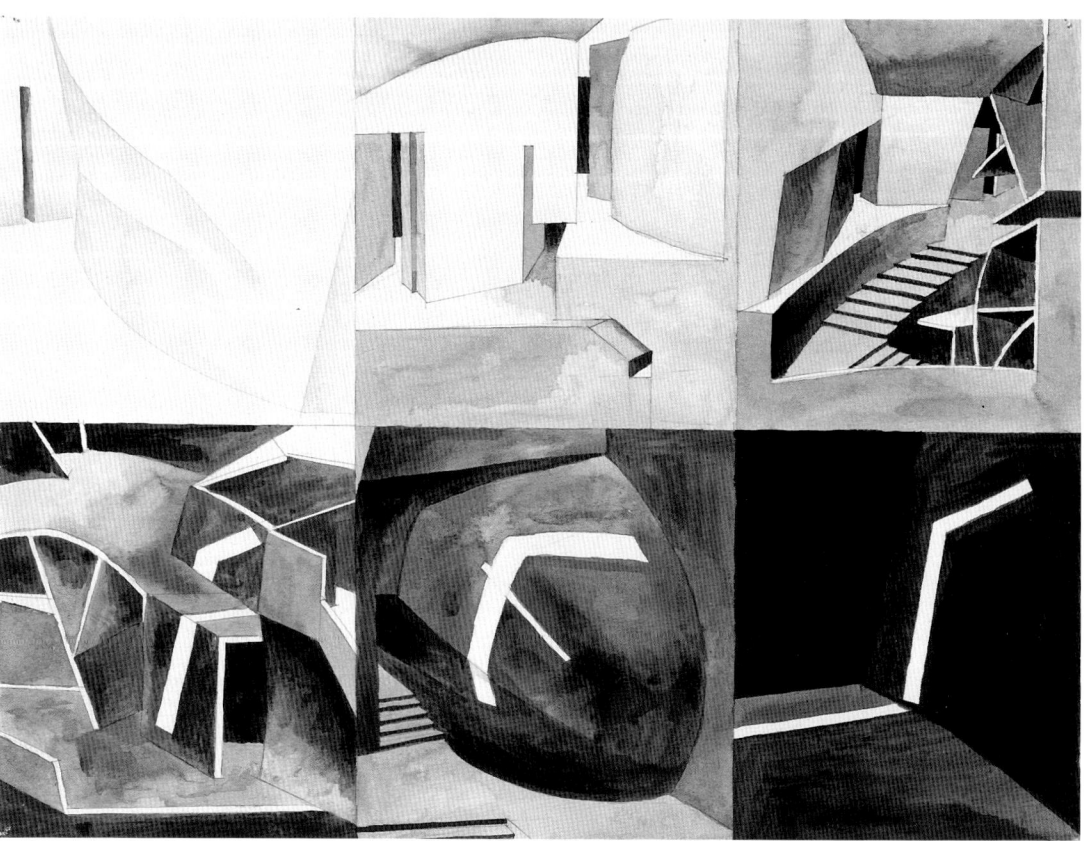

A vessel for "filmic time" and "filmic space," the building's perimeter is bottle-shaped with the mouth open to the lagoon towards Venice. The cinemas interlock within this frame, creating essential crevices and fissures that allow sunlight to the water below. In section, like interlocking hands, the cinemas turn slightly, changing their interior and exterior aspects of space.

The lobby at the end of the covered boat basin joins arrival from the east with arrival from the west. Escalators take ticketed people to the upper level lobby, which has a cafe and a horizonal view of the Adriatic. The escalators pass through the lobby space in sections like the weave of theaters over the lagoon. The main facade of cable-reinforced, sandblasted acrylic responds to this warp and weave.

The main structure is of concrete in "planar" form. Metal formwork for the concrete is retained on the exterior facade. Made of a brass alloy, this metal acquires a red patina.

In some areas the cinema screens can be withdrawn, and the cinema images projected onto warped concrete planes of the structure; the images appear as dissected colors and light on the exterior. The monolithic red patina of the exterior is interrupted by these warped projection zones. Here cinema burns holes in architecture.

パラッツォ・デル・チネマ
ヴェネツィアのリド島にあるヴェネツィア映画祭の建物を建て替えるための指名コンペである。指名された10人の中には、イタリアのアルド・ロッシ、スペインのラファエル・モネオ、ノルウェイのスヴェーレ・フェーン、イギリスからジェイムズ・スターリング、フランスのジャン・ヌーヴェルなどがいた。スティーヴン・ホールがアメリカを代表することになった。

リド島の大地とヴェネツィアの水による結びつきは、干潟に面する空間に堂々と舟を乗りつけることで強調される。上を蔽う映画館の狭間から漏れ落ちる、透けるような光に満たされるこの空間——ヴェネツィアへの賛歌——は、同時にリド島のコミュニティのための場所でもある。映画祭の行われない何ヵ月もの間は、出入りの自由な、この岩屋のような空間にはアーケード沿いに店が並ぶのもいいし、パラッツォ・デル・チネマと併設されるマリーナで利用されるのもいい。

時間をいろいろな形で抽象化するという点で、建築と映画には通じるところがあるのだが、このプロジェクトでは、空間の中の時間と光について3つの解釈がとられている。

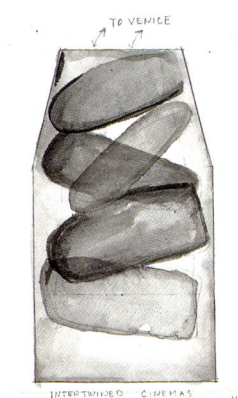

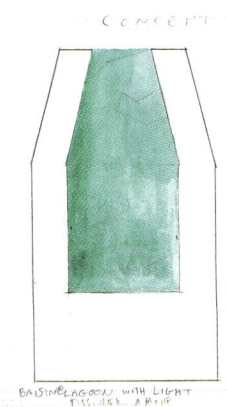

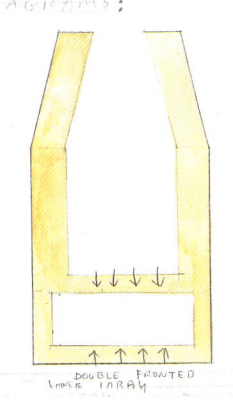

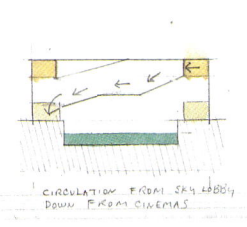

Model and sketches

137

1）映画では時間が縮んだり伸びたりするが，それが建築のゆがみや引き伸ばしという形で表現される。それは，時間を圧縮したり（20年を1分に），のばしたり（4秒を20分に）することの可能な映画のアナロジーなのである。

2）稀薄な時間は，映画館の間のすき間から干潟の水面に落ちる日の光に反映される。小波とそれに反射する光が，広い岩屋に生命を吹き込む。

3）絶対的時間は，ロビーの「キュービック・パンテオン」に射しこむ光の移動によって計られる。

空間に鋭く射し込む光，反射光，影の中を舞う微妙な光は，機能的な側面を解決することと平行して考えるべきものとみなした。

「映画のような時間」と「映画のような空間」を満載した船であるこの建築は，外から見ればヴェネツィアの方向に向いて干潟に口を開いた瓶のようでもある。この外殻の中に映画館をいくつも組み合わせて，ところどころに裂け目やすき間を生じさせ，そこから太陽の光を下の水面に導くのである。断面は，手を組み合わせたような形になっているので，映画館は少しずつ向きを変えながらその内部と外部の空間の様相を変化させる。

建物に蔽われた船着場の奥にあるロビーで，東から来る人たちと西から来る人たちが一堂に会することになる。入場券を手にした人たちはエスカレーターによって，その上の階のロビーへ運ばれる。そこには，水平線に消えるアドリア海を望むカフェがある。このエスカレーターは，ロビーの空間を浮んで上昇し，さながら干潟とその上に浮ぶ映画館とを編みこんでいるようだ。金属線で補強されたアクリルにサンドブラストした正面ファサードは，空間のこのようなねじれと編まれ方を表わしたものだ。

主要な構造体は「プラナー」型枠を使ったコンクリートである。金属製の仮枠はそのまま外壁に残される。真鍮の合金で作られた金属仮枠は赤い緑青を生じる。

一部には，映写スクリーンを取り外すとねじれたコンクリートの構造壁に映画を映すことができるところがある。色と光が外壁を切り裂いたかのように映像が外壁に映し出されると，大きな塊として見える赤い緑青の外壁には，ところどころこのようなねじれた映写ゾーンがはさみこまれる。ここは，映画が建築にあけた焼け焦げ穴というわけだ。

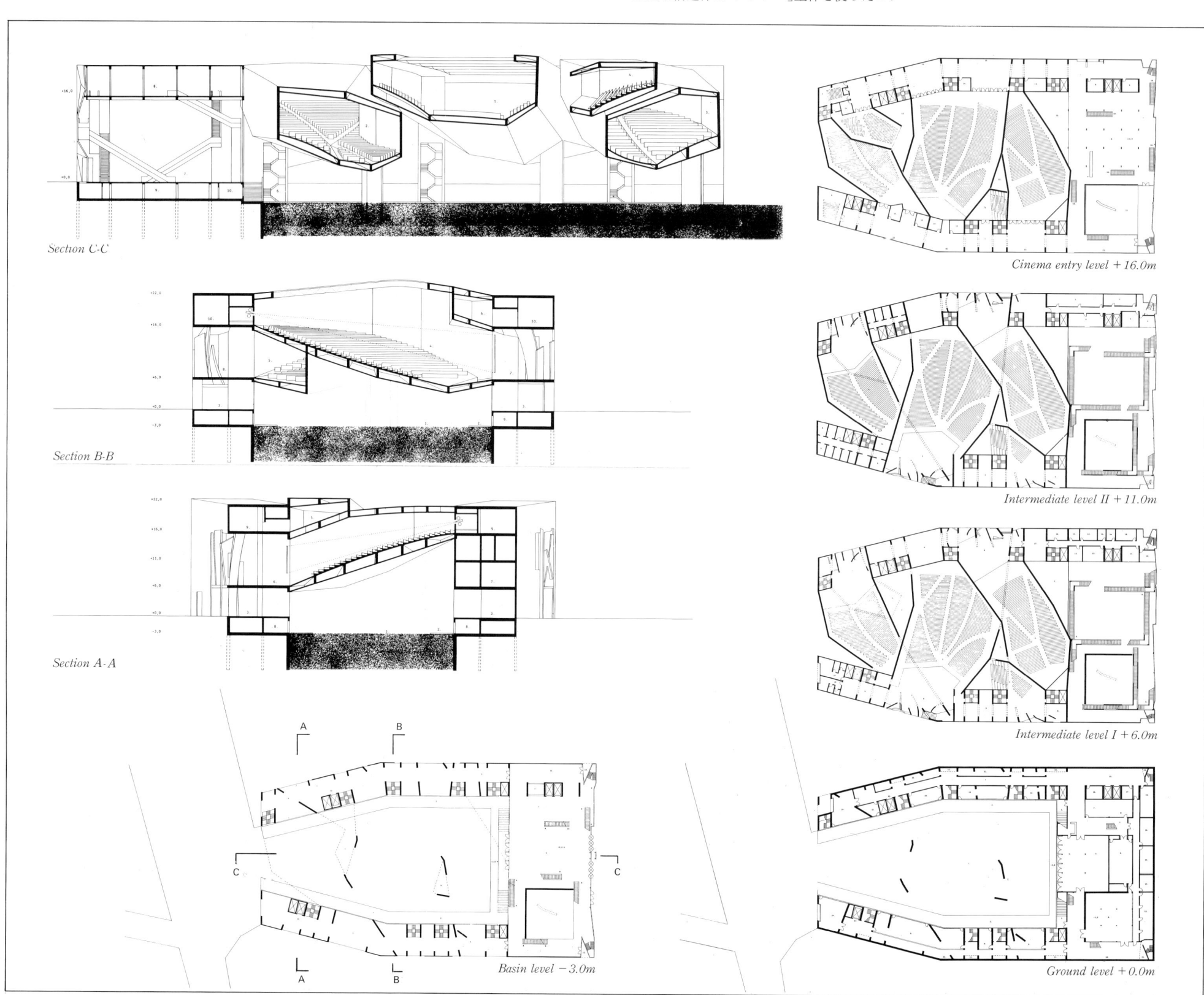

Section C-C

Section B-B

Section A-A

Basin level −3.0m

Cinema entry level +16.0m

Intermediate level II +11.0m

Intermediate level I +6.0m

Ground level +0.0m

Theater

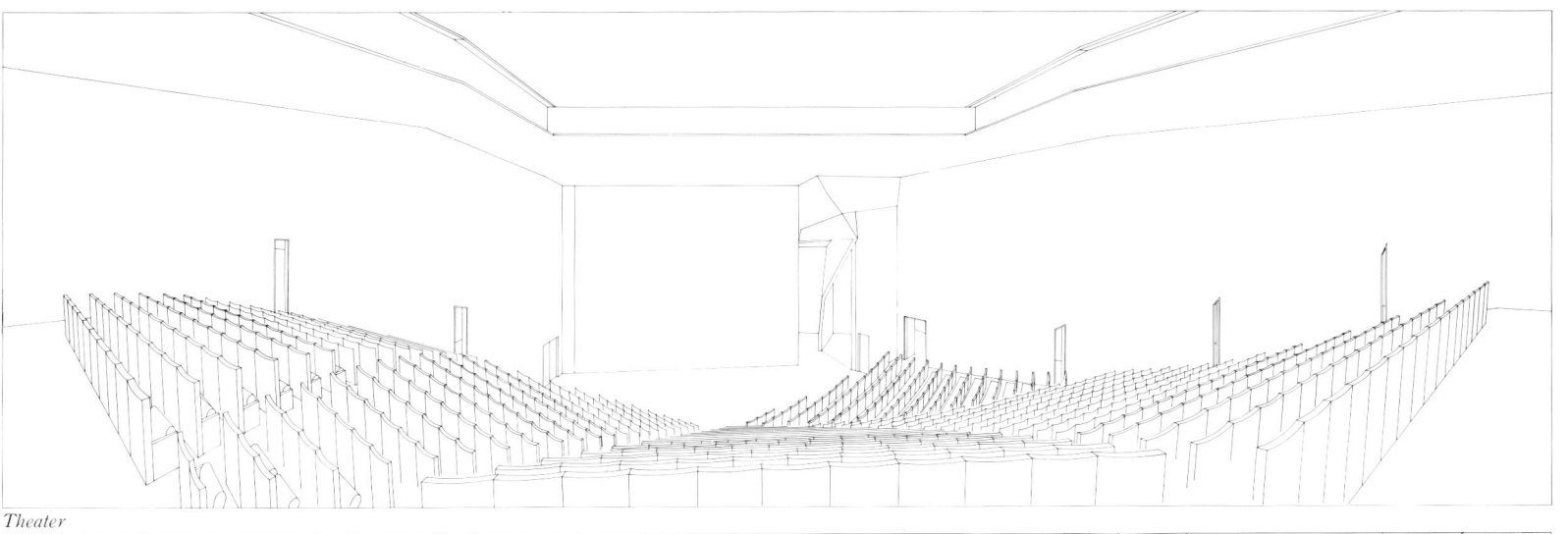

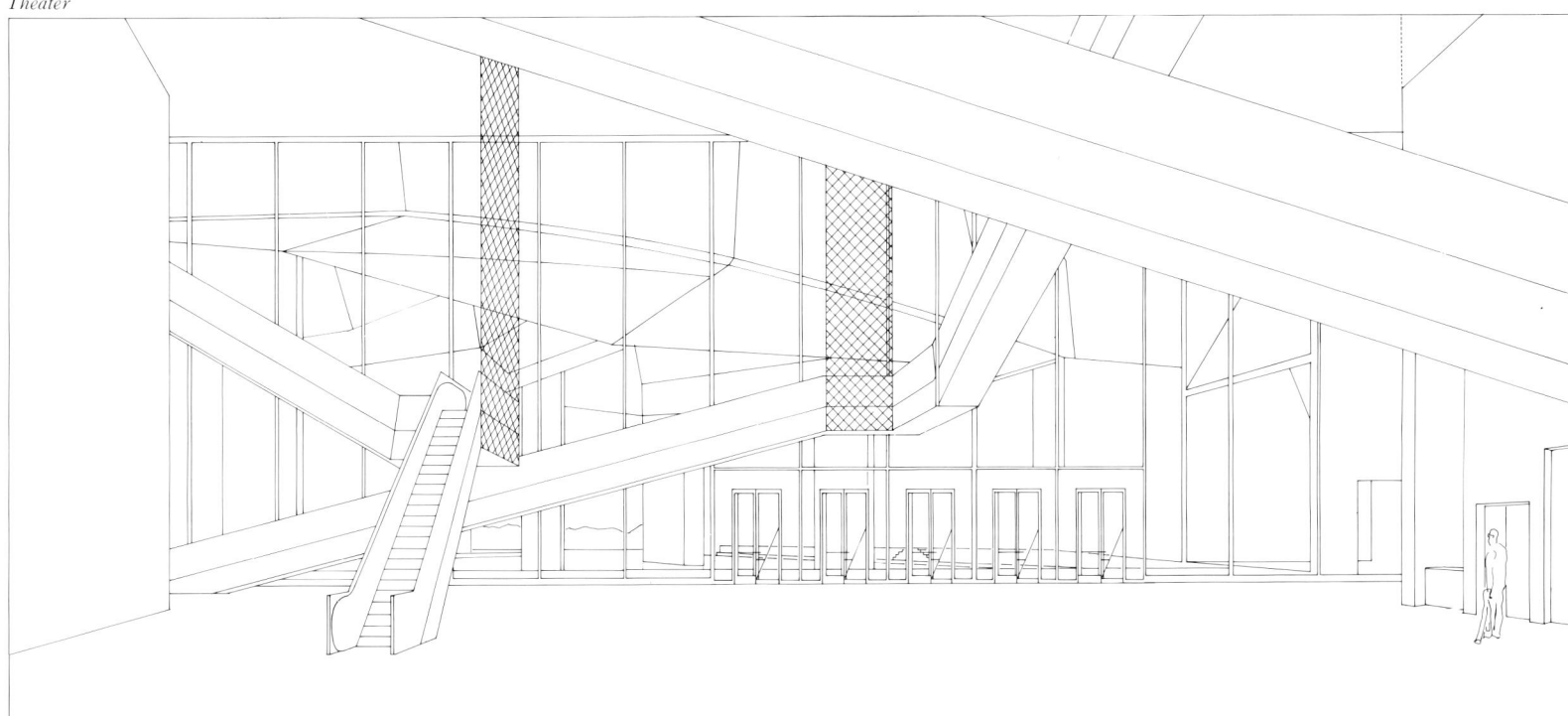

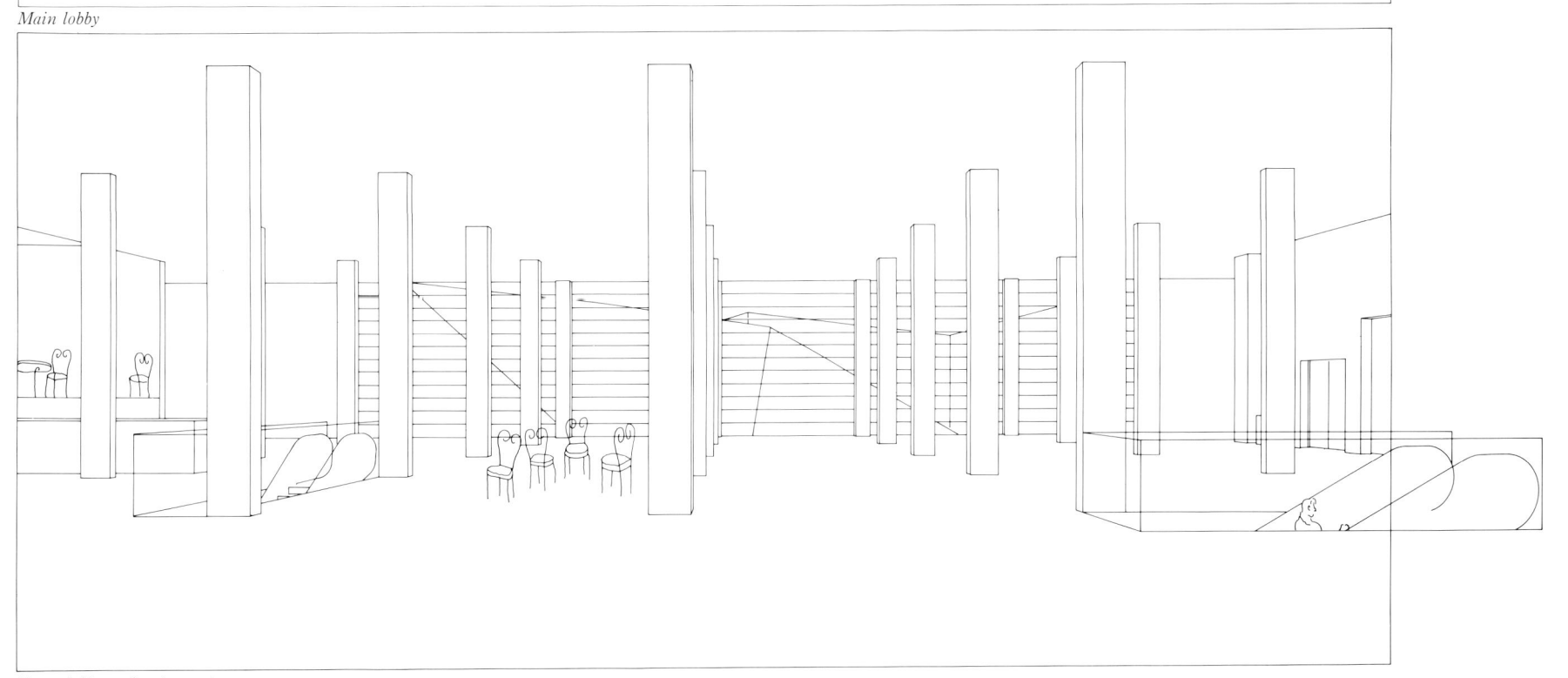

Main lobby

Upper lobby and restaurant

139

*Kemper Museum of
Contemporary Art
Kansas City, Missouri
1991*

The program for this small museum for the Kansas City Art Institute calls for its division into three basic areas: 1) a gallery for the Kemper collection, 2) a large reception area and lobby, and 3) a gallery for temporary exhibitions.

Each area is defined by a different type of light: 1) the permanent collection with cool north light, 2) the entry and reception area with a Hall of Shadows, topped with a shadow trap which rotates according to seasonal sun angles, and 3) the temporary collection with warm light from a faceted skylight which mixes north and south light.

The "L" form of the museum defines a south-facing campus green which is also a sculpture garden. A lower level of services provides a foundation for the building. Its steel-framed structure is skinned in specially treated dull finish aluminum or zinc on a limestone base. The museum is surrounded by a stone terrace and stone garden walls.

ケンパー現代美術館

カンサス・シティー美術研究所に付属するこの小さな美術館計画は，大きく3つのエリアに分割することを求められている。1）ケンパー・コレクション展示ギャラリー。2）広い受付エリアとロビー。3）特別展のためのギャラリー。

各エリアはそれぞれ別のタイプの照明計画を持っている。1）パーマネント・コレクションには北からの落ち着いた光。2）入口・受付エリアには，四季により変わる太陽の高度に合わせて回転するシャドー・トラップが天井に付いたシャドー・ホールがある。3）特別展用のギャラリーには，北と南の光を融合させる小さく面取りされたスカイライトから暖かな光が差し込む。

L字型の建物は，彫刻庭園ともなっているキャンパスの南向きの緑地を縁どっている。サービス施設の置かれた低層レベルは建物の基礎を構成している。鉄骨の構造体は，石灰岩の基礎の上にのった，特別に鈍く仕上げられたアルミや亜鉛の被膜で包まれる。建物の周囲は石敷きのテラスと石の庭塀で囲まれている。

Concept sketch

Concept sketch

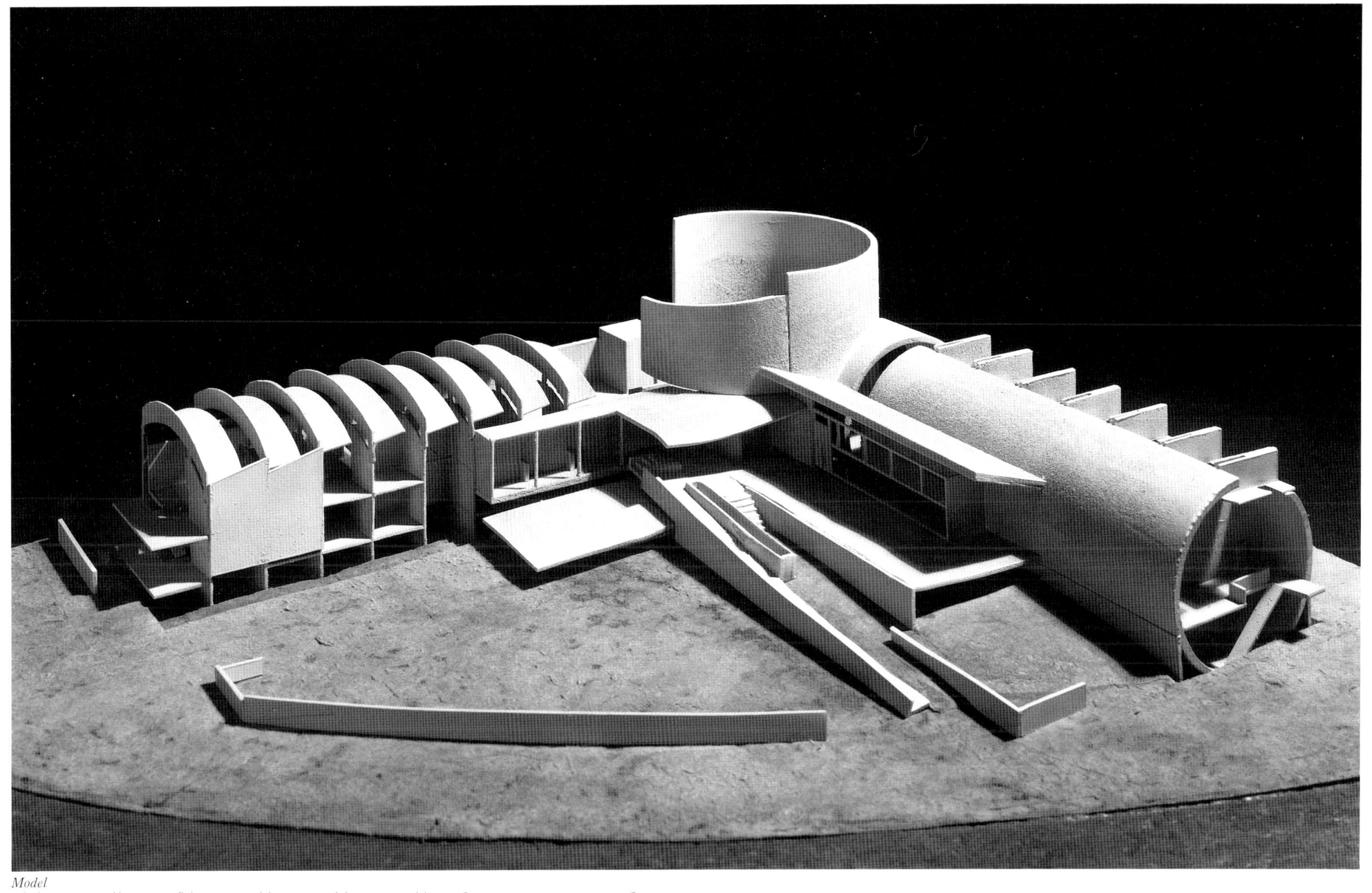

Model

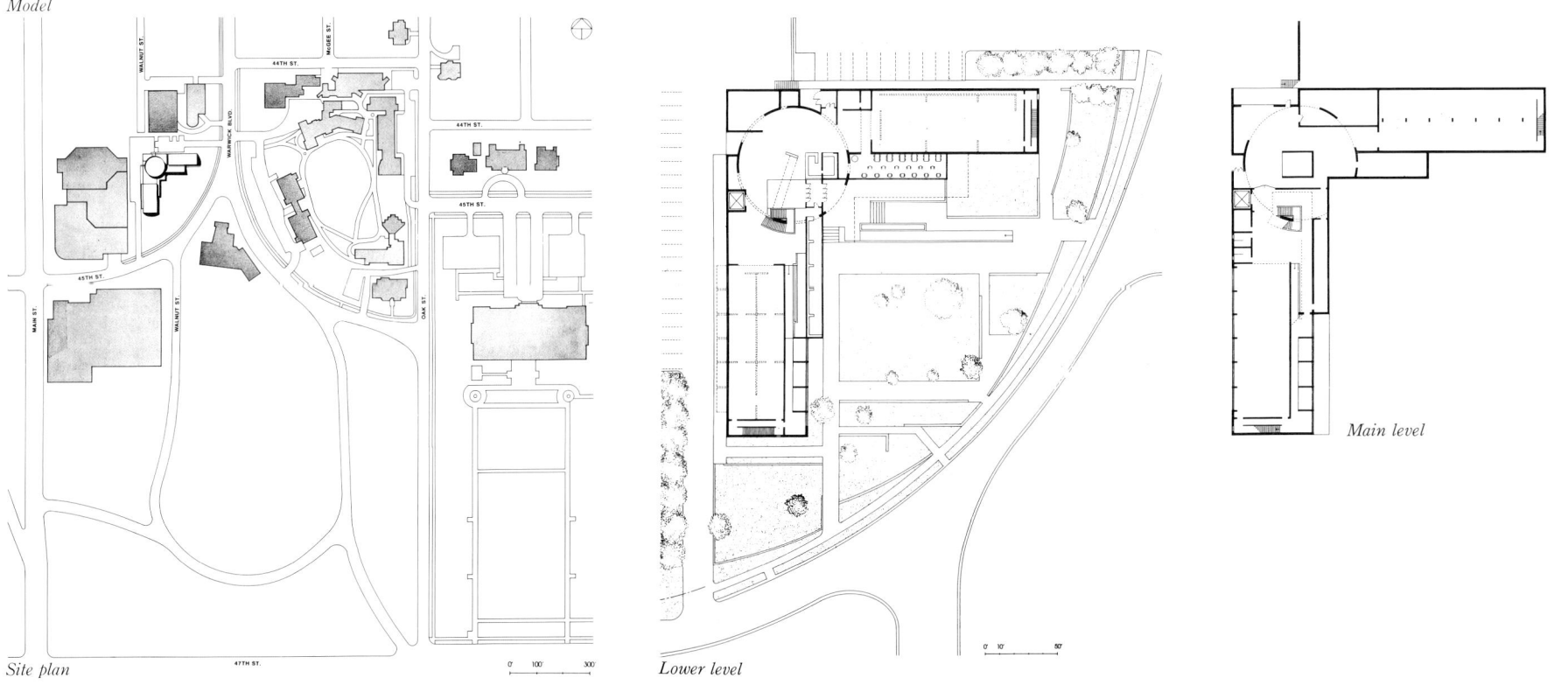

Site plan

Lower level

Main level

5 Edge of a City
都市の周縁

The health of the eye seems to demand a horizon. We are never tired so long as we can see far enough.
—Ralph Waldo Emerson

On the fringe of the modern city, displaced fragments sprout without intrinsic relationships to existing organization, other than that of the camber and loops of the curvilinear freeway. Here, the "thrown away" spreads itself outward like the nodal lines of a stone tossed into a pond. The edge of a city is a philosophical region, where city and natural landscape overlap, existing without choice or expectation. This zone calls for visions and projections that delineate the boundary between the urban and the rural. Visions of a city's future can be plotted on this partially spoiled land, liberating the remaining natural landscape, protecting the habitats of hundreds of species of animals and plants that are threatened with extinction. What remains of the wilderness can be preserved; defoliated territory can be restored. In the middle zone between landscape and city, there is hope for a new synthesis of urban life and urban form. Traditional planning methods are no longer adequate. Looking back at the city from the point of view of the landscape, these projects consider untested programs and new kinds of urban spaces.

The exponential changes brought about by air travel over this century exemplify how experiences of space and time change from city to city. Within hours we are transported from one climate and time zone to another. Formerly, entering a city occured along the earth via a bridge or a portal. Today, we circle over then jet down to an airstrip on a city's periphery. Consequently, in making plans and projections for new city edges, it is necessary to discard old methods and working habits and begin with basic research.

The exploration of strategies to counter sprawl at the periphery cities—the formation of spaces rather than the formation of objects—are primary aims of the *Edge of a City* projects. The expanded boundary of the contemporary city calls for the synthesis of new spatial compositions. An intensified urban realm could be a coherent mediator between the extremes of the metropolis and the agrarian plain.

In each proposal, living, working, recreational and cultural facilities are juxtaposed in new pedestrian sectors that might act as social condensers for new communities. From "spatial retaining bars" that protect the desert at the edge of Phoenix, Arizona, to "spiroid sectors" that densify suburban settlement, preserving the natural landscape, the proposals presented here entwine a new social program with existing circumstances. Though they differ in form, these proposals share a "pre-theoretical ground" of psychological space, program, movement, light quality and tactility.

(S.H.)

「目の健康には水平線が必要なようだ。遠くが見えるかぎり私たちは疲れを覚えることはない。」
——R・W・エマーソン

現代都市の周縁では、あちらこちらで、既存の周辺環境との関わりを無視した新しい建物への建て替えが進んでいる。それはまた、高速道路の曲線の描く傾きやループとも別種のものなのだ。そこでは、これらの「投げ捨て」建築が、池に投じられた石のつくりだす波紋のように外へ外へと広がってゆく。こうした都市の周縁は、都市と自然の景観が混在し、選択の自由もなく将来の期待ももてない、根源的な考察を要する地域である。このような一帯には、都市と田園地帯の境界についての輪郭を描くようなヴィジョンと提案が待望されている。破壊されかけているこの土地に、残された自然景観を保存しながら、絶滅の危機に瀕した何百という種の動植物が生息する環境を護るような形で、都市の未来像を描くこともできるはずだ。残る未開の土地は保護し、枯れた土地は回復させる。自然景観と都市の間に横たわる中間地帯には、都市生活と都市形態のあいだに新たな統合を生みだせる望みがある。そこでは伝統的な計画手法はもはや適合しない。ここにあげるプロジェクトは、ランドスケープという視点から都市を見直して、未だ試みられたことのない計画や新しい種類の都市空間について考察したものである。

今世紀に入って、飛行機旅行によってもたらされた変化の代表的なものは、都市から都市への空間と時間を移動する時の体験である。今では、数時間のうちに、気候も時刻も違う所へ移動するが、かつては、よその都市に入ってゆくといえば地上を移動して橋を渡り、門をくぐってゆくものだった。それが今日では、ジェット機が空を旋回して、都市の郊外にある空港の滑走路めがけて下降するのだ。だとすれば、都市の周辺部に新たな計画を作り提案するには、古い方法や現行の慣習を捨て去り、根本的な調査からはじめなければならないだろう。

都市の周縁部のスプロールに対処する戦略を練るにあたって、オブジェを配するという形ではなく、空間をどう配置するかが、「エッジ・オヴ・シティ」の諸計画の目標である。現代都市の、外へ広がり続ける境界地域では、新たに空間を構成する統合の方法を求めている。都市の膨脹部は、大都市のいちばん外れと農業地帯の間を一体に結び付ける仲介者に転ずるに違いない。

ここにあげたどの提案をとっても、生活、労働、余暇や文化のための施設が、新しいコミュニティのための「コンデンサー」となる新たに構成された歩行者地域と並んでいる。アリゾナ州フェニックス市の外れに広がる砂漠を保護する「スペイシャル・リテイニング・バー」から、郊外地の居住密度をあげつつ自然を残そうという「螺旋形地区」に至るまで、これらの提案は、新しい社会政策と既存の環境との調和を示すものだ。それぞれ形は違っているにしても、心理的な空間、プログラム、動き、光の質、触感という、「理論以前の領域」を共有しているのである。

(S.H.)

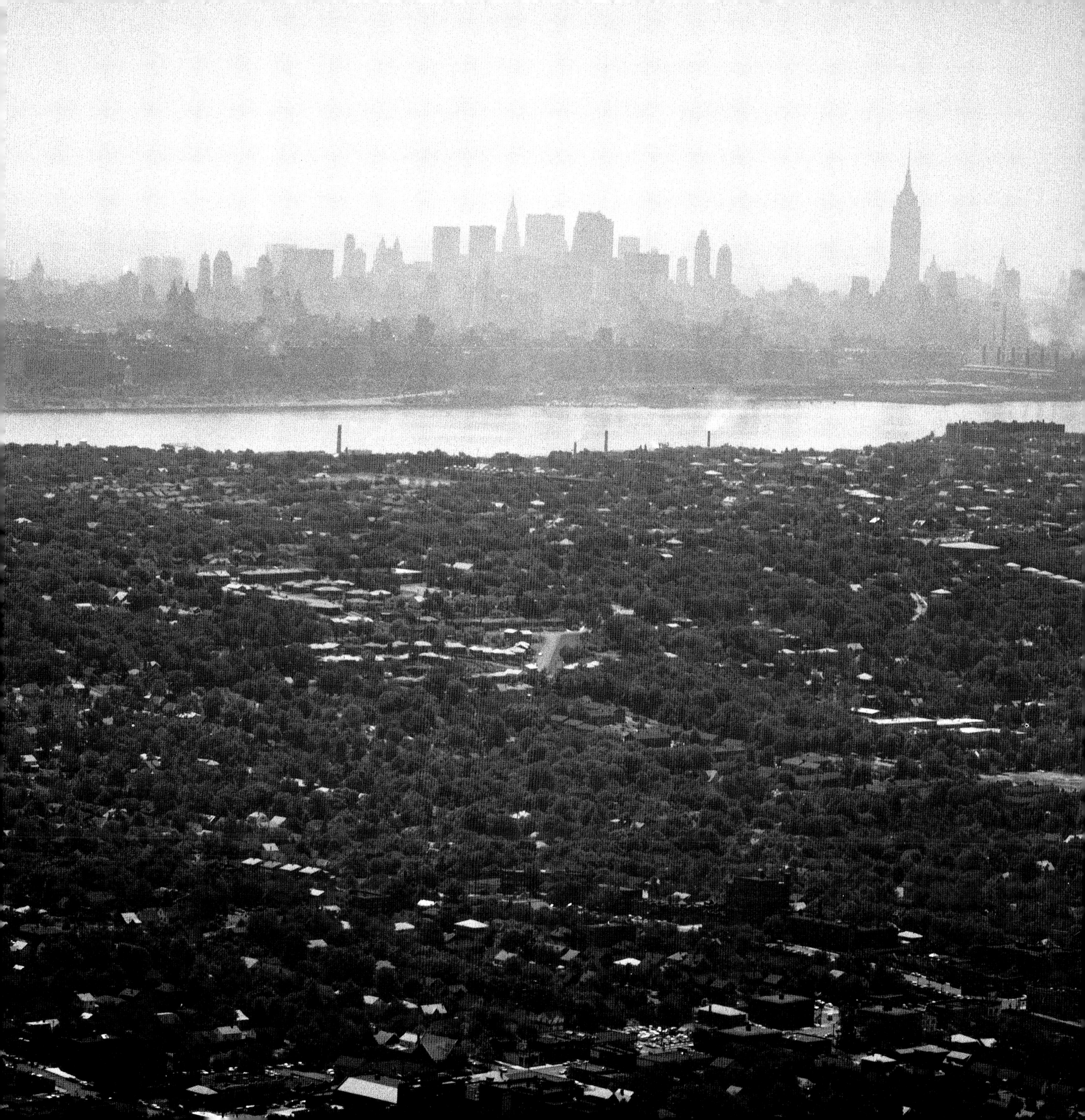

Porta Vittoria Competition
Milan, Italy
1986

The site for this project, commissioned by the 17th Triennale of Milan, is a disused freight rail yard (part of Milan's old railroad belt) bordered by blocks of different housing types. It is in the nineteenth-century gridded portion of Milan, outside the historical center.

The program required keeping only the new "Passante" subway station, provoking the redevelopment of the area. Other functions to be located at the site include a bus station and garage for thirty buses, an air terminal station, hotels, offices, and housing. The proposal is also meant to provoke consideration of other programs for the reclamation of this metropolitan site.

The conviction behind this project is that an open work—an open future—is a source of human freedom. To investigate the uncertain, to bring out unexpected properties, to define psychological space, to allow the modern soul to emerge, to propose built configurations in the face of (and fully accepting) major social and programmatic uncertainty: this is our intention for the continuation of a "theoretical Milan."

From a dense center, Milan unfolds in circles ringed by a patchwork grid that finally sprawls raggedly into the landscape. Against this centrifugal urban sprawl (from dense core to light periphery), a reversal is proposed: light and fine-grained toward the center, heavy and volumetric toward the periphery. This proposal projects a new ring of density and intensity, adjoining the rolling green of a reconstituted landscape.

Three traditional urban strategies were rejected. The flexible planning device of the grid was suspended, because of its tendency to render everything as a measure of block-by-block infill. Secondly, the method that organizes historically modeled building types according to the existing morphology of the city was suspended. Finally, the whole method of drawing a plan layout, followed later by a three-dimensional form, was rejected.

The strategy used reverses the usual method of design in architecture (from plan to section, elevation, perspectival space). Instead, perspective sketches of spatial conditions are cast backward into plan fragments, which are then reconciled in an overall layout.

By its nature the perspective drawing implies associations between elements. These spatial configurations are taken as evidence of a particular activity, clues for reconstructing a program. Images of human activity, collected from diverse sources, are held alongside the perspective views to provoke the analysis.

For the existing park, Largo Marinai d'Italia, a giant pond is proposed to reconcile the park with its name. The Palazzina Liberty is restored as the Dario Fo Pavilion and is accessible by rowboat only. A series of floating walkways connects a seaman's exhibition. Residential apartments hover over tiny objects: an oar, a horn, a carving. Old sailors discuss the artifacts with passing visitors; stories are the material of the floating exhibition.

At the edge of the pond is a large metronomelike Monument to Toil, in memory of the loading and unloading of goods that once filled this site. As the slow movement of each pipe beam reaches the end of a beat, a drop of water is emitted from its top. Nearby, an aviary housing two white doves juts out of the park, bringing light to an underground assemblage.

Across Viale Umbria, in a Garden of Sounds, the park infiltrates the urban area. Within the garden is a seasonal children's zoo whose animals require a variety of cages and enclosures (the goat, the chicken, the cow, etc.). Other little programs are implied by the titles of the various areas: The See-Saw, Fishing, The Picnic, The Water-Chute, The Sleigh, La Commedia Italiana, The Octopus, Hunting, Fireworks, Bocci Ball.

To the south of the site is a large public Botanical Garden with glass-roofed forms in a sprouting diversity parallel to the vegetation within. Over the sloping earthen floor of the interior are areas for experimental botany, checker and chess tables, and meeting tables. These are scattered throughout the green density of the vegetation. On the ground of the eastern portion is a darkened hall containing a cinema that dissects its interior. The public is exposed to back-projection on constructed objects, multiple separation, and other cinematic experiments.

Bounding the Botanical Garden is a large public fountain that is negotiated via stone steps and passages interwoven with cascades of water. The fountain opens onto a long basin for aquatic activities and barge-borne theatrical events. At the edge of this opening is a hotel for unhappy lovers. The plan has no interior corridors, setting the rooms of the hotel back-to-back. One large glass corridor belts the building. At the top is a crooked cafe-lounge and a wiry truss containing a footbridge to a suspended chapel. On the northwest portion of the site, a water channel is flanked by rudimentary housing for the homeless. Nearby, a public gymnasium is organized in a strip interwoven with spectator areas. To the east is a school of the humanities. Its central block of lecture rooms is banded by study room towers; visiting professors live in the upper portions. From the main building, a walkway connects to two wedge-shaped interrelated workshop-studios. To the west, a ramp cycles through a two-part correlating facility, leading upward into spaces more and more remote, arriving at a mechanical rooftop simulating teleological suspension.

Near Via F. Rezzonico is a sanctuary of the muses filled with ancient stone fragments. A modern cinema is inserted from the east. The public can move back and forth from celluloid simulation to stone materiality.

The new subway station opens to the west onto an elongated gap. Here the visitor passes through several activities, rising through an elliptical passage to the Garden of Sounds. Bureaucratic and administrative activities (formless and always in flux) are given specific urban character in a thin tower, a four-sided pentagon, a double-flux slab (whose section can be altered), and large galleries along the water basin. The three lobbies of these work areas are connected by a central neckshaped space.

Across Viale Mugello, to the east, larger programs fit into the existing city fabric. The airport connection station sits here; adjacent is the bus garage, housed below a public arena and velodrome.

Of these specific ideas, several might be realized, and yet the overall strategy and intention depends on none of them. They serve only as examples for the figure in the landscape of this city for which the unknown is a source of optimism. To affirm the joy of the present, to find lines of escape, to subvert an overall urban plan from within—via architecture—is part of projecting an open future as a source of freedom.

ポルタ・ヴィットリア計画
ミラノの第17回トリエンナーレに依頼されたこの計画の敷地は、使われなくなった貨物線の鉄道駅の跡地で(ミラノの旧鉄道の一部)、それぞれに表情を異にする住宅の建つブロックで周囲を固められている。このあたりは19世紀になって、格子状に区画された地域で、ミラノの歴史的な中心部からははずれた所である。

この計画では、新しい地下鉄「パッサンテ」の駅を、あたりの再開発の起爆剤として取り込むことだけは必要だった。敷地内に作る施設の概要は、バスの駅と30台のバスを収容するガレージ、空港の駅、ホテル、オフィス、それに住宅である。提案には、この都市の再開発を計る他の諸々の計画にも目を向けさせようという意図も込められている。

この計画の背後には、ひとつの信念がある。開放的な働き方——開放的な未来——は、人間の自由の根源をなすものであるということだ。不確かなものに投資すること、思いがけない資質に日の光を浴びせるようにすること、精神的な空間とは何であるかを示すこと、時代の魂を目に見えるものにすること、建物を配置することで、重要なものではありながら社会的にはまだ認定されていない計画を目の前に(充分に受入れ可能な形で)提示することである。これが、「あるべきミラノ」像をどう伝えるべきかということについての、私たちの意図である。

高密度の中心部から外にゆくにつれて、現在のミラノは密度がゆるやかになり、やがて周囲の景観の中に不揃いに食い込んで終る。このような遠心的なスプロール(濃密な中心部から稀薄

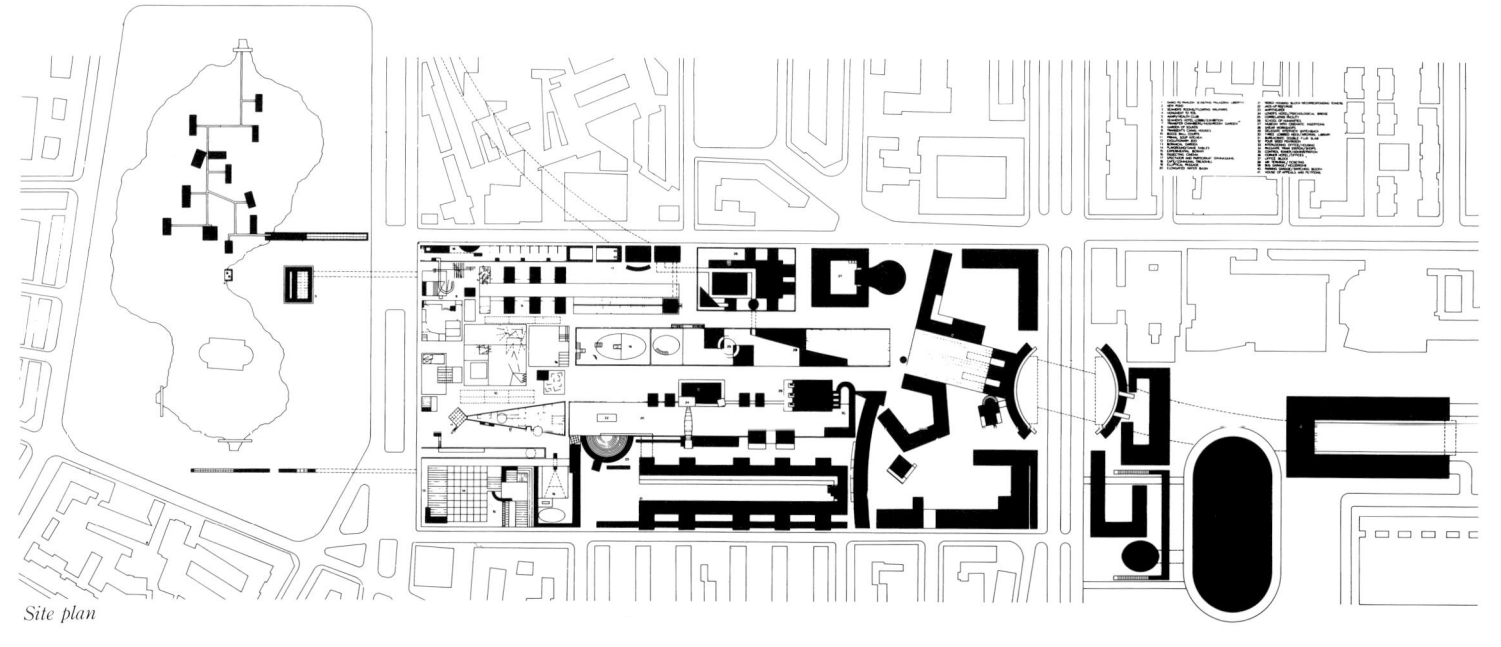

Site plan

Axonometric

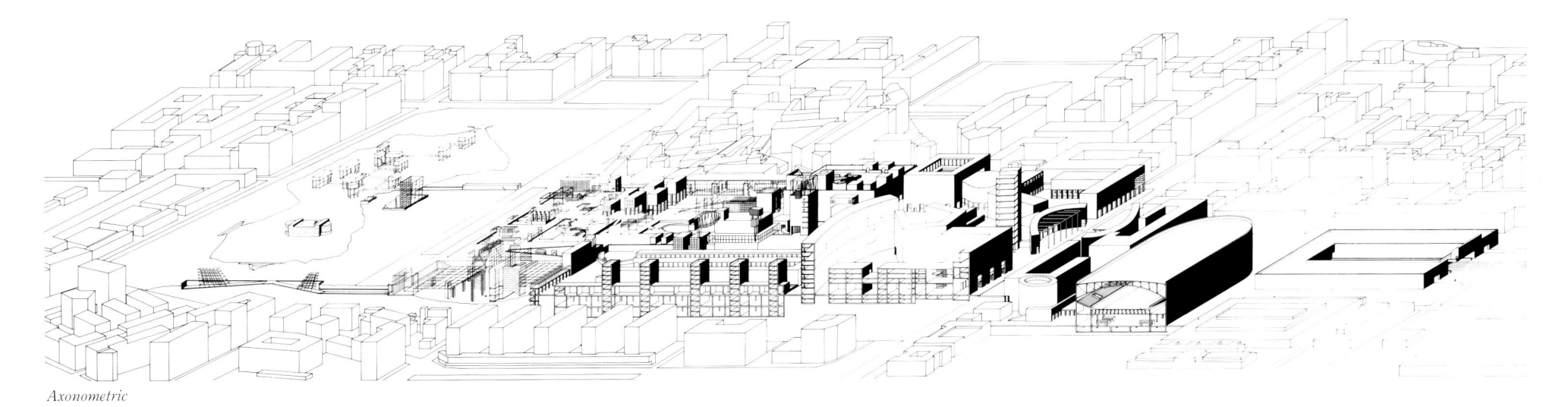

な周辺部へ)とは反対の形を私たちは提案したのである。中心に向うにつれ、小さなものを疎らに配し、周辺を大規模な建築が高密度に占めるのだ。ここでは、高密度で強い性格をもつ環状の地帯を新たに作り、景観にも手を加えて、なだらかに起伏する緑を加える。

私たちは都市計画の3つの常套手段を退けた。まず、格子によるプランニング手法は控える。とかく、何もかもブロック単位で量りながら空間を埋めてゆき、それだけで満足することになりがちだからである。次に、この都市をなぞるようにして歴史的な形の建築を作るという手もとらない。また全体のプランを描いて、その後で3次元の形態を作るという方法も退けた。

この方法は建築デザインの常道(平面図から断面、立面、パースペクティヴな空間へ)の逆をゆくものであった。つまり、空間の状況を示すパースペクティヴなスケッチからとりかかって、部分的な平面に進み、その後で全体の配置と調整をはかるのである。

その性質上、パースは様々な要素の相互のかかわり方を伝える。したがって、こうした空間上の配置は、ある特定の行動を示すものとなり、それが、何らかのプログラムを組立てる糸口になるのだ。広く集められた人間の行動のイメージは、パースに基づいて把握されて分析を促すことになる。

在来の公園、ラルゴ・マリナイ・ディターリア(イタリアの船員達の広場)にはその名に恥じぬように大きな池を提案にとりいれた。パラッツィーナ・リベルティは修復してダーリオ・フォー・パヴィリオンに名を改める。これは池の中にあるので、ボートを漕いで行くほかに近づけない。船員に関するものを納める展示場は、浮桟橋伝いに結ばれる。こまごまとした物たち、たとえばオール、霧笛、彫刻などを展示するフロアの上の階にはアパートメントが置かれる。年老いた船員たちがここを訪れる人々を相手に、展示された物について言葉をかわす。彼らの語る物語も水上の展示物の一部なのだ。

池のふちに、巨大なメトロノームを思わせる形をした、かつての重労働のモニュメントが建ってこの地を埋めつくした貨物の揚卸の作業を偲ばせるよすがになっている。それぞれのパイプが、ゆるやかな動きで受持範囲の端にゆくと、その先端から水が流れ出るというしかけだ。その傍らには、2羽の白い鳩を入れる鳥小舎が公園の上に突き出して、そこからは地下の集会場に光を届ける。

ウンブリア通りを横切って、ガーデン・オブ・サウンドに入ると、公園は、あたりが都市の様相を帯びる。庭の一部には、季節によって開かれる子供動物園があるので、様々な檻や囲いが必要だ(山羊、にわとり、雌牛などがいるのだ)。その他のこまごまとしたものは、それぞれの呼び名で内容がわかるだろう。たとえばシーソー、魚つり、ピクニック、ウォーターシュート、ソリ、イタリア喜劇、オクトパス、狩り、花火、ボッチボールといった具合だ。

敷地の南には広い植物園があって、中の植物に応じた様々な形のガラスの屋根がある。傾斜を残したままの土の床には、植物学上の実験に使われる一帯もあれば、チェッカーやチェスのテーブルや談笑するためのテーブルなどの置かれるところもある。これらが、鬱蒼と生える植物の間に点在しているのだ。東側には、内部が細分された映画館を納めた暗いホールがある。入場者は背面映写のマルチスクリーンなどの実験的映像に目を奪われる。

植物園の縁には、石の階段や歩道が滝とともに織りなされた噴水池があって、それが細長い池に向って開いている。ここでは水上の催し物や、船上のように作られた舞台での催しが繰り広げられる。そのほとりに、幸せになれない恋人たちのためのホテルがある。ホテルの平面は、内部に廊下というものがない。客室はみな、背中合せに並んでガラス張りの長い廊下が周りを囲むからだ。その屋上に、カフェラウンジがあって、さらにそこからはトラスのブリッジが延びてゆき、その先端に吊られたチャペルへ導く。敷地の北西部には、水路のふちにホームレスのための住居がある。その隣に、観客席と組合わされた体育館が帯状に並ぶ。その東には人文科学の学校がある。中央に位置する講義室棟を囲むようにして塔状の研究室棟が建つ。客員教授たちは、その上部を住居にすることになる。中央棟からは、くさび形を組合わせた平面の工作室スタジオへ通路で結ばれる。その西では、螺旋形をなすスロープが2つの建物を行きつ戻りつして、次々と空間を経て昇りつづけると、屋上で行き止まる。本来、原因に達することなどできはしない目的論的思考が、いずれ中断せざるをえないのを表現したものだ。

F・レッツォニコ通り沿いの瞑想のための聖域には古代の石の破片が豊富にある。その東側には、現代映画館が挿し込まれるようにして続いている。映画という虚像と石の実像との間を行き来できるというわけだ。

新たに作られる地下鉄駅は西の方にも出入口があって、そこからは細長い広場に続く。ここで様々な仕掛けに出会いながら長円形をなす通路を経てガーデン・オブ・サウンドに至る。役所や管理組織(固定せず常に流動的な形式にする)のためには、それぞれにふさわしい都市的な形態が与えられる。細い塔状や、辺の欠けた5角形もあれば、2層ごとに床を可変にしたり(断面の形が変えられる)、あるものは水に沿って長いギャラリーがある。これらオフィス部分の3つのロビーは中央の首のような形のスペースで結ばれる。東側、ムジェッロ通りを挟んだ向い側には、既存の都市の機能につなぐための大規模な計画もある。空港の駅がここに来るし、隣にはバスの車庫があって階下には体育館と自転車の競技場が含まれる。

これら数々のアイディアのうちで、いくつかは実現するかもしれないが、この都市全体の戦略や意図がそのうちのどれかによって左右されることはないかもしれない。ただ、これまで思いもしなかったものが楽天的な気分の源になれるような、ミラノの都市景観の一例として役立てればいいと思う。現在の喜びを確実なものにしたり、あるいは別の世界へ脱出する拠り所を提供したり、都市計画をすっかり転覆させたりすることが内側から——建築を通じて——できるなら、それは、自由の源泉としての解放された未来を、その一部なりとも人々に示せたということだ。

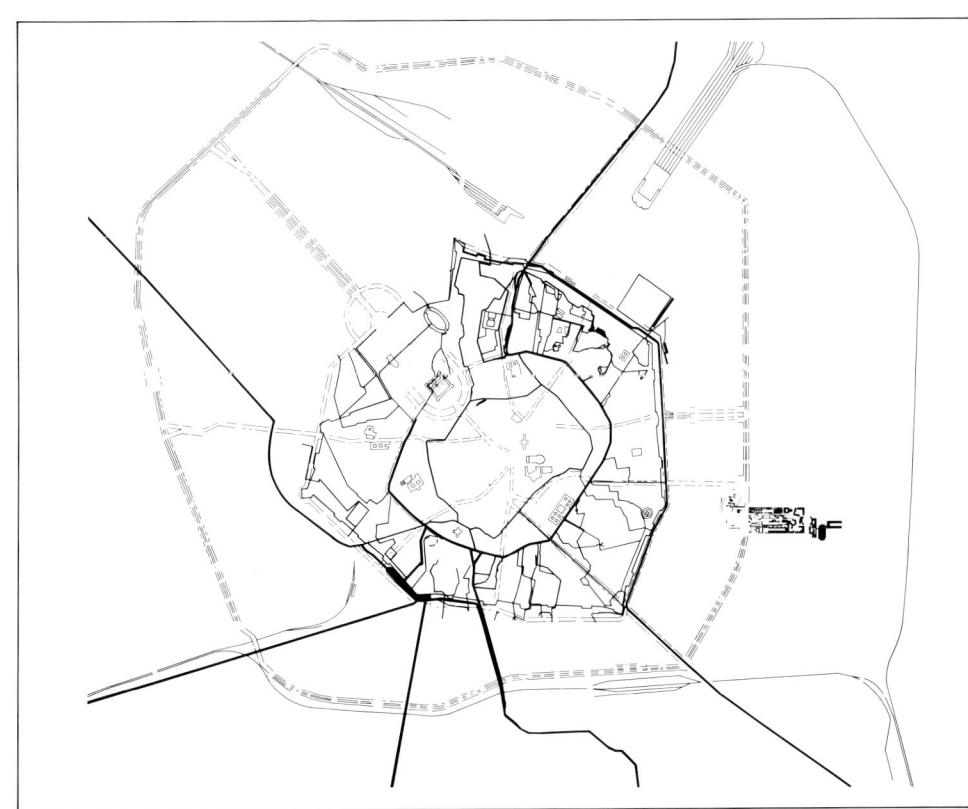

Site with plan of Milan

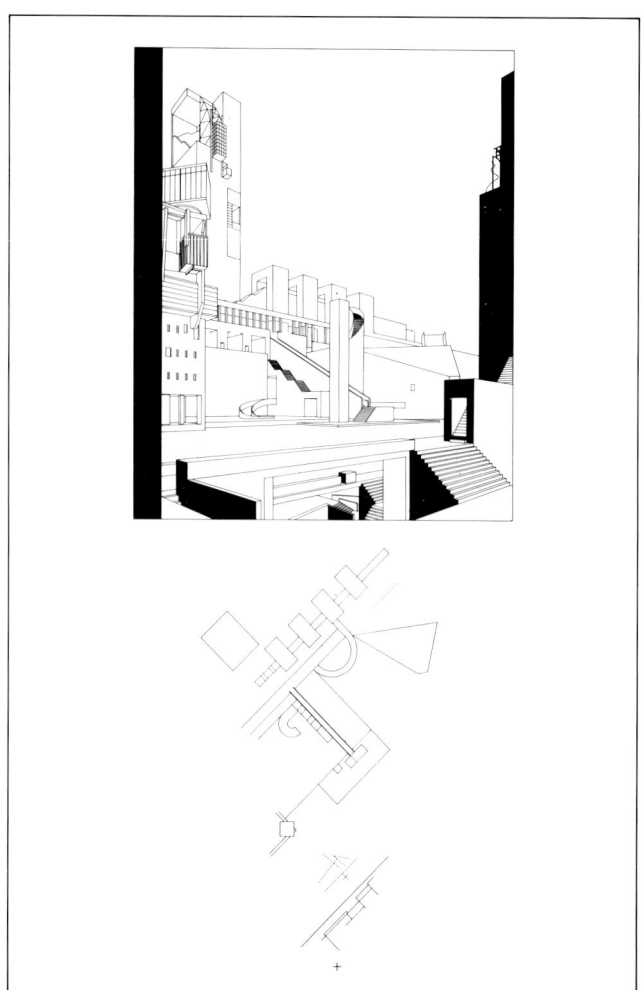

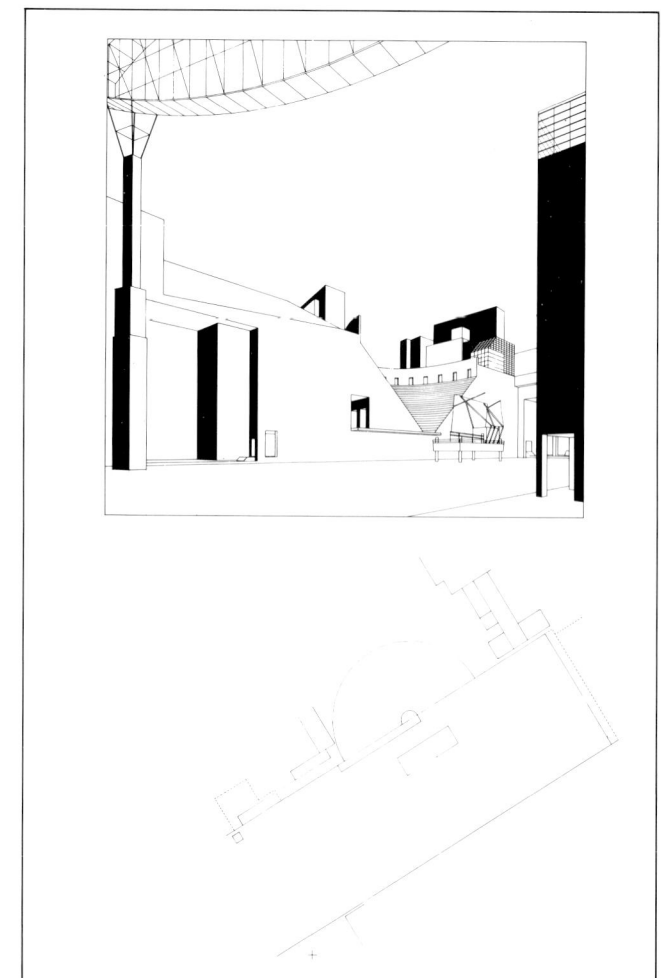

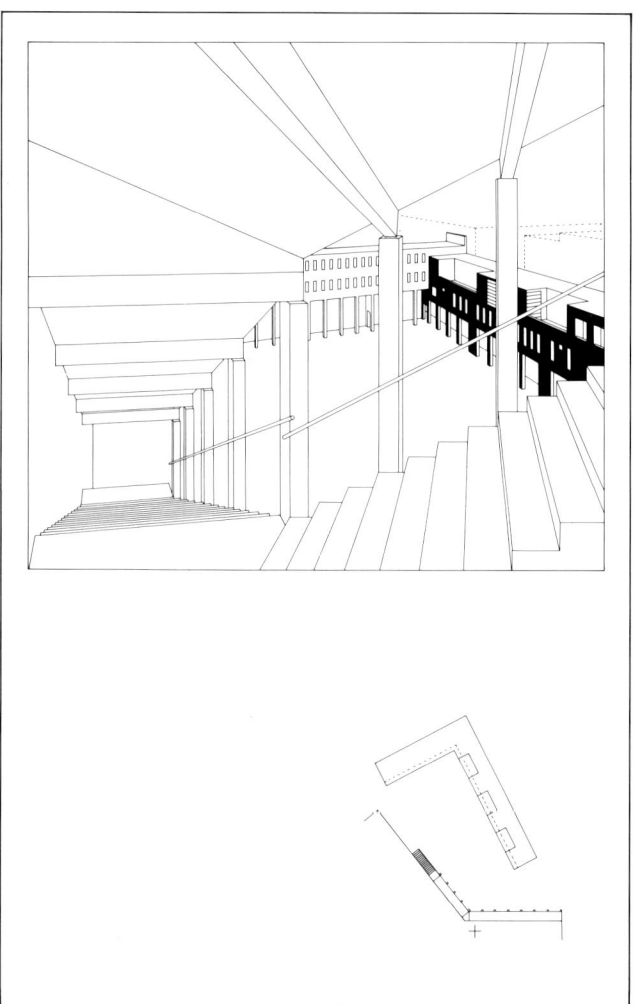

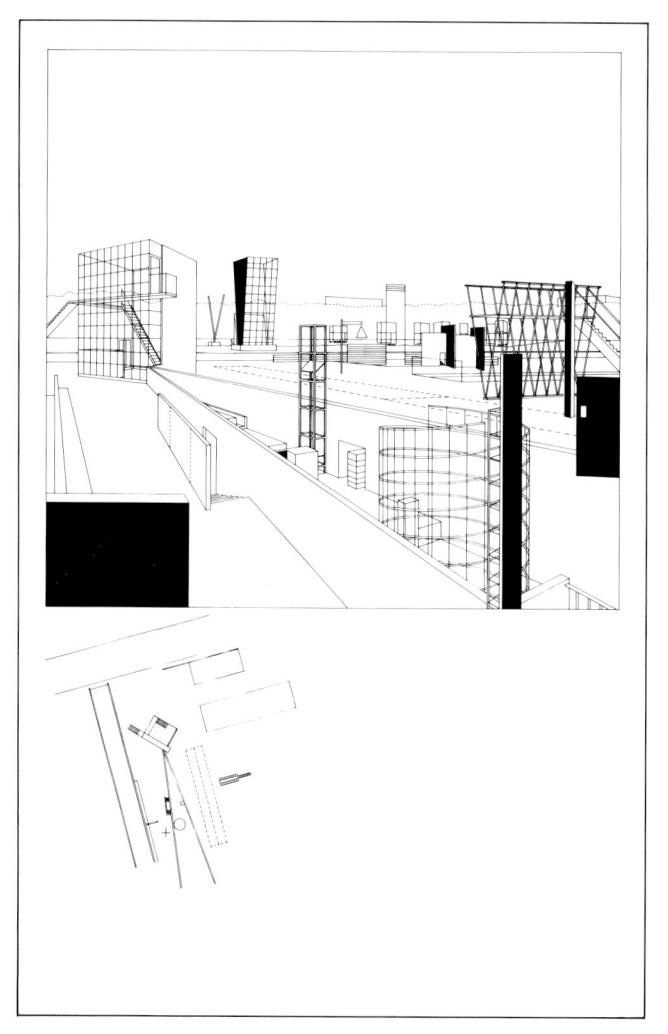

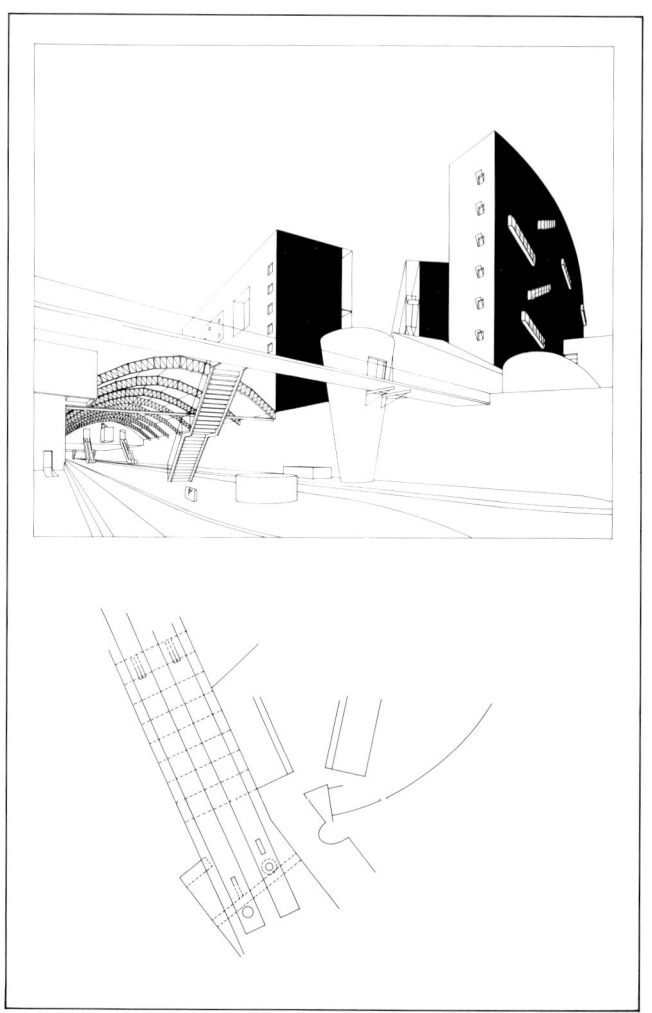

Perspectives

Water color drawings

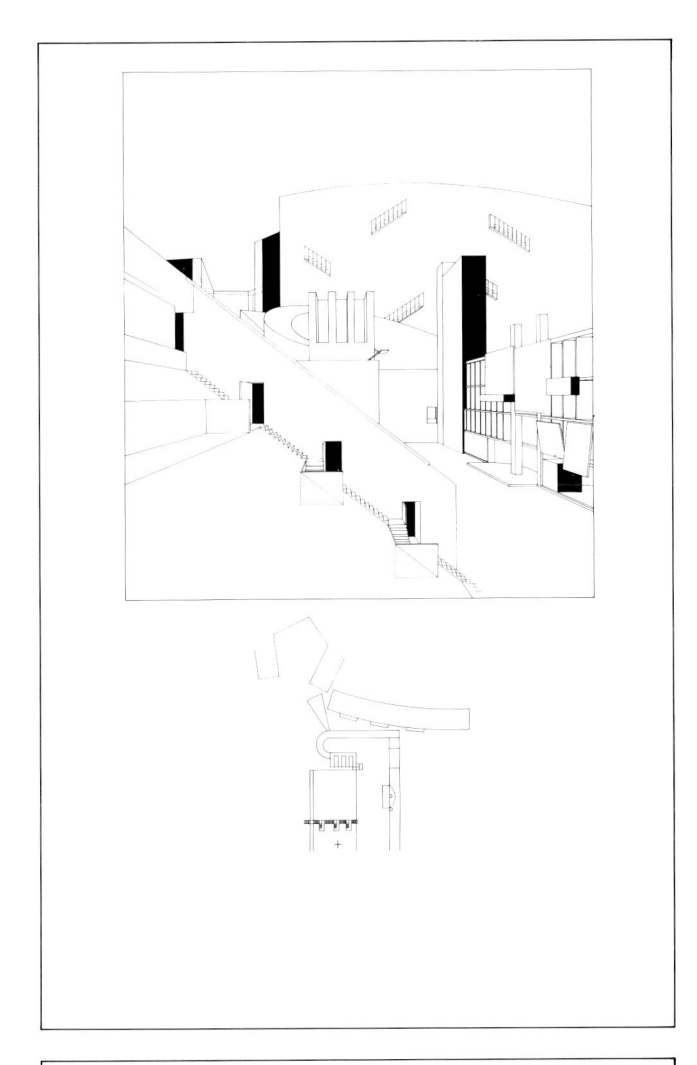

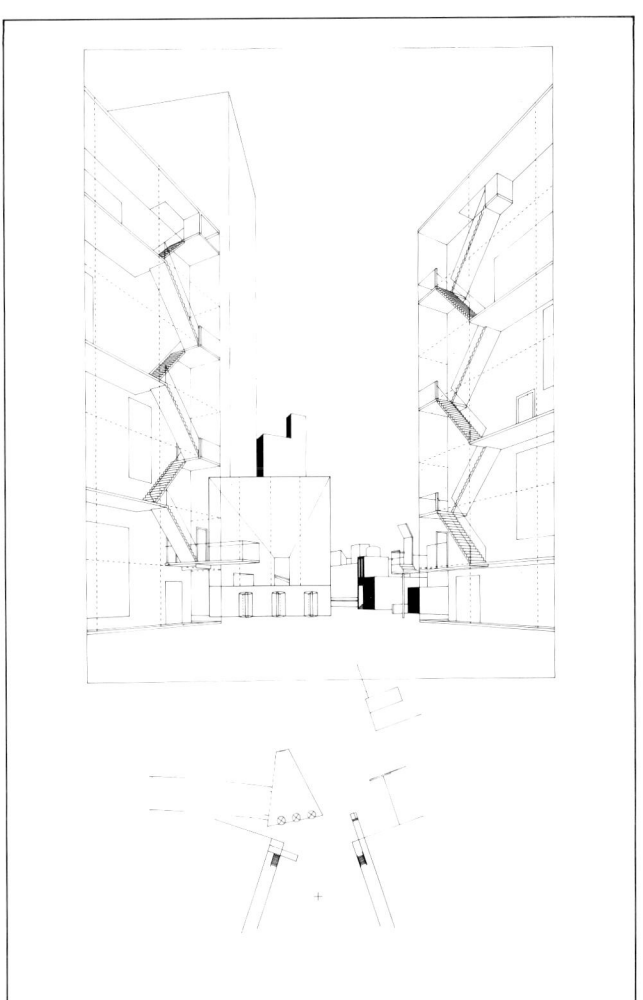

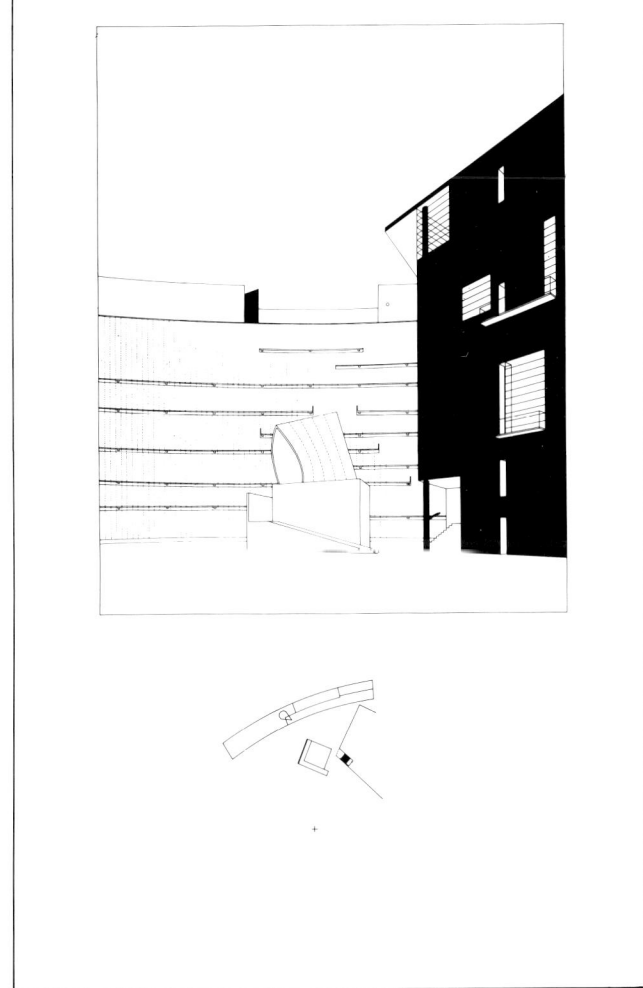

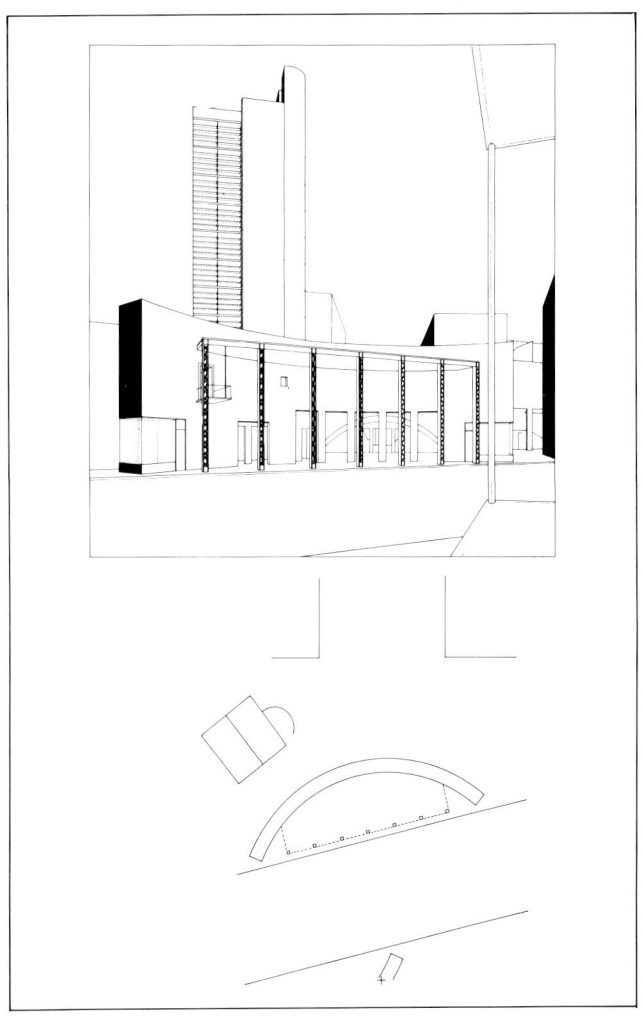

147

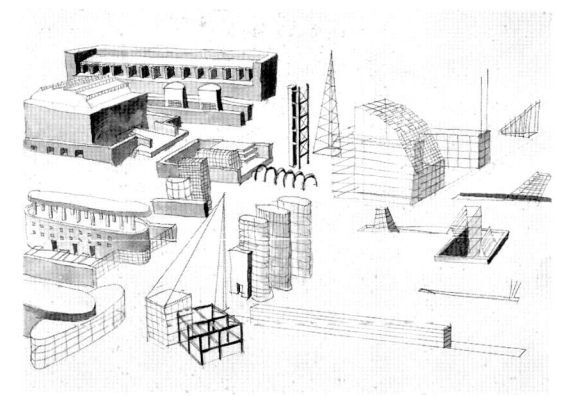

Concept sketch

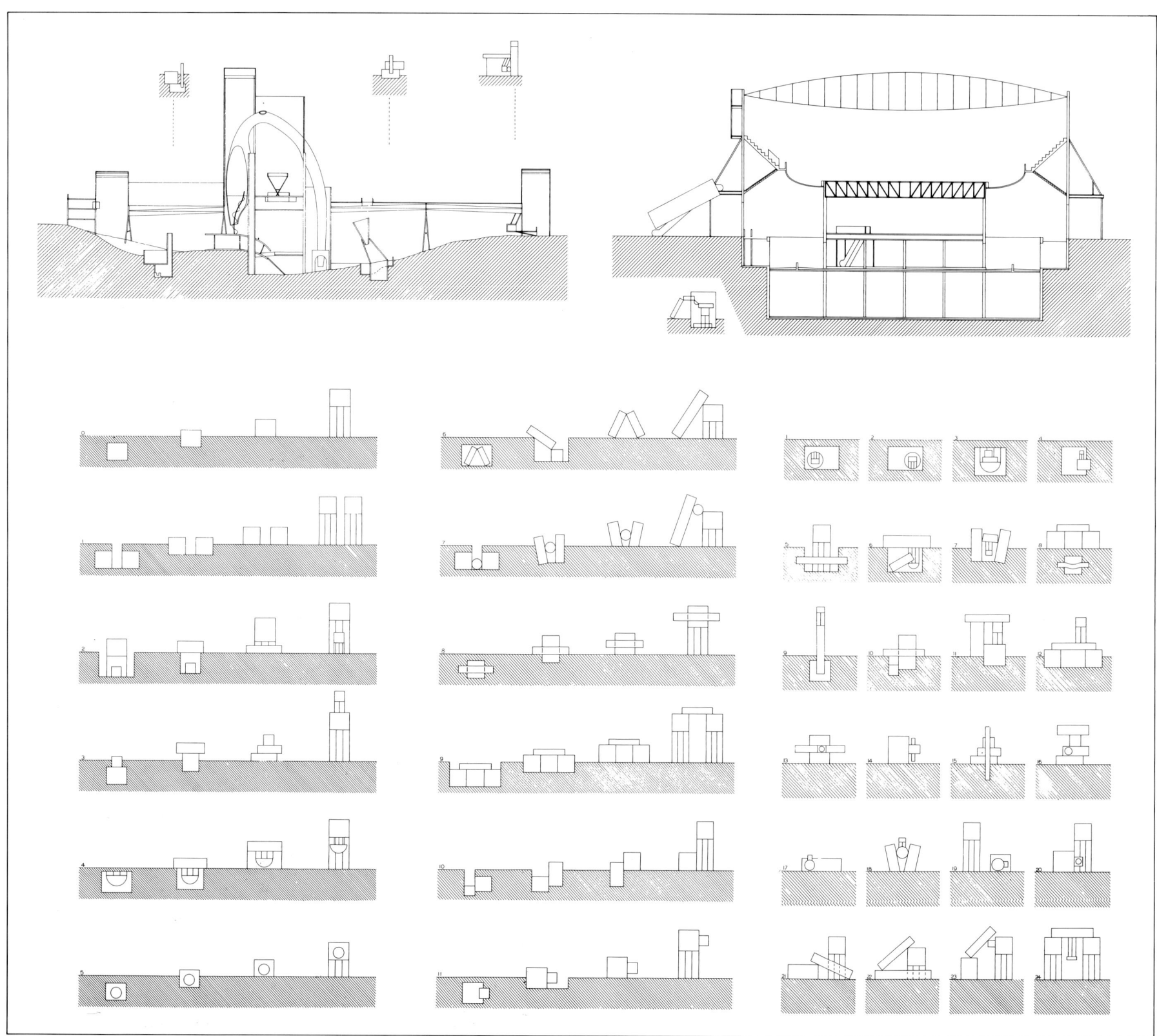

Diagrams

Concept sketch   *Model*

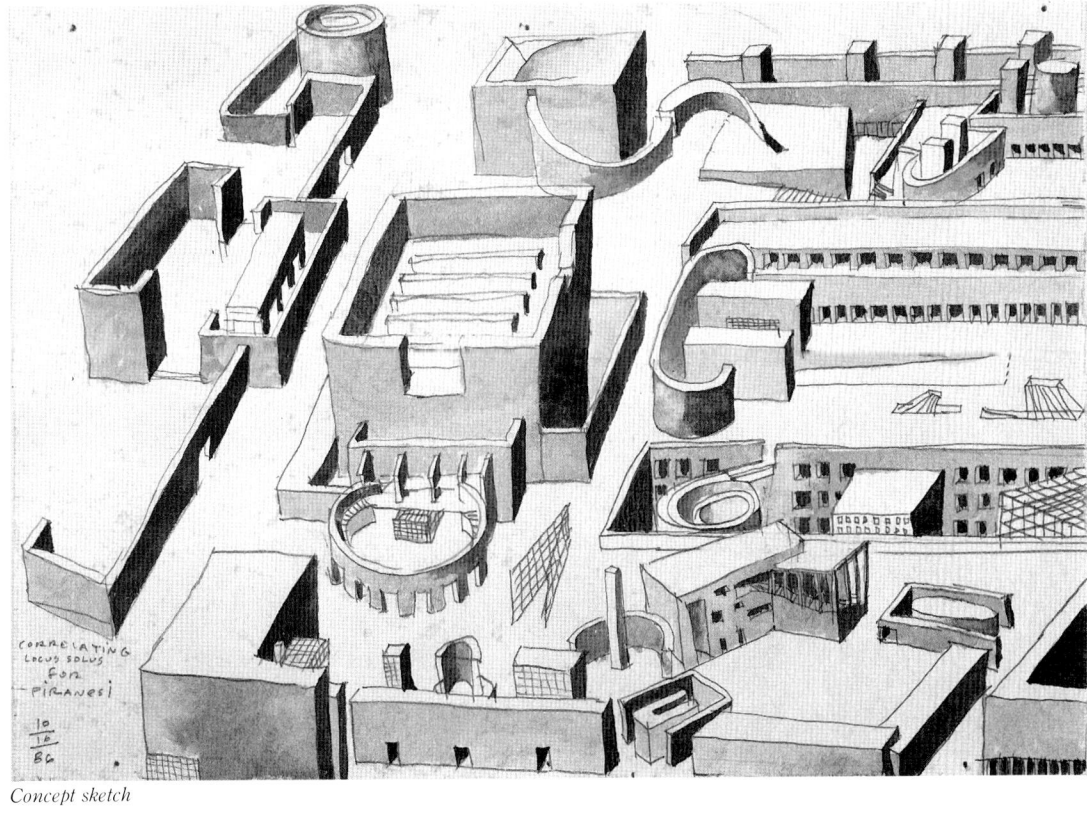

150

Models

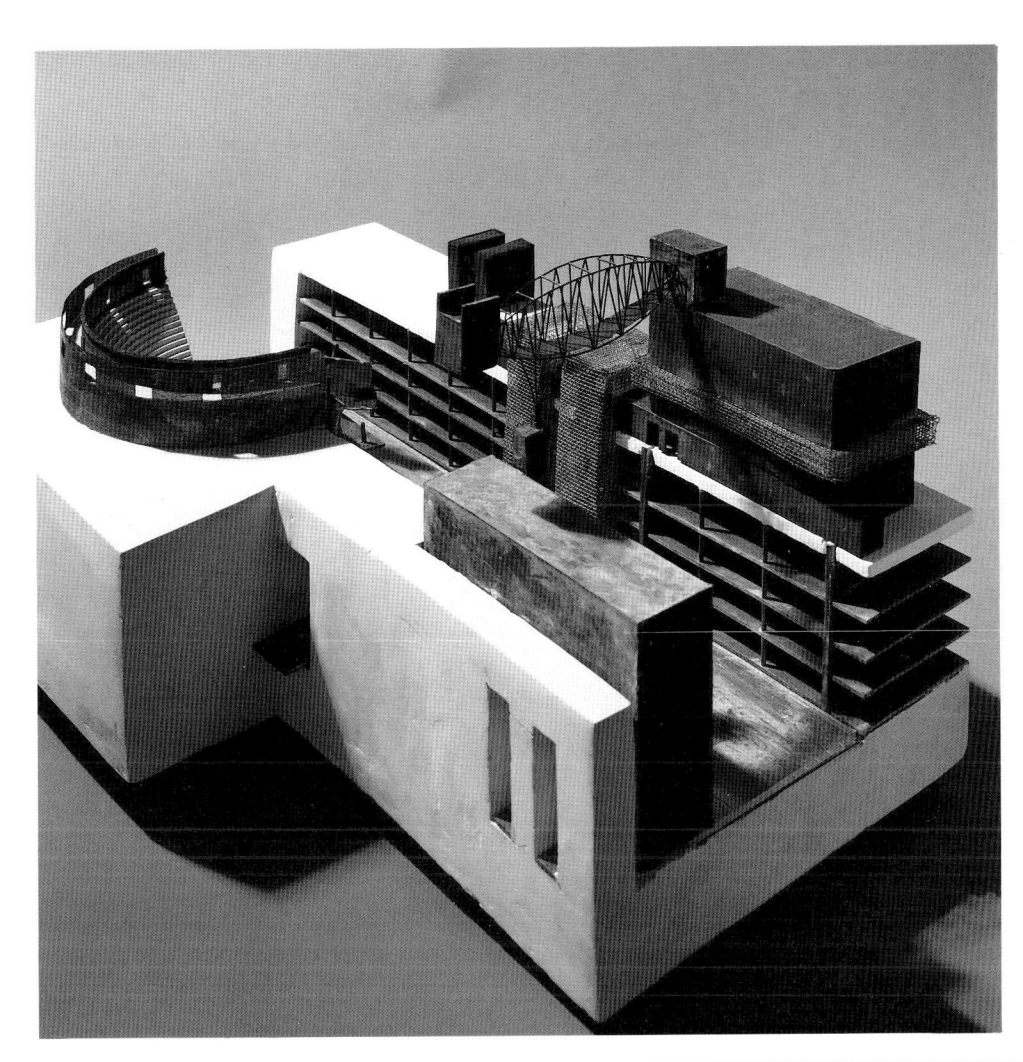

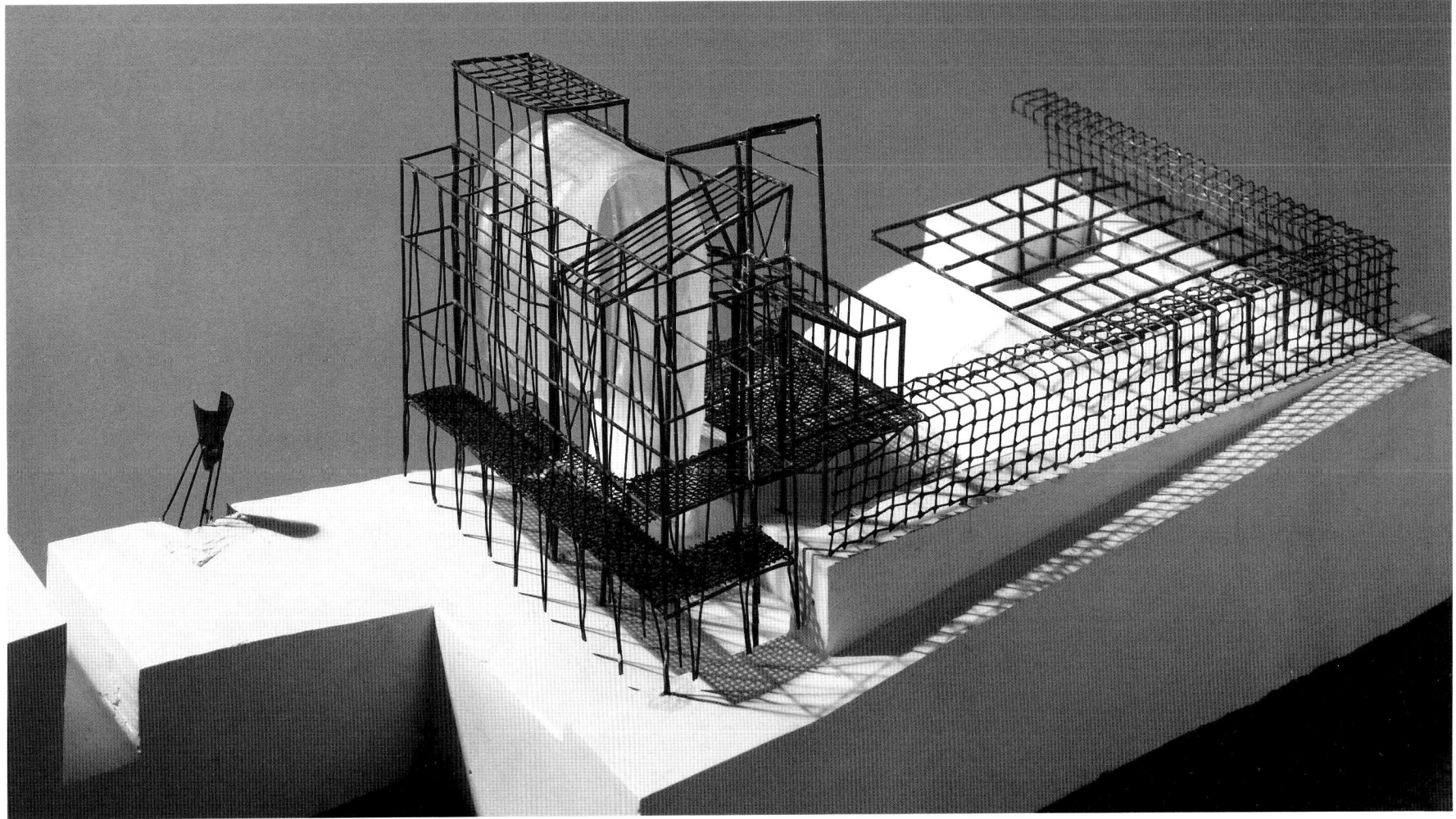

Erie Canal Edge
Rochester, New York
1988

The Erie Canal, a grand work that secured the growth of New York and of cities along its route, is now an undistinguished trench to the south of Rochester. The project is a cross-sectional study which redefines the canal and reinforces the city edge.

"Canal House" types rest on the top and bottom of the embankment, like dogs at the dinner table. On the north side of the canal, the houses form a continuous wall and an intermittant arcade; on the south, they are dis-aligned and open to the rural.

The northern urban edge is characterized by a workplace building, which anticipates new programs not requiring horizontal floors. Operation occurs via walkway beams analogous to the former work walks along the Erie Canal.

Between the work building and the canal houses are a series of social and cultural facilities: a group of cinemas, a music school, and housing for the elderly with a connecting cultural gallery.

エリー運河畔計画
これまでニューヨークと運河沿いの都市の成長を護って来たエリー運河だが、それが今ではロチェスターの南を縁どるだけの目立たぬ堀にすぎない有様だ。これは、運河を見直して都市の周縁部を強化しようと、運河の両岸にわたる計画である。

「カナルハウス」タイプの住宅が堤防の上下に、さながらダイニングテーブルに前足をかけている犬のように置かれる。運河の北側には住宅の連続する壁を作り、そのところどころにアーケードが設けられる。南岸では住宅は疎らに並ぶので、背後の田園に対して空間は開かれている。

運河の北の、都市の縁を形成する側に特徴的なものはワーク・プレイス・ビルディングである。水平の床を必要としない新しい計画が生まれることを予測して、かつてエリー運河沿いに作られていた作業用の通路になぞらえた歩行用の梁が渡されている。

ワークビルディングとカナルハウスの間には社会文化施設がある。映画館、音楽学校、それに文化ギャラリーを備えた老人用のハウジングなどだ。

Site plan, axonometric and plans

Model

Model

*Spatial Retaining Bars
Phoenix, Arizona
1989*

スペイシャル・リテイニング・バー

フェニックスの歴史の上で,何より際立つのは,幅30フィートの運河を延べ250マイルにわたって巡らして,山あいの平地を耕作していたホホカム・インディアンの文明が千年の長きにもわたって栄えながら,忽然と消え去ってしまったというミステリーである。フェニックスの外周部に位置する,中に空間を抱いた,柱と梁だけで構成されたような建築の連りは,そこが都市の端であり,砂漠の始まりであることを伝える。ひとつの単位がそれぞれ180フィート平方の土地を囲み,それが垂直方向にも立ち上って,彼方の山並みと砂漠のつづく景色を,さながら額縁のように切りとる。

ロフトのような生活空間が,静寂と孤独の中に宙に浮び,砂漠の日の出と日没を従えた,新たな地平線を形づくる。コミュニティの一員として生活しているという思いは,地表に並ぶ広場を通り抜けて出入りするたびに高められる。設備の操作は,住居に隣接するロフトのスペースから電気的な操作によって行われる。文化的な施設は壁のないフレームの中に吊られるようにして置かれる。

30フィート角の断面を持つ建物全体が,中空の鉄筋コンクリートで作られ,下面はつややかに磨かれるので,明け方や夕暮れ時ともなれば,その下側の面は砂漠に赤く輝く太陽に照り映えて,かつてホホカム運河の水面で反射された光が中空に現出したかのように見える。

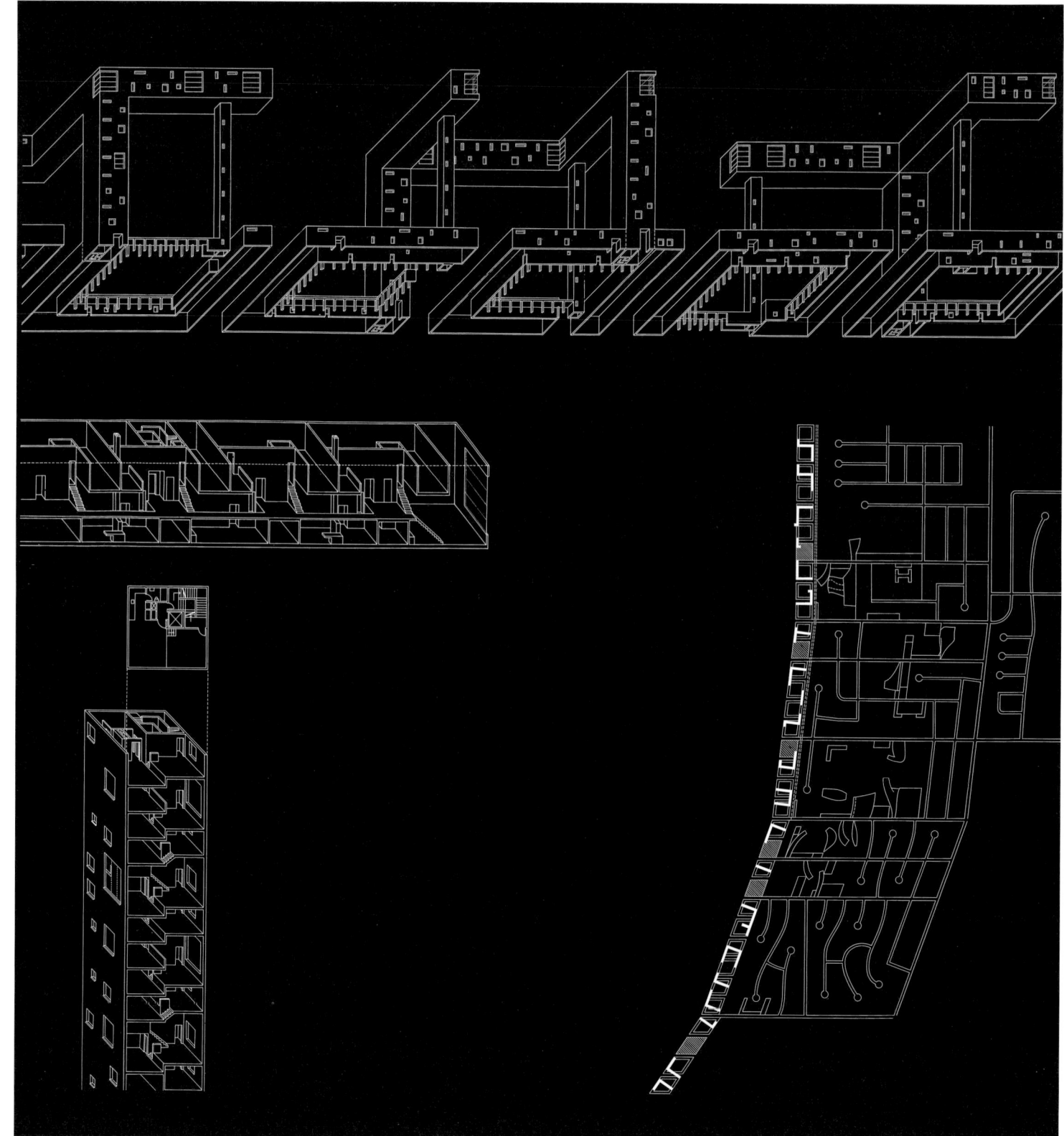

The most prominent aspect of the history of Phoenix is the mysterious disappearance of the Hohokum Indian civilization after their cultivation of the valley with 250 miles of thirty-foot canals for 1,000 years.

Sited on the periphery of Phoenix, a series of spatial retaining bars infers an edge to the city, a beginning to the desert. Each structure inscribes a 180-foot-square space while it rises to frame views of the distant mountains and desert.

Loftlike living areas hang in silent isolation, forming a new horizon with views of the desert sunrise and sunset. Communal life is encouraged by entrance and exit through public squares at grade. Work is conducted electronically from loft spaces adjoining dwellings. Cultural facilities are suspended in open-frame structures.

The thirty-foot-square building sections act as hollow, reinforced concrete beams. Exteriors are made of pigmented concrete with the undersides of the arms polished to a high gloss. In the morning and evening these undersides are illuminated by the red desert sun—a hanging apparition of light once reflected by the water of the Hohokum canals.

Site map

Axonometrics and plan

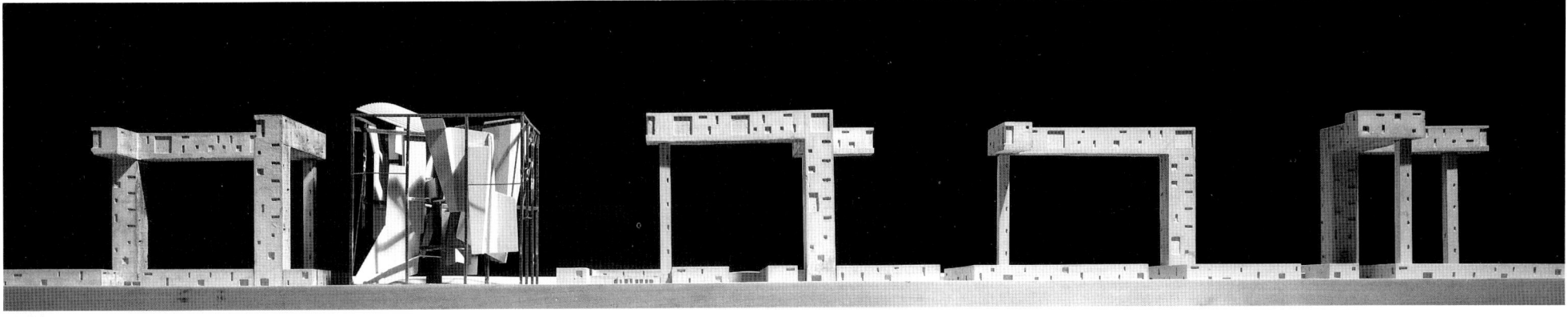

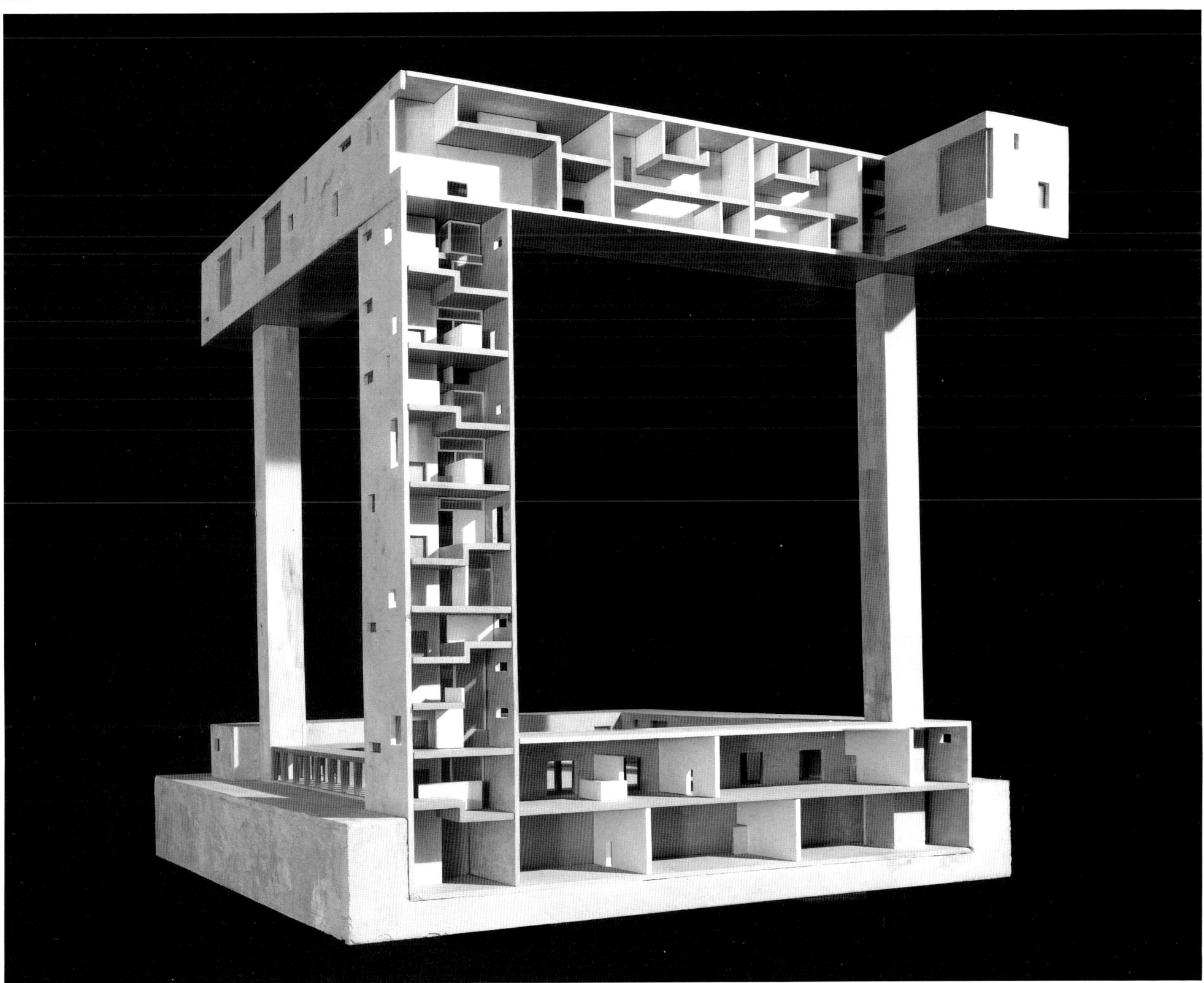

Model

Model

*Stitch Plan
Cleveland, Ohio
1989*

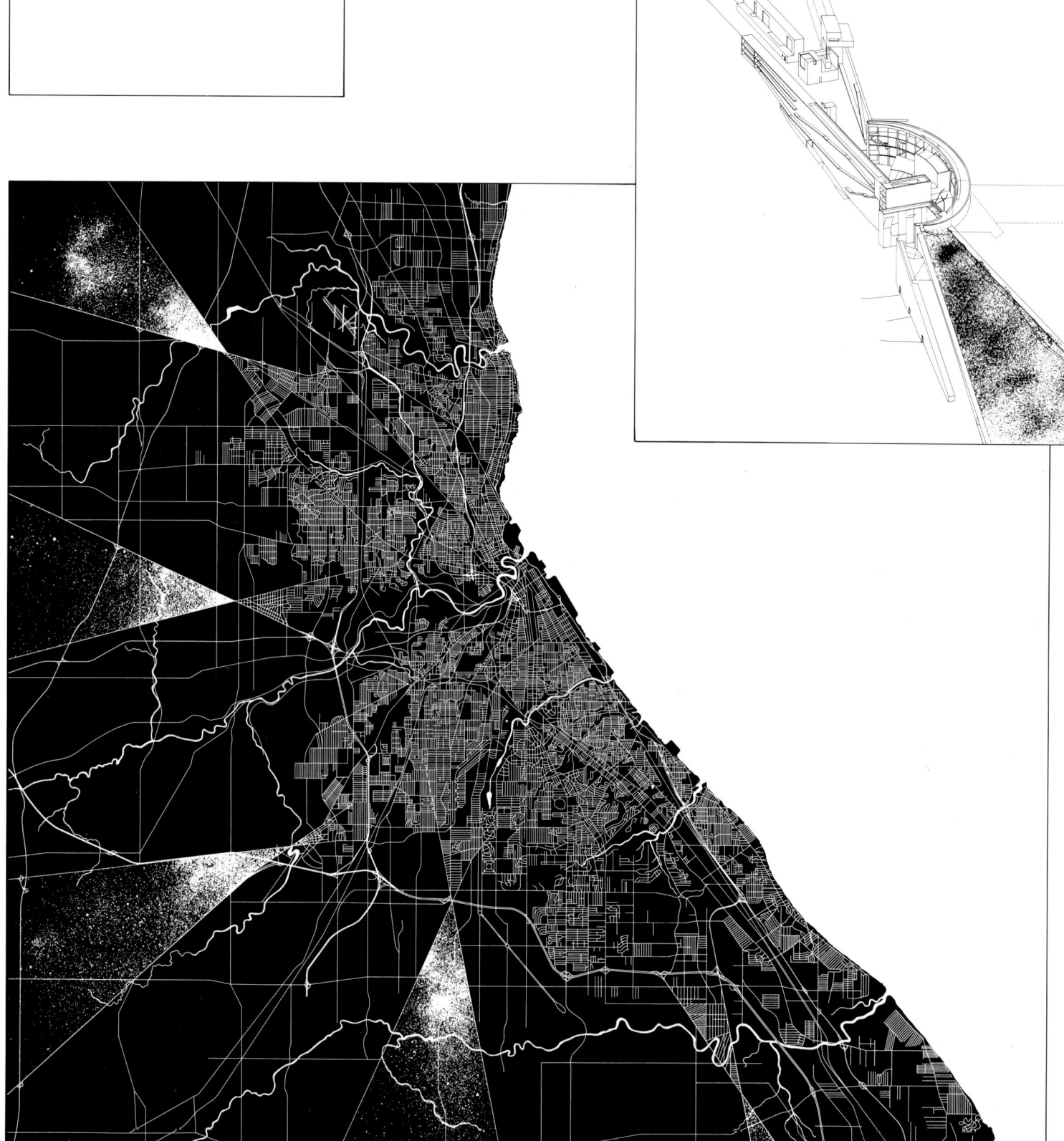

Five *X*s spaced along the inland edge of Cleveland (the northern edge is formed by Lake Erie) define precise crossover points from new urban areas to a clarified rural region. These newly created urban spaces are girded by mixed-use buildings.

At one *X* the crossover is developed into a dam with hybrid functions. The urban section contains a number of buildings including a hotel, a cinema, and a gymnasium. The rural section contains public programs related to nature, including a fish hatchery, an aquarium, and botanical gardens.

The artificial lake formed by the dam provides a large recreational area and extends the crossover point into a boundary line. Taken together, the *X*s imply an urban edge.

ステッチ・プラン
クリーブランドの内陸側の周縁部（北側の端はエリー湖に面する）に沿って，間隔をおいて並ぶ5つのX型は，新興の都市域から田園地域へと変わる交差部を明確に定めている。5つのX型の内側につくられる新しい都市域側には，種々の用途をもつ建物が建ち並ぶ。

X型のひとつは，その交差部に様々な機能を複合させたダムになる。その都市側には数多くのビルが建ち並び，ホテル，映画館，体育館などがある。それに対して，田園地帯側は，自然を生かした公共的な計画，たとえば魚の孵化場，水族館，植物園といったものである。ダムが形づくる人造湖は，広いリクリエーション地域となるので，交差部は引き伸ばされて，点ではなく境界線を形成する。また，X型をひとつながりとして見ると，それは都市の縁を暗示するものとなる。

Site map/axonometric and diagram

Section

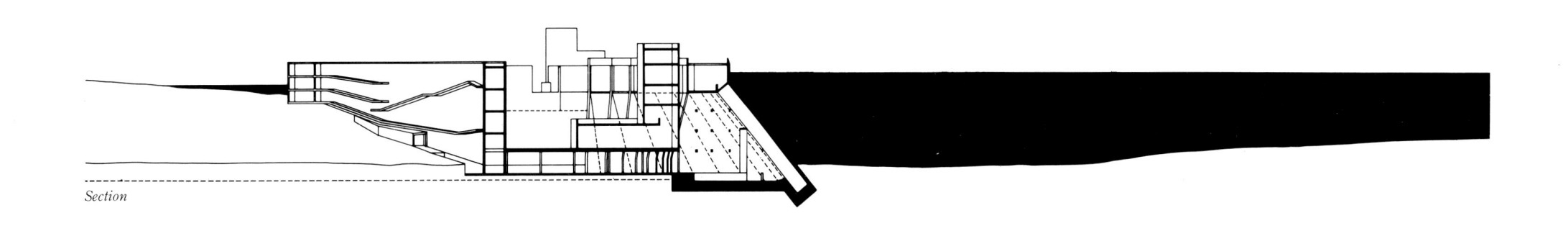

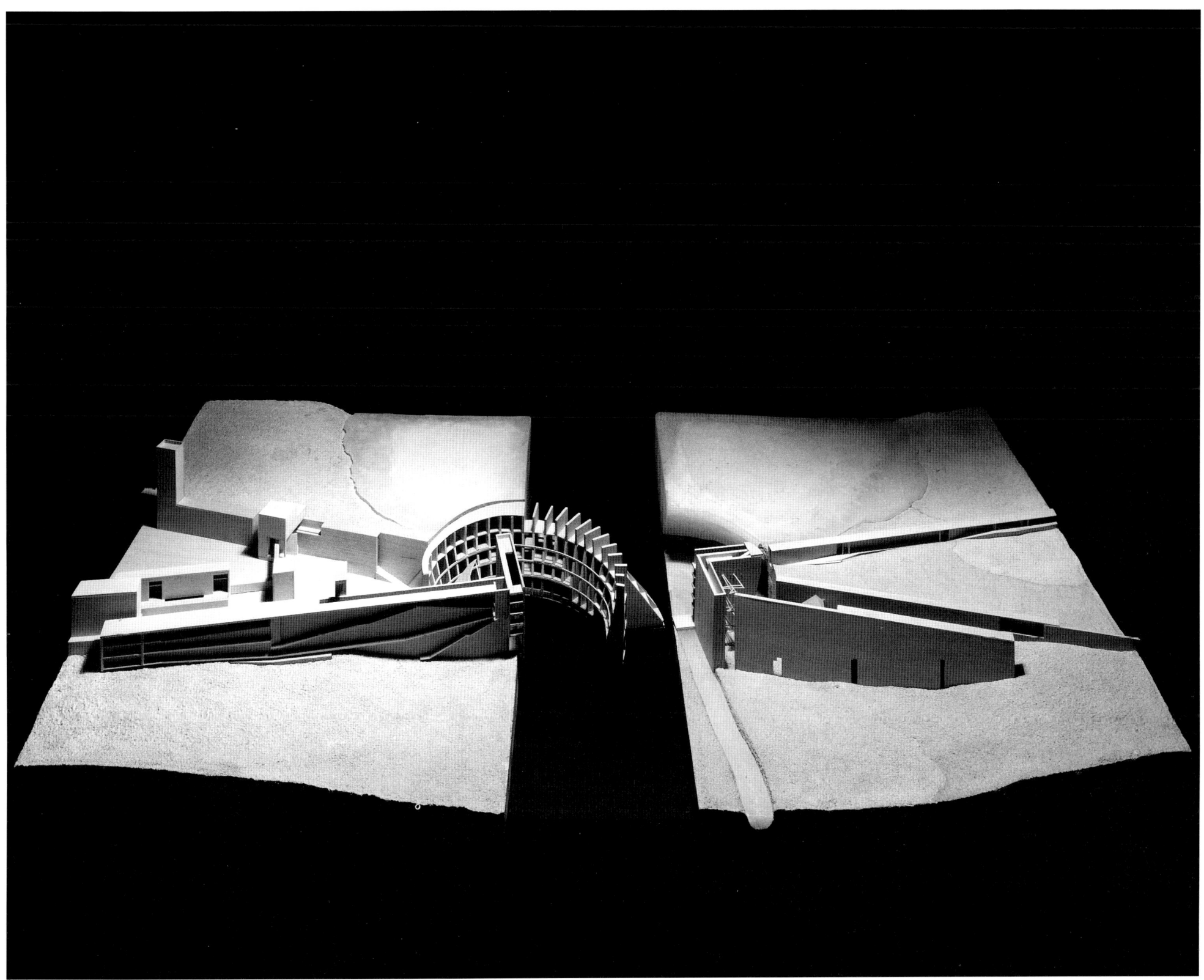

Model

Parallax Towers
New York, New York
1990

In this proposal, the existing 72nd Street train yards would be transformed into a new city-edge park in the spirit of Frederick Law Olmsted. The existing dense development to the east looks out over this new open park, which extends to the Hudson River's edge.

On the river, ultrathin skyscrapers bracket the view and create a new kind of framed urban space over water. Hybrid buildings with diverse functions, the towers are linked by horizontal underwater transit systems that connect underwater parkside lobbies to high-speed elevators serving upper transfer lobbies. Occupants are within walking distance of the 72nd Street subway entrance or express ferries to the Jacob K. Javits Convention Center, Wall Street, and La Guardia Airport.

In counterbalance to the ultrathin towers, an ultrathick floating public space is used as a concert stadium, large-screen movie theater complex, or grand festival hall.

パララックス・タワー
この計画は72丁目の鉄道操作場の敷地を，フレデリック・ロウ・オルムステッドの精神を承け継ぐ，シティ・エッジ・パークに生まれ変わらせようというものだ。東側の高密度に開発された区域から見ると，ハドソン河岸までひろがるこの新しい公園越しの景色が広がる。川面に極細型の高層ビル群が景色を包み込むようにして建ち並ぶと，水面に新しい種類の都市空間が浮ぶ。様々な機能を内包した複合ビルである複数のタワーを地下で水平方向に結び，これがやはり水中にある公園側のロビーに続いて，そこから高速エレベーターによって上階の乗換ロビーと結ばれる。ビルの利用者は72丁目の地下鉄の入り口をはじめ，ジェイコブ・K・ジェイヴィッツ・コンヴェンションセンターやウォールストリート，ラガーディア空港などへ行く高速フェリーの乗り場へも歩いて通える。

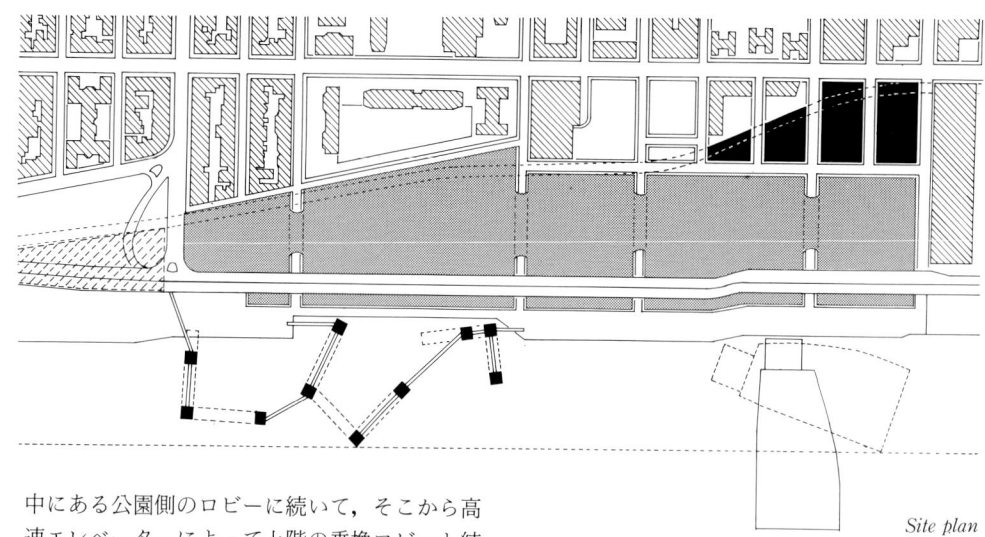

極細型の高層ビルと対比させるように，ヴォリュームのある水上パブリック・スペースは，コンサート・スタジアムや巨大スクリーンの映画館，グランド・フェスティヴァル・ホールなどとして使われる。

Site plan

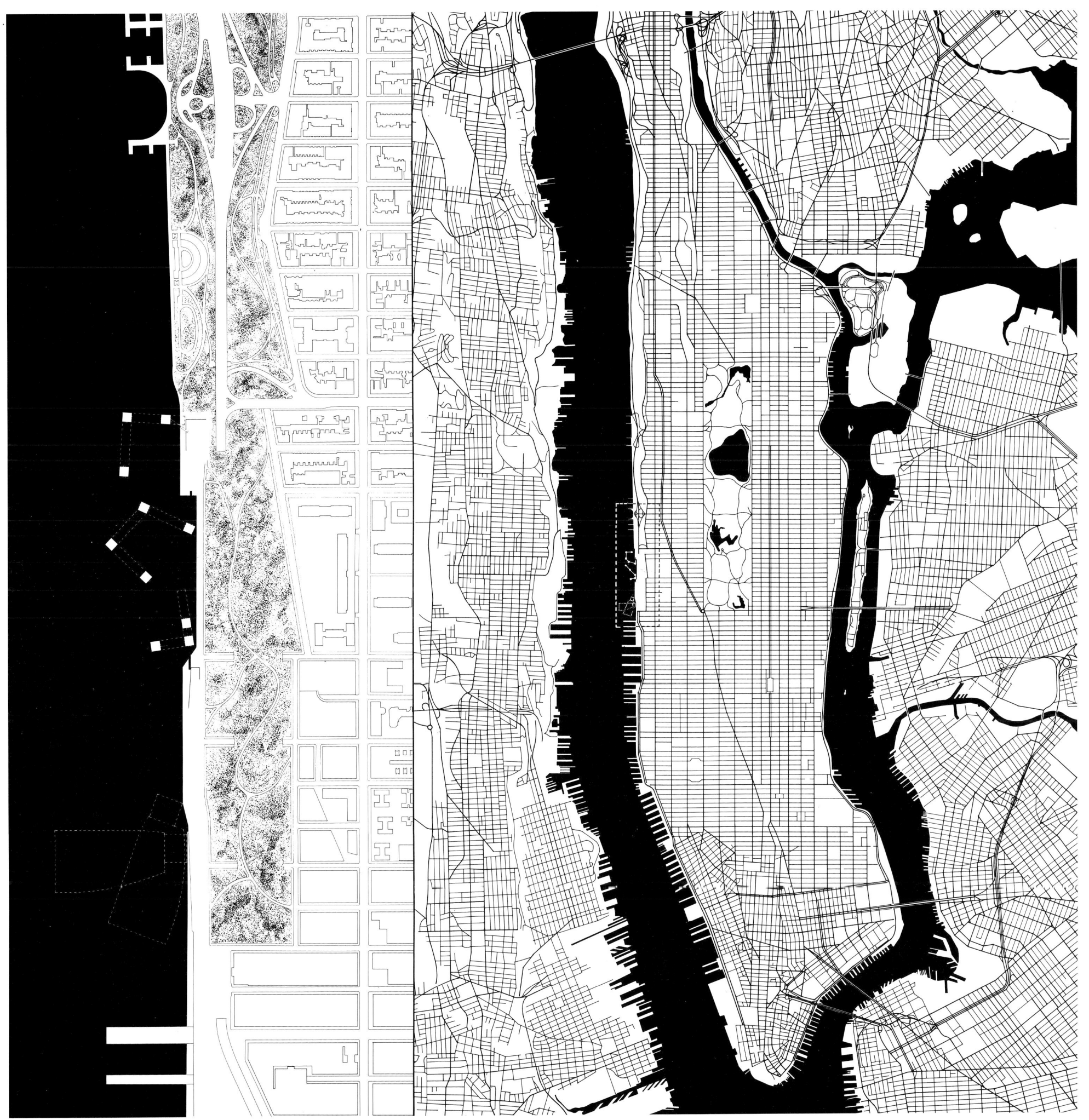

Site map

Spiroid Sectors
Dallas/Fort Worth, Texas
1990

Concept sketch

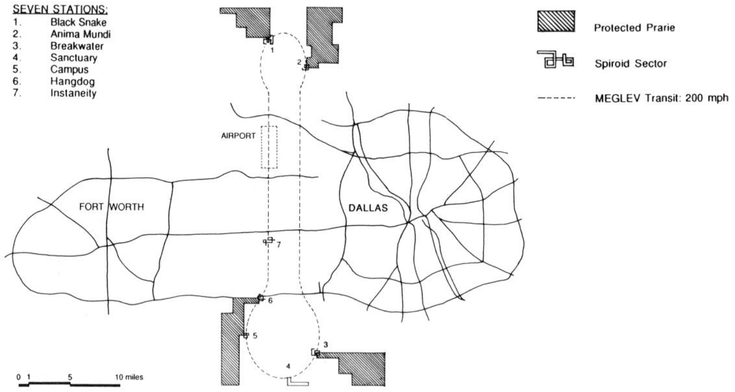

SEVEN STATIONS:
1. Black Snake
2. Anima Mundi
3. Breakwater
4. Sanctuary
5. Campus
6. Hangdog
7. Instaneity

Protected Prarie
Spiroid Sector
MEGLEV Transit: 200 mph

Site

Concept sketch

Exploded axonometric

Protected Texas prairie is framed by new sectors that condense living, working, and recreational activities. Future residents are transported to new town sectors by a high-speed MAGLEV transit from the Dallas/Fort Worth Airport.

A new hierarchy of public spaces is surrounded by armatures knotted in a continuous space-forming morphology. Various public passages along the roof afford a shifting ground plane, invigorating the interconnected experience of the sector's spaces.

The coiling armatures contain a hybrid of macroprograms: public transit stations, health clubs, cinemas, and galleries, with horizontal and vertical interconnected transit. Microprograms of domestic activities are in smaller adjacent structures. The smallest spiroids form low-cost courtyard housing in experimental thin/thick wall construction.

スパイロイド・セクター

テキサスで保護地域に指定されているプレイリーのまわりの一帯は，住居やビジネスやリクリエーションなどの施設で埋められようとしている。将来の住民たちは，ダラス／フォートワース空港からマグレヴ高速鉄道でニュータウン地域に帰る。

ここではパブリック・スペースを構成する新しいハイアラーキーは，連続的な空間を作る建築を随所に配して周囲を囲むという形をとる。種々の交通ルートが高架で設けられるために，地上面の動きが自由になって，各区域を結ぶ活動を促すことになる。

螺旋形をなす建物の中には広い地域を対象にする施設が混在する。たとえば鉄道の駅，ヘルスクラブ，映画館，ギャラリーなどが入り，それらが，文字通り縦横に結ばれる。小さな範囲の活動のための近隣計画は隣の小規模な建物が引き受ける。最も小さい螺旋形は，薄壁と厚壁による実験的な壁構造のローコストのコートハウスである。

Montage

List of Works 1975-92
作品リスト

1974–75
Residence
Manchester, Washington

Program: two square ground plans with a pair of courtyards between them organize mass which is sheathed in cedar boards weathering to silver gray; finishes are rough gray on the exterior and smooth cream on the interior with a curved stair connecting 3 levels; volumes and openings are organized according to harmonic proportions
Client: Helen and Myron Holl
General contractor: Myron Holl
Major materials: wood, plaster
Cost of construction: $60,000

1975
Manila Housing
Daga Dagatan, Manila

Program: proposal for an international competition for housing in Daga Dagatan
Client: International Architecture Foundation
Project team: James Tanner, John Cropper
Major materials: concrete
Site area: 147 hectares

1976
Sokolov Retreat
St. Tropez, France

Program: an underwater retreat, anchored onto an existing house at the edge of the harbor in St. Tropez
Client: Michelle Sokolov
Major materials: concrete, glass
Total floor area: 780 sq ft

1976
St. Paul Capitol Competition
St. Paul, Minnesota

Program: project for the State Capitol consolidating a museum for collecting and preserving the records of the past with governing functions in a subterranean structure
Client: State of Minnesota
Project team: James Tanner, William Zimmerman
Major materials: concrete, glass, granite, marble
Total floor area: 300,000 sq ft
Cost of construction: $57 million

1977–78
Gymnasium Bridge
South Bronx, New York

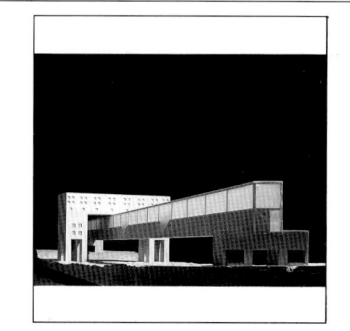

Program: hybrid building combining a gymnasium and bridge that condenses the activities of meeting, physical recreation and work into one structure while simultaneously forming a bridge from the community to the park on Randall's Island
Client: Wave Hill Center
Structural system: steel truss, concrete abutments
Major materials: steel, glass
Total floor area: 50,400 sq ft

1978–79
Telescope House
Still Pond, Maryland

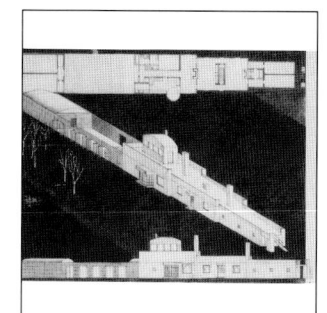

Program: residence for a retired couple who wanted a versatile home that could be opened up or closed off according to the number of guests
Client: Gene Wyble
Project team: Joseph Fenton
Major materials: concrete, wood
Site area: 160 by 493 ft
Total floor area: 4300 sq ft
Cost of construction: $280,000

1978–79
Millville Courtyard
Millville, New Jersey

Program: the sunny side of an empty lot is organized into a courtyard
Client: an advertising agency
Design years: 1978–79
Construction year: 1979
Project team: Joseph Fenton
General contractor: Russel Sturgis
Major materials: concrete block, exterior cement plaster
Site area: 4,000 sq ft
Cost of construction: $55,000

1977–78
Minimum Houses
Hastings-on-Hudson, New York

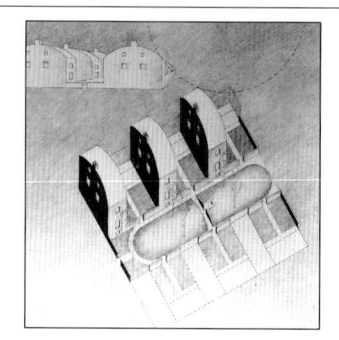

Program: a proposed alternative to high-rise housing near Manhattan; each house has a small garden and a back porch
Project team: Steven Holl; Rick Bottino, model
Major materials: single-span wood joists, concrete block walls, and rubber membrane roofing and wall covering
Total floor area: 1300 sq ft each
Cost of construction: $50,000 each

1979
Les Halles Competition
Paris, France

Program: housing, and an international meeting place on the former site of Les Halles pavilions of Baltard; trees are planted in the place of iron columns, walls are lined with arcades made of sandblasted glass
Client: City of Paris
Project team: Joseph Fenton, Ron Stiener, Stuart Diston
Structural system: concrete frame
Major materials: concrete, steel, marble slabs, sandblasted glass

1979
Bridges of Melbourne
Melbourne, Australia

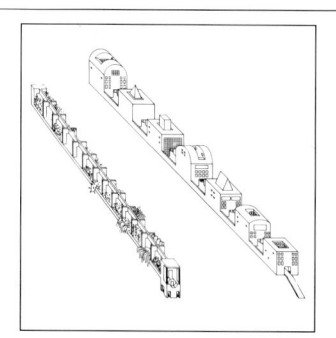

Program: designed for a Melbourne competition for a landmark to be built on a vast railroad yard dividing the central area of the city from the Yarra River, Bridge of Houses was part of an entry consisting of seven bridges proposed as "urban arms" extending the streets of Melbourne across the yards to the river; in this proposal the houses function as an ornate collection of urban villas with 4-6 apartments per block, facing green internal courts
Architects: Steven Holl with Joseph Fenton

1979–82
Bridge of Houses
New York, New York

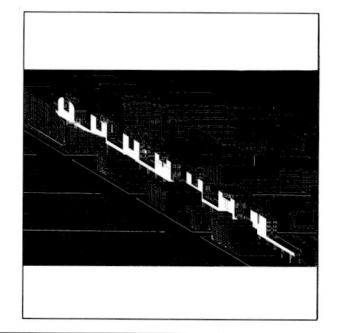

Program: a variety of housing types and a public promenade on an abandoned elevated railroad
Project team: Mark Janson, Joseph Fenton, Suzanne Powadiuk, James Rosen
Consultant: Paul Gossen Structure
Major materials: lightweight metal frame, metal siding acid treated, wood doors with sandblasted glass
Total floor area: 147,500 sq ft
Cost of construction: $9,587,500

1980–81
Metz House
Staten Island, New York

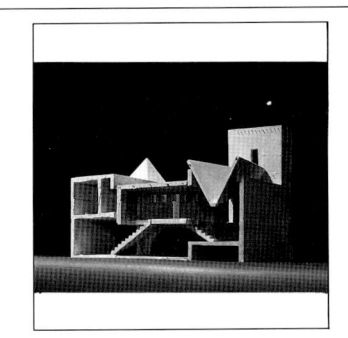

Program: a small house as a dwelling/working space for two artists and their daughter; conventional living/dining spaces are replaced by studios for sculpture and painting
Client: Mike Metz
Project team: Joseph Fenton, Mark Janson, James Rosen, Paola Iacucci, Melita Prieto
Major materials: concrete block, pine, wood frame, slate, white marble
Total floor area: 2350 sq ft
Cost of construction: $90,000

1980–81
Pool House and Sculpture Studio
Scarsdale, New York

Program: a sculpture studio and bathhouse are sited next to an existing pool; the bathhouse provides an area for changing and refreshing; the sculpture studio that doubles as a guest room
Client: Rosen
Project team: Mark Janson, James Rosen
Major materials: concrete block, stucco, marble
Total floor area: 682 sq ft
Cost of construction: $80,000

1982–83
Guardian Safe Depository
Fair Lawn, New Jersey

Program: renovation of an existing concrete building into a safe depository bank including a new facade, lobby, offices and security system
Client: Guardian Safe Inc.
Design years: 1982–93
Construction years: 1982–83
Project team: Joseph Fenton, Mark Janson
Consultants: Paul Gossen
Major materials: concrete, steel, exterior cement plaster
Total floor area: 10,000 sq ft
Cost of construction: $1 million

1982–83
Van Zandt House
East Hampton, New York

Program: year-round weekend house with lap pool and guest bedroom
Client: Van Zandt
Project team: Joseph Fenton, Mark Janson, Peter Shinoda, Charles Anderson
Major materials: stucco, wood frame, terne metal, double glazed windows
Total floor area: 1,600 sq ft
Cost of construction: $260,000

1982–83
Cohen Apartment
New York, New York

Program: apartment interior
Client: Cohen
Design years: 1982–83
Construction year: 1983
Project team: Mark Janson, Joseph Fenton
General contractor: Purdy Construction Company
Major materials: wood, plaster
Total floor area: 2,500 sq ft
Cost of construction: $350,000
Additional information: all custom made fixtures, furniture, and carpets

1980–84
Autonomous Artisan's Housing
Staten Island, New York

Program: an existing warehouse converted into housing and common workspace for artisans, including roof terraces and private gardens between each house
Design years: 1980–84
Project team: Mark Janson, David Kessler, Paola Iacucci
Major materials: concrete, wood
Total floor area: 9,828 sq ft
Cost of construction: $1,500,000

1984
Ocean Front House
Leucadia, California

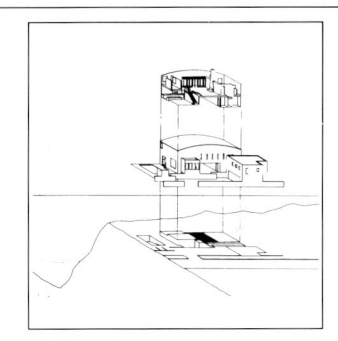

Program: the central portion of this private residence is open onto the oceanic horizon; the body of the house bridges this opening with a section of overlapping volumes topped by an arced roof
Project team: Mark Janson, Peter Lynch, Suzanne Powadiuk
Structural system: wood frame
Major materials: wood and integral color stucco
Total floor area: 2,288 sq ft
Cost of construction: $275,000

1984–88
Berkowitz-Ogdis House
Martha's Vineyard, Massachusetts

Program: private residence
Client: Steven Berkowitz, Janet Odgis
Design years: 1984–88
Construction years: 1986–88
Project team: Peter Lynch, Ralph Nelson, Peter Shinoda, Stephen Cassell
General contractor: Doyle Construction Company
Major materials: wood
Total floor area: 2,600 sq ft
Cost of construction: $275,000

1984–88
Hybrid Building
Seaside, Florida

Program: building combining retail, office and residential uses
Client: Robert Davis
Design years: 1984–85
Construction years: 1986–88
Principal-in-charge: Steven Holl, Stephen Cassell, Lorcan O'Herlihy
General contractor: New Creation Builders
Major materials: concrete, stucco, metal, wood
Total floor area: 17,665 sq ft
Cost of construction: $2 million

1985–86
Pace Collection Showroom
New York, New York

Program: commercial showroom
Client: Pace Collection
Design years: 1985–86
Construction year: 1986
Project team: Peter Shinoda, Peter Lynch, Paola Iacucci, Donna Seftel, Tom Van Den Bout
General contractor: C. Clark Construction Company
Major materials: steel windows, integral color plaster
Total floor area: 1,200 sq ft
Cost of construction: $110,000

1986
Objects, Swid Powell
New York, New York

Program: in the series of objects designed for Swid Powell, which includes plates, candle sticks, and a picture frame, programs are imposed on the objects to explore new relationships between lines, planes, and volumes
Client: Swid Powell
Major materials: brass with green patina finish, glazed porcelain china

1986
Carpets, V'Soske
New York, New York

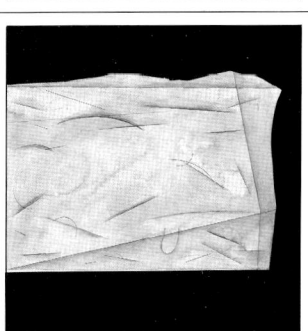

Program: each of these carpets were designed to uniquely express the concepts of the individual projects for which they are made
Client: V'Soske, New York
Design year: 1986

1986
Porta Vittoria
Competition
Milan, Italy

Program: mixed-use buildings for an open project that required forward-looking, experimental urban plans
Client: XVII Triennale of Milan
Principal-in-charge: Steven Holl, Peter Lynch
Project team: Jacob Allerdice, Laurie Beckerman, Meta Brunzema, Stephen Cassell, Gisue Hariri, Mojgan Hariri, Paola Iacucci, Ralph Nelson, Ron Peterson, Darius Sollohub, Lynnette Widder

1986–87
Apartment, Museum of
Modern Art Tower
New York, New York

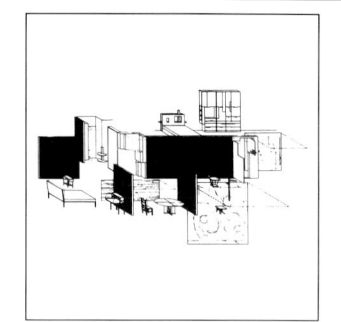

Program: apartment interior
Design years: 1986–87
Construction year: 1987
Principal-in-charge: Steven Holl, Peter Lynch
Project team: Ralph Nelson, Stephen Cassell
General contractor: C. Clark Construction Company
Major materials: integral color plaster
Total floor area: 1,800 sq ft
Cost of construction: $180,000

1987
Giada Showroom
New York, New York

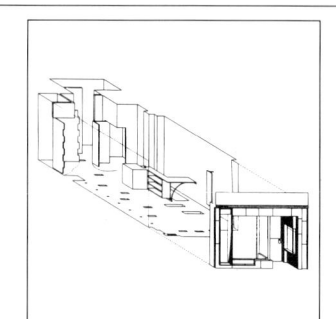

Program: retail showroom
Client: Giada
Design year: 1987
Construction year: 1987
Principal-in-charge: Steven Holl, Peter Lynch
General contractor: C. Clark Construction Company
Major materials: integral color plaster, brass, glass, terrazzo
Total floor area: 800 sq ft
Cost of construction: $190,000

1987–88
45 Christopher Street
Apartment
New York, New York

Program: residential apartment
Design years: 1987–88
Construction year: 1988
Principal-in-charge: Peter Lynch
Project team: Steven Holl, Peter Lynch, Adam Yarinsky
General contractor: Clark Construction Company
Major materials: plaster, steel, concrete
Total floor area: 2,000 sq ft

1987–88
Apartment,
Metropolitan Tower
New York, New York

Program: residential apartment
Design years: 1987–88
Construction years: 1987–88
Principal-in-charge: Steven Holl, Stephen Cassell
Project team: Lorcan O'Herlihy, Atsushi Aiba
General contractor: Woodworks Construction
Major materials: terrazzo, plaster
Total floor area: 1,200 sq ft

1988–90
Residence
Cleveland, Ohio

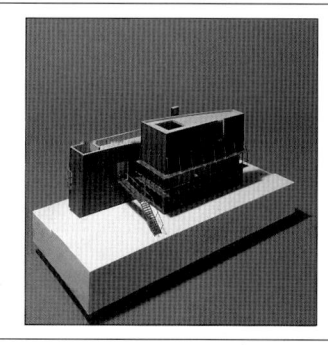

Program: private residence for a lawyer and his wife, a painter
Principal-in-charge: Steven Holl, Adam Yarinsky
Project team: Peter Lynch, Thomas Jenkinson, Lawrence Davis, Kent Hikida, Pier Copat, Thomas Gardner, Stephen Cassell
Major materials: steel, wood
Total floor area: 3,500 sq ft

1988
Abrams Residence
Oxnard, California

Program: private residence
Client: Abrams
Principal-in-charge: Steven Holl, Lorcan O'Herlihy
Project team: Richard Warner, Peter Lynch, Elizabeth Lerer, Pier Copat, Kent Hikida, Thomas Gardner, Patricia Bosch
Consultants: Robert Lawson, structure
Major materials: concrete, steel
Total floor area: 2,000 sq ft
Cost of construction: $250,000

1988
Erie Canal Edge
Rochester, New York

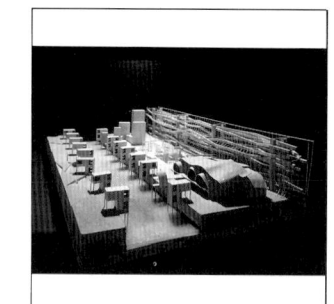

Program: new urban sector at canal edge providing housing, work space, cinemas
Project team: Pier Copat, Ben Frombgen, Bryan Bell
Major materials: steel frame, concrete frame

1988
Berlin AGB Library
Competition
Berlin, Germany

Program: open-stack library
Client: America Gedenk Bibliothek
Principal-in-charge: Steven Holl, Peter Lynch
Consultants: Guy Nordensen, structural
Structural system: concrete frame, steel truss
Major materials: concrete, sandblasted glass
Total floor area: 94,000 sq ft
Cost of construction: $32 million

1988–91
College of Architecture &
Landscape Architecture
University of Minnesota
Minneapolis, Minnesota

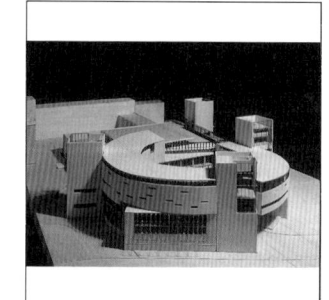

Program: 90,000-square-foot addition to School of Architecture
Client: University of Minnesota
Principal-in-charge: Steven Holl, Thomas Jenkinson, Peter Lynch, Adam Yarinsky
Project team: Stephen Cassell, Kent Hikida, Michael Dant, Bryan Bell, Anne Marx, Hideaki Ariizumi, Ben Frombgen
Consultants: Ellerbe Beckett, Inc., structural and HVAC
Major materials: concrete, steel, aluminum

1989
Spatial Retaining Bars
Phoenix, Arizona

Program: new city edge
Use of buildings: housing, work space, shops
Project team: Peter Lynch, Pier Copat, Ben Frombgen, Janet Cross
Structural system: concrete
Major materials: concrete

1989
Stitch Plan
Cleveland, Ohio

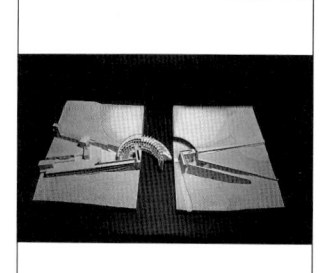

Program: urban community (housing and commercial) at city edge
Project team: Peter Lynch, Patricia Bostch, Pier Copat, Ben Frombgen, Bryan Bell

1989
Exhibition, Museum of
Modern Art
New York, New York

Principal-in-charge: Steven Holl,
Stephen Cassell
Project team: Peter Lynch, Pier
Copat, Ben Frombgen, Bryan Bell,
Marsha Davis

1989–91
Void Space/Hinged Space
Housing
Fukuoka, Japan

Program: mixed-use complex with
mostly residential apartments
Client: Fukuoka Jisho Co.
Design years: 1989–91
Construction years: 1990–91
Principal-in-charge: Steven Holl,
Hideaki Ariizumi
General contractor: Shimizu Corp.
Structural system: concrete
Major materials: concrete, aluminum
Total floor area: 4,243 m²
Cost of construction: $7.8 million

1989
Paris Tolbiac Competition
Paris, France

Program: a project for urban ideas
for the re-use of the Tolbiac rail
yards in Paris explores new types
of urban space; a section relational
experiment; it was characterized by
experiential phenomena with programmatic lines and correlation
Architects: Steven Holl with Peter
Lynch and William Wilson

1989–92
Stretto House
Dallas, Texas

Program: private residence
Local Architect: Max Levy
Design years: 1989–91
Construction years: 1991–92
Principal-in-charge: Steven Holl,
Adam Yarinsky
Consultants: Datum Engineering
General contractor: Thomas S.
Byrne Co.
Structural system: concrete block,
steel pipe
Major materials: concrete, metal
Site area: 1 acre
Total floor area: 6,500 sq ft

1989–91
Strand Theater Facade
Renovation,
New York Experimental
Glass Workshop
Brooklyn, New York

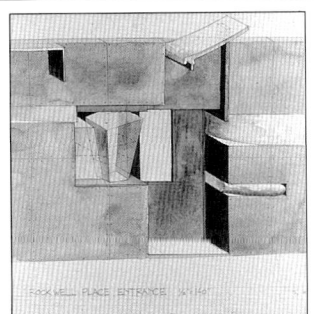

Program: facade renovation for a
glass workshop studio
Client: E.D.C. New York
Principal-in-charge: Steven Holl,
Janet Cross
Project team: Peter Lynch, Hideaki
Ariizumi
Major materials: Cast glass, blown
glass, bent glass, patinaed brass,
aluminum

1990–91
Palazzo del Cinema
Competition
Venice, Italy

Program: competition for cinema
complex
Client: City of Venice
Project team: Peter Lynch,
Stephen Cassell, William Wilson,
Thomas Jenkinson, Janet Cross,
Jun Kim, Lucinda Knox
Consultants: Guy Nordenson
Structural system: concrete
Major materials: concrete, metal
alloy, sandblasted acrylic, cork,
plaster, metal fabric
Total floor area: 25,200 m²
Cost of construction: $28 million

1990–91
Showroom,
Anne Klein A-Line
New York, New York

Program: retail showroom
Client: Anne Klein
Design year: 1990
Construction years: 1990–91
Principal-in-charge: Steven Holl,
Mark Janson, Adam Yarinsky
Project team: Ingar Staggs,
Hal Goldstein, Janet Cross
General contractor: C. Clark Construction Company
Major materials: plaster, terrazzo,
sandblasted glass
Total floor area: 10,000 sq ft
Cost of construction: $1.1 million

1990
1995 World Expo
Competition
Vienna, Austria

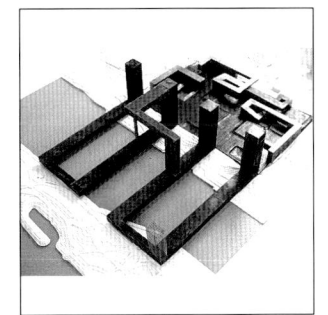

Program: exhibits, public services,
cafes, shops, hotels for a World Expo
Client: City of Vienna
Principal-in-charge: Steven Holl,
Peter Lynch
Project team: Romain Ruther
Structural system: steel frame

1990
Parallax Towers
New York, New York

Program: an alternative proposal for
Manhattan's 72nd Street Railyards
including offices, apartments, hotel
rooms, and the extension of Riverside Park
Project team: Peter Lynch, Steven
Holl, Romain Ruther
Structural system: steel tube truss
Major materials: steel, glass

1990
Spiroid Sectors
Dallas/Fort Worth, Texas

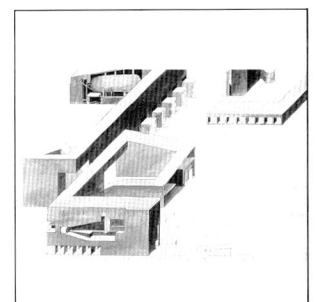

Program: a proposal for a new hybrid building type sited in the partly
settled area between Dallas and
Fort Worth; these sectors would
allow a densification of living quarters and workplaces, while enclosing and protecting large areas of
Texas prairie
Project team: Tod Fouser, Peter
Lynch, Scott Enge, Hal Goldstein,
Chris Otterbein, Laura Briggs, Janet
Cross

1990
Edge of a City Exhibition
Walker Art Center
Minneapolis, Minnesota

Program: an exhibition exploring
the limits of landscape and urban
growth as developed in 6 projects
with different locations; each project develops a different strategy
Principal-in-charge: Janet Cross
Project team: Hideaki Ariizumi,
Laura Briggs, Stephen Cassell,
Sarah Dunn, Scott Enge, Tod
Fouser, Hal Goldstien, Thomas
Jenkinson, Peter Lynch, Chris Otterbein, Adam Yarinsky

1991
Kemper Museum of
Contemporary Art
Kansas City, Missouri

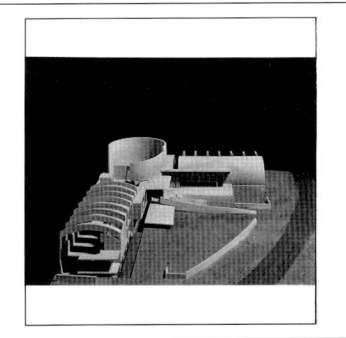

Program: this proposal for a new
art museum explores the problem
of controlling and utilizing natural
light by developing three alternate
skylighting systems; diffused north
light in a curved space and faceted
south light in the two main gallery
halls, and a "Laboratory of Light
and Shadow" in the central atrium
Client: Kansas City Art Institute
Local architect: Divine Architects
Project team: Chris Otterbien,
Janet Cross

1991
D. E. Shaw & Co. Offices
New York, New York

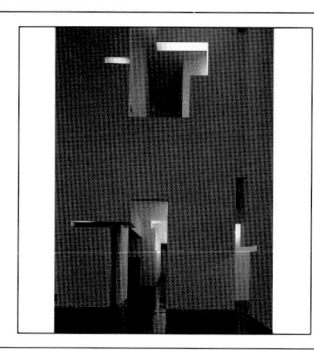

Program: offices for 65 employees on two floors of a 40-story midtown Manhattan tower
Client: D.E. Shaw & Co.
Principal-in-charge: Steven Holl, Thomas Jenkinson
Consultants: Robert Director Associates (MEP), Scott Feuron (Technologies)
General contractor: Clark Construction Company
Major materials: drywall on metal studs, paint
Total floor area: 16,000 sq ft

1991–92
Town Square, Four Houses and Chapel
Port Ludlow, Washington

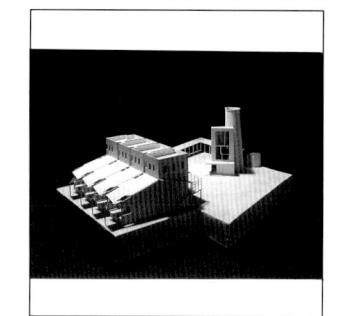

Program: a new town square in the shape of a parallelogram was proposed at the center of a new community on the site of a former saw mill; four houses are on one side of the square, while the chapel form expressed the duality of its function as a meeting house and a place of silence and reflection
Client: Port Ludlow Development
Project team: Janet Cross, Scott Enge, Todd Fouser, Adam Yarinsky, Thomas Jenkinson
Structural system: wood frame

1991–92
Shop and Office
Langley, Washington

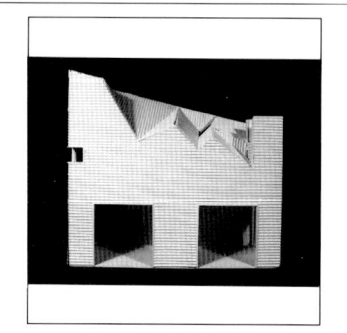

Program: a two level experiment in corrugated metal accommodates a seed shop with shopkeeper's apartment upstairs; on the uppermost level an attic "dream space" is formed by the interior consequences of the "crumpled roof"
Principal-in-charge: Janet Cross
Project team: Adam Yarinsky, Terry Surjan
Major materials: wood, corrugated aluminum
Total floor area: 1600 sq ft
Cost of construction: $180,000

1991–92
Tower of Silence
Manchester, Washington

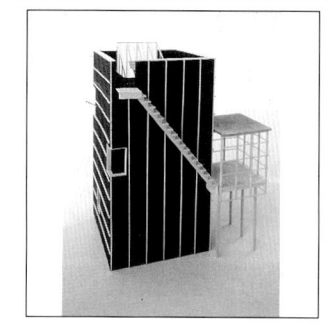

Program: this building was planned as a silent retreat and architecture studio sited in a forested area overlooking the Puget Sound in Manchester
Project team: Tod Fouser, Janet Cross
General contractor: Myron Holl
Total floor area: 256 sq ft
Cost of construction: $20,000

1992
Villa Den Haag
The Netherlands

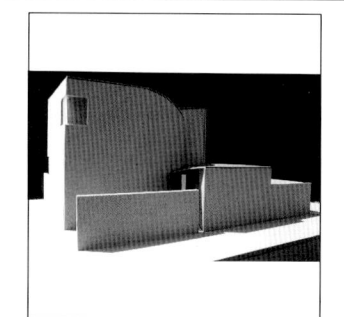

Program: private residence
Client: Geerlings Vastgoed B.V.
Principal-in-charge: Steven Holl, Adam Yarinsky
Project team: Tomoaki Tanaka, Mario Gooden, Janet Cross, Terry Surjan
Structural system: brick, concrete
Major materials: stained concrete bricks, wood windows, plaster
Site area: 248 m^2
Total floor area: 270 m^2

1992
Cranbrook Institute of Science
Bloomfield Hills, Michigan

Program: this new addition to the existing Institute of Science by Eliel Saarinen will explore the phenomenal connection between architecture and science
Client: Cranbrook Educational Community
Principal-in-charge: Stephen Cassell, Adam Yarinsky
Project team: Terry Surjan, Janet Cross

1992
Art and Architecture Buildings,
Andrews University
Barrien Springs, Michigan

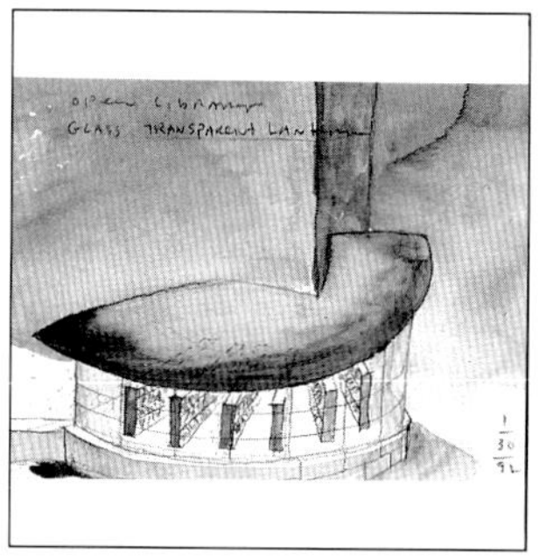

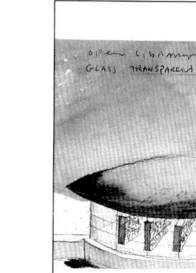

Program: this project creates new art and architecture buildings on the campus of Andrews University
Client: Andrews University
Principal-in-charge: Steven Holl, Thomas Jenkinson, Adam Yarinsky
Project team: Tomoaki Tanaka, Stephen Cassell, Mario Gooden, Terry Surjan

1992–
Makuhari Housing
Chiba, Japan

Program: 180 units of housing and retail shops
Client: Mitsui Group
Project architect: Tomoaki Tanaka
Project team: Mario Gooden, Tom Jenkinson, Janet Cross
Site area: 8,415 m^2

STEVEN HOLL ARCHITECTS

Atsushi Aiba
Jacob Allerdice
Hideaki Ariizumi
Laurie Beckerman
Bryan Bell
Stephen Cassell
Pier Copat
Janet Cross
Lawrence Davis
Scott Enge
Joseph Fenton
Tod Fouser
Ben Frombgen
Thomas Gardner
Annette Goderbauer
Hal Goldstein
Mario Gooden
Friederike Grosspietsch
Kent Hikida
Steven Holl
Paola Iacucci
Mark Janson
Thomas Jenkinson
Matthias Karlen
David Kessler
Jun Kim
Lucinda Knox
Peter Lynch
Anne Marx
Ralph Nelson
Lorcan O'Herlihy
Suzanne Powadiuk
Melita Prieto
James Rosen
Justin Rüssli
Florian Schmidt
Peter Shinoda
Darius Sollohub
Terry Surjan
Tomoaki Tanaka
Philip Teft
Tom Van Den Bout
Lynnette Widder
William Wilson
Adam Yarinsky

AWARDS

1982 Progressive Architecture Citation. Metz House & Studio, Staten Island, NY.
1984 Progressive Architecture Citation. Van Zandt Weekend House, East Hampton, NY.
1985 AIA New York Chapter Award. Andrew Cohen Apartment, New York, NY.
1986 AIA New York Chapter Award. Pace Collection Showroom, New York, NY.
1986 Progressive Architecture Citation. Berkowitz-Odgis House, Martha's Vineyard, MA.
1987 Progressive Architecture Citation. Hybrid Building, Seaside, FL.
1988 AIA New York Chapter Awards. Urban Proposal, Porta Vittoria District, Milan & Giada Clothing Shop, New York, NY.
1988 NEA, Graham Foundation & NYSCA Grants. M.O.M.A. Exhibit, New York, NY.
1989 AIA National Honor Award. Berkowitz-Odgis House, Martha's Vineyard, MA.

1990 Progressive Architecture Awards. College of Architecture and Landscape Architecture, University of Minnesota & American Memorial Library, Berlin, West Germany.
1990 Arnold W. Brunner Prize in Architecture. American Academy and Institute of Arts and Letters.
1991 Progressive Architecture Award. Void Space/Hinged Space Housing, Fukuoka, Japan.
1991 AIA National Honor Award. Hybrid Building, Seaside, FL.
1991 NYC Art Commission Excellence in Design Award. Renovation of the Strand Theater, Brooklyn, NY.
1992 AIA New York Chapter Honor Award. Void Space/Hinged Space Housing, Fukuoka, Japan.
1992 AIA National Honor Award. Offices for D.E. Shaw & Co., New York, NY.

EXHIBITIONS
Yale School of Architecture Gallery: "Young Architects." New Haven, Connecticut, Feb. 1980.
Cooper Union: "Window, Room, Furniture" (group show). New York City, Dec. 1981.
Architectura Arte Moderna: "Bridges" (one man show). Rome, Dec. 1981.
White Columns Gallery: "Bridge of Houses". New York City, Sept. 1982.
Whitney Museum Downtown: "Metamanhattan." New York City, Jan. 1984.
Facade Gallery: "Cultural Connection and Modernity" (one man show). New York City, June, 1984.
"Architecture in Transition." Berlin, Germany, Oct. 1984.
Princeton School of Architecture: "Anchorage" (one man show). New Jersey, Spring 1985.
Whitney Museum: "High Styles, American Design." New York City, 1985.
XVII Triennale of Milan, "Urban Section." Milan, Italy, 1987.
John Nichols Gallery: "House/Housing." New York City, Oct.–Nov. 1987.
GA Gallery: "The Emerging Generation in USA." Tokyo, Japan, Nov.–Dec. 1987.
Museum of Modern Art. New York City, Feb.–April 1989.
Werkebund Gallerie. Frankfurt, Germany, 25 July–27 Aug. 1989.
Fukuoka Jisho Gallery. Fukuoka, Japan, 30 May–1 Sept. 1989.
Aedes Gallery. Berlin, 19 July–1 Sept. 1989.
Harvard Graduate School of Design. Cambridge, Massachussets, Jan.–Feb. 1990.
Walker Art Center. Minneapolis, Minnesota, 1991.
Venice Biennale. Venice, Italy, 1991.
Henry Art Gallery. Seattle, Washington, 1992.
Canadian Center for Architecture. Montreal, Canada, 1992.
GA Gallery: "Steven Holl." Tokyo, Japan, June–July 1992.
GA Gallery: "Contemporary Architectural Freehand Drawings" (group show). Tokyo, 1992.

PUBLISHED WRITINGS
"IAUS Report: A New Wave of European Architecture." *Architecture and Urbanism* (Aug. 1977).
Bridges. Pamphlet Architecture Series #1. New York: Princeton Architectural Press, Dec. 1977.
"Review of Blue Mountain Conference." *Skyline* (Nov. 1978).
"The Desert De Retz." *Student Quarterly* (Dec. 1978). Syracuse School of Architecture.
"USSR in the USA." *Skyline* (May 1979).
The Alphabetical City. Pamphlet Architecture Series #5. New York: Princeton Architectural Press, March 1980.
"Conversation with Alberto Sartoris." *Arcade* (Oct. 1981).
Bridge of Houses. Pamphlet Architecture Series #7. New York: Princeton Architectural Press, July 1981.
Cities: "Anatomy of a Skyscraper." Cooper-Hewitt Museum, 1982: pp. 68-69.
Urban and Rural House Types. Pamphlet Architecture Series #9. New York: Princeton Architectural Press, Dec. 1982.
"Foundations, American House Types." *Precis IV.* Columbia University, 1983: pp. 36-37.
"Teeter Totter Principles." *Perspecta 21.* The Yale Architectural Journal, 1984: pp. 30-51.
"Within the City: Phenomena of Relations." *Design Quarterly* (Spring 1988): Walker Art Center.
Anchoring. New York: Princeton Architectural Press, 1989.
Edge of a City. Pamphlet Architecture Series #13. New York: Princeton Architectural Press, 1991.

PHOTOGRAPHIC CREDITS
Yukio Futagawa, © RETORIA:
pp. 4–5, 19, 43,48, 50, 51, 53, 54, 57, 59, 61, 63, 78–88, 91, 94, 95, 98, 103, 106, 112, 123, 125–127, 130, 133, 135, 141, 143, 149–151, 153, 155, 157, 162 (left 3, left 5), 163 (left 1, left 2, left 4, right 3, right 5), 164 (left 1, left 5, left 6, right), 165 (left 4, right 6), 166 (left 1, left 2)
Wayne N. T. Fujii, © RETORIA:
pp. 23, 24, 25 (left), 26, 27, 44–47, 62, 64, 65, 67–69, 70 (top left), 71–73, 104, 105, 107–111, 162 (left 5, right 2)
Yoshio Takase, © RETORIA:
pp. 114, 115, 118–121, 165 (left 2)
Paul Warchol:
pp. 29–31, 33, 35 (right), 41 (top second left)
Mark C. Darley:
pp. 34 (bottom right), 35 (left), 41 (top left, right middle, bottom left, bottom right)
Jon Jensen:
pp. 40 (top right), 41 (bottom second left)
Provided by Steven Holl Architects:
pp. 21, 22, 25 (right), 28, 34 (top left, bottom left, top right), 35 (second left, second right), 37, 39, 40 (top left, bottom left, bottom right), 41 (top right), 70 (bottom left, top right, bottom right), 76, 77, 101, 158, 160, 161, 162 (left 1, right 2, right 4), 162 (left 3, left 6, right 4), 163 (right 6), 165 (left 1, right 1, right 2, right 3, right 5), 166 (left 3, left 4, left 5, right 2)

GAアーキテクト 11
〈スティーヴン・ホール〉

1993年1月20日初版発行
1993年9月3日再版発行

企画・編集	二川幸夫
序文	伊東豊雄
文	スティーヴン・ホール
和訳	玉井一匡
英訳	渡辺洋
デザイン	細谷巖
発行者	二川幸夫
印刷・製本	大日本印刷株式会社
発行	A.D.A. EDITA Tokyo Co., Ltd.
	東京都渋谷区千駄ヶ谷3-12-14
	TEL.(03)3403-1581(代)

禁無断転載

ISBN4-87140-417-X C1352